COMPLETE CONDITIONING FOR LACROSSE

Tom Howley

Human Kinetics

Library of Congress Cataloging-in-Publication Data

Howley, Tom, 1965-
Complete conditioning for lacrosse / Tom Howley.
    pages cm
Includes bibliographical references.
1. Lacrosse--Training. I. Title.
GV989.H68 2016
796.34'7--dc23

2015015768

ISBN: 978-1-4504-4514-6 (print)

Acquisitions Editor: Justin Klug; **Developmental Editor:** Laura Pulliam; **Managing Editor:** Nicole O'Dell; **Copyeditor:** Mandy Eastin-Allen; **Permissions Manager:** Martha Gullo; **Graphic Designer:** Tara Welsch; **Cover Designer:** Keith Blomberg; **Photograph (cover):** Patrick Shanahan (www.shanahanphoto.com); **Photographs (interior):** Neil Bernstein, unless otherwise noted; **Photo Asset Manager:** Laura Fitch; **Visual Production Assistant:** Joyce Brumfield; **Photo Production Manager:** Jason Allen; **Art Manager:** Kelly Hendren; **Associate Art Manager:** Alan L. Wilborn; **Illustrations:** © Human Kinetics, unless otherwise noted; **Printer:** Versa Press

We thank Cornell University and the Friedman Strength & Conditioning Center for assistance in providing the location for the photo shoot for this book.

Human Kinetics books are available at special discounts for bulk purchase. Special editions or book excerpts can also be created to specification. For details, contact the Special Sales Manager at Human Kinetics.

Printed in the United States of America   10 9 8 7 6 5 4 3 2 1

The paper in this book is certified under a sustainable forestry program.

Human Kinetics
Website: www.HumanKinetics.com

United States: Human Kinetics
P.O. Box 5076
Champaign, IL 61825-5076
800-747-4457
e-mail: humank@hkusa.com

Canada: Human Kinetics
475 Devonshire Road Unit 100
Windsor, ON N8Y 2L5
800-465-7301 (in Canada only)
e-mail: info@hkcanada.com

Europe: Human Kinetics
107 Bradford Road
Stanningley
Leeds LS28 6AT, United Kingdom
+44 (0) 113 255 5665
e-mail: hk@hkeurope.com

Australia: Human Kinetics
57A Price Avenue
Lower Mitcham, South Australia 5062
08 8372 0999
e-mail: info@hkaustralia.com

New Zealand: Human Kinetics
P.O. Box 80
Mitcham Shopping Centre, South Australia 5062
0800 222 062
e-mail: info@hknewzealand.com

E5898

To Amanda—my wife and best friend. Without her love, support, and sacrifice for more than 20 years, this project would not have been possible.

Contents

Preface

Lacrosse is one of the fastest growing sports in the United States and Canada, and its popularity is expanding throughout the world. Coaches and players are interested not only in developing the skills, techniques, and strategies of the sport but also in learning how best to prepare mentally and physically for competition. *Complete Conditioning for Lacrosse* addresses these topics and enables readers to develop the fundamental physical skills necessary to improve lacrosse performance.

As the sport grows, the need for off-field training becomes more apparent. Athletes want to know how to improve speed, quickness, and stick-handling skills and be in great shape on game day. *Complete Conditioning for Lacrosse* shows athletes of all skill levels the best strategies for making those gains possible. Training improves game skills and helps athletes avoid injury, and with added strength, power, and speed, the athlete's confidence level will grow to new heights. This book gives the athlete all the tools needed for success, including fundamental program design, exercise techniques, speed and agility drills, scientific recovery strategies, and tips for avoiding physical breakdown.

Many young athletes have access to camps and other opportunities for skill instruction, but few resources help the athlete with off-field development. This practical, methodical guide helps make training as simple as possible so that anyone who applies the principles can improve lacrosse performance. Being such a young sport on the international scene, lacrosse has not had the benefit of developing a culture of training. Training knowledge from other sports has been adopted and modified to fit into the lacrosse mold, but few resources are truly specific to the training needs of lacrosse players. This book fills that void and will inspire future lacrosse players so a strong culture of intense, hard work will exist in the next generation.

Complete Conditioning for Lacrosse is a practical guide for any user of any age or experience level. With the knowledge gained, players can design both off-season and in-season workouts that address the specific needs and individual weaknesses of all lacrosse players. With sufficient hard work, intensity, and proper recovery, great gains can be realized.

This is also a guide for coaches. Coaches with experience in the sport will find this book beneficial for understanding team preparation away from the field and enhancing future player development. Due to the explosive growth of the sport over the past 20 years, many youth coaches are new to the sport and are trying to learn as much as possible about skills, strategy, and technique. This book will help these individuals learn how to develop players away from the field and help them reach their full potential.

Throughout my career at Cornell University and being part of a lacrosse program with a history of great accomplishments, I have grown to truly appreciate the skill, athleticism, and commitment of the players involved in the sport. From the great players in the early part of the 20th century, when lacrosse first became an intercollegiate sport, to the championship teams under legendary head coach Richie Moran and into the modern era with numerous Ivy League champions and Tewaaraton Trophy winners, the men and women involved in Cornell's program have been a tremendous inspiration to many. Their exploits have been inspirational to me as well, and many of the lessons learned from them over the years are included in this book. These practical lessons can be passed on to the next generation of great players who will follow in their footsteps.

As the reader begins to digest the information in this book, a few tips are in order:

- Keep the training practical. The information contained in this book is a means of improving skill and gaining the skills necessary to improve one's game and isn't so complex that training becomes frustrating or overwhelming.

- Keep it simple! Always keep in mind the resources available and think about the best ways to design the program to suit your needs.

- Think about individual or team needs. What does the athlete or team need to do to get better? What are the athlete's or team's strengths and shortcomings? Pay particular attention to those areas that need the most work.

- Have fun! Training should be exciting and inspirational. Learn to embrace the daily challenges of training so that long-term success may be enjoyed. The gains made in training today are an investment that can be withdrawn in the heat of battle on game day!

Acknowledgments

This book is a product of more than 25 years in the strength and conditioning profession. I have the greatest respect and admiration for the amazing professionals who influenced me, challenged me, and supported me along the way. My time in the profession has been an incredible journey and I truly stand on the shoulders of giants.

Coach Fred Roll, my strength coach at Tulane University, was the first to encourage me to pursue the strength coaching profession, and his efforts made my future career possible. Under his leadership, I learned just how much influence a strength and conditioning professional could have in the life of a young person. He and his amazing staff (Jay Omer and Kyle Pierce) had a significant effect on my life and I am grateful for their investment! While in graduate school at Auburn University I had the privilege of working under Coach Paul White, who taught me the art of coaching and exposed me to what it means to be a servant-leader. His kindness, hospitality, and encouragement will always be fondly remembered. The single greatest influence on my professional life is Coach Jeff Connors. His thorough understanding of training principles, discipline, work ethic, and passionate service to others are just some of the characteristics he instilled. I will forever be indebted to him for taking a chance on hiring me at East Carolina University and helping to mold me into the man I am today. My coworkers at East Carolina University (Jay Butler, Sonny Sano, and Jack Midyette) are incredible professionals! During those years together, we learned a lot, laughed a lot, and worked hard to improve our coaching skills.

My time at Cornell University has been a great blessing. Since arriving in July of 1995, I have had the privilege of working with a number of dedicated, selfless colleagues in strength and conditioning. Teena Murray, Tom Dilliplane, Leslie Johnson, Marilynn Brockman, Maghan Lunsford, Jay Andress, Jeremy Golden, and Erika Travis have all dedicated their time and talents to the athletes at Cornell. Their hard work, sacrifice, and professional service to Cornell athletics is greatly appreciated! Andy Noel (our athletic director at Cornell) has provided the leadership and resources necessary to achieve success. Without his support, our program would not be what it is today.

Throughout my time at Cornell I have had the privilege of working with some of the best lacrosse coaches in the country. Richie Moran, Dave Pietramala, Jeff Tambroni, Ben DeLuca, and Matt Kerwick patiently taught me about the sport of lacrosse but also, more importantly, about life. All of these men are not only outstanding lacrosse coaches but also great friends. In women's lacrosse, Coach Cheryl Wolf and Coach Jenny Graap have been incredibly supportive over the past 20 years. I am indebted to them for embracing my program and for allowing me to be a part of some of the special moments in Cornell Women's Lacrosse history. Jim Case, the associate head athletic trainer at Cornell University and the head trainer for men's lacrosse, has been a great friend and mentor and in our many conversations on the sidelines has taught me more about the sport of lacrosse than anyone. Jim's knowledge of the game and willingness to share his knowledge have proven invaluable. I am grateful to Jim for previewing the contents of this book and helping prepare the manuscript for final publication. His lacrosse wisdom is contained throughout. Finally, a debt of gratitude is owed to the men and women who have proudly worn the Big Red jersey. Those warriors who walked on to Schoellkopf Field and promised to give their all for Cornell have inspired me by their performance both on and off the field. Throughout these years together I have received far more than I have given, and I will forever be grateful for their support and selfless dedication to Cornell, their teammates, and the sport of lacrosse. You are a special group of people!

I would be remiss without mentioning the source of inspiration for all of us in the Cornell lacrosse program. On the afternoon of March 17, 2004, Mario St. George (George) Boiardi, our senior captain and team leader, passed away on Cornell's Schoellkopf Field while blocking a shot during a game. In the words of his teammates, George was a "passionate leader, tireless worker, selfless teammate, and loyal friend." George was God's gift to those who had the privilege of knowing him during his 22 years on this Earth, and his legacy lives beyond the lacrosse field and is carried in the hearts and lives of everyone in the Cornell lacrosse program, all of whom were affected by his life. George embodied the spirit of Cornell lacrosse, and his name will forever be associated with playing the game the way it was meant to be played—with intensity, passion, and dedication. His influence in the lives of his family, teammates, classmates, friends, and coaches will continue as we try to emulate the spirit of selfless service in which George lived. The Cornell lacrosse program changed forever after George's death. Before that incident, the goal of the team was to attain *success*, which Coach Jeff Tambroni described as "fulfilling your own mission." After that tragic day, the program's emphasis shifted to striving for *significance* through investing in the lives of others. Developing men and women of character who selflessly serve others has become the primary goal of the program. This tradition is carried beyond the walls of Cornell through the supporters of the Boiardi Foundation. This organization continues George's work by empowering the next generation through academics and athletics. You may contact the Boiardi Foundation at http://boiardifoundation.org.

Chapter 1

Training Considerations

Over the past several decades, lacrosse has grown in popularity throughout the world. Originally played as a Native American game, several native tribes throughout North America enjoyed many variations of the sport. One of the initial purposes of the sport was to provide training for warriors before combat and, it is assumed, improve their overall conditioning and mental toughness. In the Mohawk language, lacrosse was known as *Tewaaraton*, meaning "little brother of war," and was played with loosely defined boundaries and rules. In some cases, the goals were more than a mile apart and a contest could last throughout an entire day.

In order to perform successfully in such a grueling, physically demanding atmosphere, participants had to be mentally resilient and in exceptional physical condition. A high level of physical fitness remains a crucial element of the game today. Those athletes with a passionate work ethic, focused determination, and a comprehensive game plan for success are more likely to achieve their athletic goals and ultimately enjoy a greater degree of success on the field.

In modern-era lacrosse, the fast-paced style of play, agile movements, high-powered shots, and strategic personnel match-ups make for a level of excitement that is appealing to players and fans alike. Outdoor (field) and indoor (box) lacrosse have been popular, although localized, for many years in Canada, the Great Lakes region, and the Eastern United States. Over the past three decades, however, the sport has exploded in popularity, partly due to the increased exposure of National Collegiate Athletic Association, men's and women's international lacrosse competitions, and the emergence of professional leagues in North America. Schools, clubs, and leagues have been established throughout North America and the rest of the world to accommodate the surge in popularity.

This enthusiasm and new exposure increased the fan base and made what had been a hidden gem more accessible to a greater number of people. As the sport grew, the exceptional performance of great players such as Jim Brown, Mike French, Gary and Paul Gait, Eamon McEneaney, Dave Pietramala, and Mike Powell helped ignite the national popularity of the sport, especially in the United States at the collegiate level, and inspired many young people to follow in their footsteps. What had been a localized phenomenon expanded to more regions as club teams and school-sponsored programs emerged. With this increased popularity, lacrosse players and coaches sought the most effective means for improving performance both on and off the field.

Whether playing loosely organized backyard games or Major League Lacrosse games, players must have speed, agility, strength, balance, and well-proportioned energy systems to perform at their best for an extended period of time. Players who combine these physiological skills with stick- and ball-handling skills, strategic awareness, and the iron will of a warrior make the sport passionate, fun, and fan friendly. Because of the intense nature of the sport, players must have an exceptionally high level of athleticism and endurance and must be physically trained to meet and overcome the extreme physical challenges of game-day performance and avoid injury. As the sport continues to grow, coaches and athletes are looking for ways to prepare for competition and gain a competitive edge over the opponent. With some helpful hints, suggestions for exercises and drills, and a great deal of hard work, every athlete can improve his or her game!

NECESSITY OF TRAINING

Before developing a training program, coaches and athletes must clearly understand why preparation is so essential in the sport of lacrosse. From a physiological perspective, the improvement of athleticism is the most important factor in improving lacrosse performance. Athleticism can be defined as "the ability to execute athletic movements at optimum speed with precision, style, and grace in the context of the sport or activity" (Gambetta 2015). A successful performance outcome requires the integration of a wide variety of physiological characteristics related to athleticism: speed (linear and lateral), strength (upper body and lower body), balance (unilateral and bilateral), hand–eye coordination, leverage, and endurance. These physical skills, combined with strategic awareness, finesse, and ball-handling skills, will contribute to improvement in performance. These are the primary characteristics that players should seek to improve as they prepare for competition. With a dedicated game plan off the field, every player—beginner or advanced—has the ability to significantly improve.

One major consideration in physical training is preventing or minimizing the severity of injuries. Although injuries sometimes occur as a result of participation, many can be avoided altogether through the implementation of simple drills and exercises that address potential injury hazards in advance. Knowing the types of injuries that may occur while playing lacrosse, and addressing them through effective, incremental development of strength and movement skills can help athletes stay healthy and decrease the chance of injury.

Another benefit of training is that it helps instill confidence. The psychological skills gained through challenging, consistent training are just as important as the skills gained during physiological development. An athlete who has worked hard to prepare mentally and physically knows the necessary investment has been made to become a better player and therefore will perform with more confidence, energy, and enthusiasm for a longer period of time. A poised, confident player is more likely to take calculated risks and is better able to withstand the temporary setbacks that are a natural part of every contest.

The best lacrosse players tend to be those who work to develop the foundational elements of athleticism and integrate those elements into a coordinated training plan off the field in order to prepare for the rigors of game-day competition. Relying on game skills and instinct may be insufficient, especially as the level of competition escalates and players become bigger, stronger, better conditioned, and more experienced. The skillful integration of mental preparation, physical preparation (off the field), and game awareness and knowledge (on the field) is crucial to becoming a well-balanced, highly efficient lacrosse athlete. That self-assured, poised demeanor is earned through many hours of tedious training and attention to detail in working the body and mind to meet and overcome obstacles. Game-day performance is the result of pushing the body beyond self-imposed limitations and knowing that one has done everything to prepare for success.

TRAINING PROGRAM DEVELOPMENT

Some degree of analysis is required before more practical work can begin. Players must take inventory of their needs and desired outcomes by assessing current fitness levels, formulating general goals, and considering their previous training experience. In many cases, the athlete's coach is a great resource for feedback. What characteristics does a player need to work on to attain optimal results on the field? For some, the specific deficiency may be linear or lateral speed. This may be a defensive player who has trouble covering an opponent in a one-on-one match-up situation or an attacker who may need to accelerate more quickly through the defense. For other players, a lack of total-body strength may be a deficiency that, if addressed properly, can result in significant improvement in power, balance, and body control. Whatever the deficiencies, an off-season devoted to training will help the athlete address weaknesses and become a better player. In addition, a comprehensive physical testing profile will enable the athlete to discover areas of performance that should be corrected. Without the valuable information gained during these initial steps, the remainder of the physical preparation process leading up to competition will be unclear and the outcomes will be uncertain.

Establishing a Foundation

Regardless of an athlete's training status, strategies can be implemented to develop the physical skills necessary for future success. The first step in building any structure is to lay a solid foundation. In preparation for lacrosse, that foundation consists of basic skills, drills, and movements that gradually increase in intensity and complexity. For beginner or intermediate athletes (up to five years of training experience), a successful program begins with a lower level of intensity (e.g., reduced complexity or resistance) and volume (e.g., reduced number of drills, sets, or reps) and gradually escalates as the athlete's work capacity and adaptability improve and overall athleticism increases. This will help instill confidence and allows for steady gains to be realized.

Initially, athletes should perform simple resistance exercises and movement drills two to three days per week to allow for sufficient neurological adaptation. The program at first should emphasize introductory strength development, flexibility, movement-skills orientation, and conditioning, and then it should evolve steadily to encompass all of the fitness parameters that are specific to the development of lacrosse skills. The game plan should cover all the components of training, and its application must be consistent, not sporadic. Athletes who do not work toward developing all of the fitness parameters (strength, power, speed, flexibility, balance, body control, and conditioning) concurrently will not see significant, substantial physiological gains and may quickly lose most, if not all, short-term gains. If training is consistent, improvements will be made.

In addition, short-term and long-term goals should be set along the way so coaches and athletes can adequately assess progress and evaluate the training program to determine whether the desired outcomes are being met. Without these objectives in place, training has little purpose and may lead to an imbalanced result. Athletes are by nature highly competitive, and feedback based on testing and goal attainment is an outstanding motivational tool. Progress in performance or goal achievement will give athletes additional motivation for future accomplishments. It should also be mentioned that in many cases, gains do not occur in a linear fashion. Improvements may be realized quickly in one area while in other performance categories, gains may occur more slowly. Over time, however, hard work will yield positive results.

Many interrelated variables are involved in developing a successful lacrosse player. Linear and lateral speed, strength, power, flexibility, game skill and knowledge, endurance, desire, and mental toughness all play significant roles in successful performance. Regardless of one's position on the field, every athlete must be fully prepared for competition. The success of the team is determined by how well each player builds himself and how dedicated he or she is to achieving individual goals. When the individual players are united in their willingness to train and pursue physical improvement, the team has a better chance of attaining success.

A balanced, multidimensional approach to training is crucial to ensure that each athlete can compete at the desired level with minimal skill deterioration. When addressing athletic development, strength is the foundation for movement-skill development and injury prevention. Strength may be defined as the maximal force a muscle or muscle group can generate at a specified velocity (Knuttgen and Kraemer 1987). Without adequate total-body (upper, lower, and core) strength, the athlete's potential for maximal force production, particularly in the areas of shot speed, stick control, and acceleration, may be compromised and the risk of injury may be increased. This total-body strength base will enable the lacrosse player to excel at many other (often more advanced) skills. Acceleration, top-end speed, and agility all depend on the athlete's ability to produce force. In some instances, younger, inexperienced athletes desire to be fast, powerful, and well conditioned but choose to skip the strength-development component necessary for achieving those skills due to the dedication required.

In addition to strength, it is recommended that players develop a comprehensive, preparatory level of conditioning before other movement skills (e.g., speed, agility) are introduced. The establishment of an aerobic foundation allows the cardiorespiratory system to adapt more effectively when transitioning to lacrosse-specific anaerobic endurance training and allows for quicker recovery from bouts of anaerobic activity. Again, many novice athletes choose to skip this step and may not have an adequate base of aerobic endurance.

Finally, recovery strategies play a crucial role in the potential success of any training plan. If recovery is neglected or ignored, the training program will likely be less effective. Recovery strategies are as much a part of the training process as the actual workouts themselves. Without consistency in both the breakdown (workout) and recovery (refueling) phases, the success of the training process may be compromised.

Designing a Program

Before the program-design process begins, several factors must be taken into consideration. What goals would the individual or team like to attain? Improved lateral speed? An increase in lean muscle mass to provide more body armor to withstand intense contact? Overall improvement in stick- or ball-handling skills via the enhancement of upper-body and grip strength? These are all valid, lacrosse-specific objectives. How should the training influence on-field performance? Ultimately, the testing or development protocol used must affect on-field performance in a positive manner. Without this link, training will not be as effective. The answers to these specific questions regarding lacrosse performance are crucial in deciding which training system is most appropriate for a team or an individual player.

When designing a program, the athlete should begin with a vision of the desired outcome and work forward. What are the athlete's specific performance goals for the future? What performance variables must be addressed so that lacrosse skills can improve? Each athlete, in consultation with his or her coach, must perform a needs analysis in order to identify weaknesses and areas of performance to address in order to improve game skills in the future. A needs analysis must take into consideration the strengths and weaknesses of the individual in each of the performance categories. Upper- and lower-body strength, power, linear speed, lateral speed, flexibility, and conditioning should be assessed as part of this process. Specific strategies for testing each of these are discussed in chapter 2. When designing a program, special attention must be given to areas of weakness while maintaining those performance characteristics that are considered strengths. For example, an athlete with excellent mobility skills (e.g., linear or lateral speed) but poor upper-body strength may wish to focus on strength development while maintaining mobility skills during a particular training phase.

Specific short-term and long-term goals for both the team and the individual should then be set and incorporated into the training plan. For example, an athlete with a goal of improving upper-body strength should set incremental goals during each four- to six-week training cycle. If the goal is to improve bench press performance by 20 pounds (9 kg) during the off-season, the athlete should set smaller goals (e.g., 5-10 pounds, or 2-4.5 kg) for each four- to six-week training period. This will build reasonable strength and help her see gains throughout the off-season. The ultimate outcome should be a stronger, more powerful, well-conditioned player who is able to transfer off-field improvement to lacrosse-specific skills.

GENDER DIFFERENCES IN TRAINING FOR LACROSSE

Lacrosse is gaining popularity throughout the world for both men and women for good reason. The excitement, fast-paced style of play, and limited equipment needs have made the sport very popular with schools, clubs, and universities. Although some differences in rules and strategies exist between men's and women's lacrosse, the objectives remain the same: increased athleticism, improved skill development, and injury prevention. Both male and female players also strive to improve movement proficiency, strength, power, flexibility, and endurance. Although there are subtle differences in training schedules (e.g., the start of the season, practice and competition schedules), the overall preparation cycles for men's and women's lacrosse are comparable.

More physical contact is permissible in the men's game; therefore, male lacrosse players are required to have balance, strength, and joint integrity in order to deliver and receive body checks. Overall, females tend to have less absolute strength than their male counterparts with 40 to 60 percent of the upper-body strength of men and 70 to 75 percent of the lower-body strength. (Ebben and Jensen 1998). However, relative strength (measuring lean body mass to strength and power ratios) are virtually identical in both female and male athletes (Ebben and Jensen 1998). Controlling the ball, making shots with tremendous velocity, resisting and administering stick checks, and maintaining positioning all require strength and stability, and virtually no physiological differences exist between men and women in the type of program used to enhance these characteristics.

Injury prevention is essential for both male and female players. However, female athletes are more susceptible to knee (typically anterior cruciate ligament) injuries, and specialized exercises may be needed to address this difference. Bilateral and unilateral strength-development exercises for both the knee and hip joints, plyometrics, and a lateral-movement training program are essential elements in preventing knee injuries because they improve connective tissue integrity, stability, and a player's ability to withstand the production of substantial force. A balanced movement-skill program focused on injury prevention should gradually increase the volume and intensity of lateral moves to allow for adaptation to rapid deceleration and change of direction.

In addition, efficient cycling of the training program allows for adequate recovery. Multiple weeks (usually three to five) of higher intensity workouts should be followed by a week of moderate to light activity to allow for recovery and adaptation. If planned recovery periods are not incorporated, breakdown may occur in the training cycle. Many coaches fail to factor mental or physical downtime into the off-season plan and therefore may not maximize the productivity of the training cycle. Although there are no guarantees that an athlete can avoid injury, a well-planned, comprehensive training program can certainly reduce the likelihood that injuries will occur.

With few exceptions, a well-designed training plan for a female athlete would be similar to that for a male athlete. Strength and power development, linear and lateral speed training, flexibility, conditioning, and recovery would differ in very few ways. The most significant difference would not be gender (i.e., male, female) but rather experience level (i.e., beginner, intermediate, advanced). The program for a beginner would be more simplistic than a program for someone who has more experience in off-field training. For this reason, this text treats the men's and women's game in like fashion when discussing training parameters and discusses any differences that are noteworthy.

TRAINING STRATEGIES

Before beginning to design the off-field workouts, it is crucial to understand the philosophical principles that support the training model. The perfect program exists only in theory. It is important to create the best possible model that addresses each athlete's specific needs. The foundations of training must be considered before beginning the planning phase. First, training must be approached in a comprehensive manner. This means that all elements necessary for competition—strength, power, speed, agility, conditioning, flexibility, and recovery—must be part of the program at some point during the training cycle (and may overlap). Neglecting some of these characteristics will produce less-than-optimal results.

Next, strength development is the key to any athletic endeavor. A stronger athlete is a better athlete. Without a foundation of strength, other areas of the training model may be compromised. For example, power gains will not be as substantial without a baseline level of strength that enables the speed component to transfer into practical skills. For most healthy athletes, the most effective way to develop strength is to perform closed kinetic chain, multijoint movements with free weights. Such movements develop joint integrity, flexibility, and specific movement patterns that are necessary for successful performance in lacrosse. In addition, resistance training must produce physiological symmetry. Athletes whose muscular structure is out of balance are less effective and may be more likely to sustain an injury. All training programs must include movements that promote joint and muscular balance from side to side, top to bottom, and left to right.

Third, all training activities must transfer to practical, lacrosse-specific skills. This is accomplished by incorporating proper linear and lateral speed mechanics (e.g., running technique) and sport-specific conditioning (e.g., speed endurance training) into the training program. Without these important links, the strength and power earned in the weight room cannot be effectively transferred to competition. A strong, powerful lacrosse player who lacks speed endurance may be effective for a short period of time but will eventually lose skill precision as the game enters the second half—when the outcome of most games is determined. A less experienced athlete in particular must learn to work on all facets of the game and not focus just on the elements that seem most appealing or comfortable.

Next, a comprehensive program must be implemented in a logical manner and broken into stages (cycles) that complement skill training and development. This type of strategic planning is known as periodization. Each stage, or cycle, must have clear objectives; the long-term goal is always improved performance. Recovery techniques must be consistently used alongside training. Proper nutrition, flexibility, and rest are crucial for success. These elements provide the means for supercompensation (i.e., elevating performance capabilities) and allow for overall growth and development.

The final and perhaps most important consideration is the manner in which training is conducted. Mental focus, determination, and willingness to break through physical barriers are characteristics that all great lacrosse players draw upon during a game. This same attitude must be present while preparing to play. Each workout must be conducted at a level of intensity that matches that of game day, and athletes should take on every training opportunity with a game-day mentality and the desire to overcome obstacles. Without these elements, training results may be lacking and the end result will be disappointing.

Lacrosse is a physically demanding, high-speed sport that requires each athlete to be physically and mentally strong, powerful, well conditioned, and disciplined. For players to best prepare to compete and succeed, off-field training must be incorporated into the training schedule, and training to develop strength, power, speed, agility, and conditioning along with lacrosse-specific skill development must take place simultaneously. There are no shortcuts! Off-the-field training requires a great deal of hard work; persistence in performing the workouts and having a logical, organized plan of attack are the most effective ways to attain goals. Each athlete must be committed to excellence, be patient in waiting for results, and—most important—*have fun* along the way!

Chapter 2

Testing and Evaluation

Lacrosse is a complex, multidimensional sport that requires the athlete to demonstrate proficiency in a wide range of performance categories. Offensive moves (e.g., dodging, setting picks, screening, stick handling, passing, shooting), defensive maneuvers (e.g., sliding, body checks), and transition execution (e.g., clearing, riding) all require the use of fundamental athletic skills that can be addressed through performance training. Speed (both linear and lateral) is required for playing all positions on the field and can mean the difference between making a play or coming up short. Rapid offensive flow, which is either initiated from the face-off or transitioned from the defensive end of the field, requires linear acceleration, deceleration, and rapid change of direction. On the defensive end, defensive man-to-man coverage, slides, and body checks require foot speed, lateral speed, and rapid deceleration. Goalie play involves hand–eye coordination, foot speed, lateral speed, balance, and body control.

Regardless of the position an individual plays, lacrosse requires strength (upper-body, lower-body, core, and grip), which is needed for stick handling, passing, shooting, checking, and clearing. Ultimately, however, lacrosse is a power sport. Power is the ability to generate force rapidly. Dodging, passing, and shooting all require explosive, powerful movements. Tying all of these elements together is conditioning, or the ability to move at a high rate of speed for as long as possible with minimal deterioration of skill.

Without adequate preparation of the cardiorespiratory system, all performance skills (e.g., power, strength, speed) are susceptible to decline. Conditioning is not only a product of genetic gifts but, more important, a product of hard work and commitment. Conditioning can be the great equalizer during competition. Teams with fewer natural talents and

THE PURPOSE OF TESTING

A number of tests may be performed, and coaches must consider many factors when deciding which tests are best for their team. What is the desired outcome of the training program? Which tests fit into the lacrosse system used? What equipment and facilities are available with the means of testing the event? For example, it would be difficult to test a 40-yard dash if a 40-yard course with sufficient room for deceleration at the end of the course is not available. How much time do the players have to devote to training considering academic responsibilities, other sport responsibilities, and organizational limitations such as league or conference rules? All of these factors must be considered when designing a training program and developing a testing baseline that best complements the program and its desired outcomes. Rather than administering numerous tests, which may not be manageable, coaches should consider narrowing the tests to a few that can be done efficiently and effectively and can be administered throughout the year. Tests must be both valid and reliable. Validity refers to the degree to which the test measures what it is intended to measure. Lacrosse-specific (or position-specific) skills are complex but may be tested via simple skills or movements that can predict performance on game day. For example, performance in a 40-yard sprint during the off-season is an excellent predictor of acceleration abilities on the playing field during the season. Reliability refers to the test producing consistent and repeatable results. In most cases, tests are reliable when testing protocols, equipment, test administrators, and techniques are consistent from one test period to the next. The specificity of testing is also important. Specificity refers to the ability of the test or training event to have a direct correlation to the demands of lacrosse. For example, the NFL agility drill is an excellent indicator of change-of-direction speed. There is a connection between an individual's time in that event and the athlete's ability to redirect during a lacrosse game. Training (and testing) specifically for this event will enable the athlete to realize improvement in the ability to execute the lateral speed demands of particular field positions. It is also crucial to appreciate the interdependence of one test event on another. In the example above, lateral movement skills (as measured by agility) are the by-product of an increase in lower-body strength (as measured by the squat test), core strength (as measured by the core hold test), explosive power (as measured by the broad jump), and improved running technique. This is one reason why it is so important to improve leg strength and power while working on technique to enable the athlete to transition weight-room gains with lacrosse skills.

physical gifts can gain a competitive advantage by outworking and outhustling others, and they do so by maintaining a higher level of conditioning. Success requires bringing all of these skills together in a cohesive manner. Deficiencies in any of these areas may result in underperformance or even injury.

Before planning a training regimen, each of these performance indicators should be assessed individually. Testing allows for honest, objective feedback about an athlete's strengths and areas that need to be improved. Initially, testing should be administered either at the end of the season or shortly before the off-season training cycle begins. This will help ensure that data are high quality and reliable. The results of testing can be used to measure the athlete's current fitness profile and to quantify progress throughout the training cycle.

In addition, coaches may use testing to assess the effectiveness of their program during the off-season training period. If certain weaknesses or specific trends in the team's performance are detected, the training program may be adjusted to address those deficiencies. For example, if periodic test results indicate that lateral speed is poor, the next phase of the training program can be adjusted to include more change-of-direction drills.

Coaches may also use testing to predict on-field performance. Results may be used to identify which athletes are best suited for certain positions and which may be the most successful at executing a specific skill. For example, an athlete with exceptional conditioning levels (speed endurance) may be more effective at playing a midfield position, which requires athletes to play in both the offensive and defensive zones. An athlete with excellent lateral movement skills, foot speed, and hand–eye coordination may be best suited for goalie—one of the most important positions on the field.

Test results may also be used for strategic planning and for making personnel decisions, and each coach should establish a system of performance standards that can be replicated with some degree of consistency throughout the training cycle. Regardless of the means used, testing should be fun, consistent, and beneficial for the athlete and, ultimately, for the team.

PERFORMANCE TESTING

Individual performance characteristics should be assessed at regular intervals during the year. Although testing is most often conducted during the off-season, there may be times when it is appropriate to test during the season (e.g., the conditioning test). Progress can be measured and the athlete can see tangible results—the benefits of hard work and consistency. Instead of choosing just one or two tests, the athlete should consider the entire range of testing categories, especially those in which he or she is deficient. Although it's not easy to face weaknesses, each athlete needs to address and overcome weaknesses in order to become a better player.

Flexibility Assessments

Flexibility is the ability to move joints effectively and efficiently through a full range of motion (ROM). Flexibility is a key element in determining joint ROM and the ability to execute skills such as acceleration and cutting. Significant range of motion in the hip flexors or hamstrings for example, will allow the athlete to move unimpeded through a greater range of motion and reduce the possibility of injury. This is especially important for lacrosse players during high-speed events such as sprinting, decelerating, checking and other contact opportunities. Athletes with functional flexibility—the ability to play with a lower center of gravity—can maintain leverage during body-contact situations.

Regardless of the physical demands of specific positions, a lacrosse player will benefit from including flexibility training in the routine. Flexibility can refer to two things: a muscle's ability to lengthen and shorten in response to the body's movements and a joint's ability to reach its full ROM. These factors affect a player's injury risk profile and influence performance. For example, greater hip mobility may contribute to lower accumulated stress, which may in turn reduce instances of groin and hip flexor strains. Performance may also suffer as a result of insufficient upper-body and torso flexibility. Limited shoulder ROM and back tightness may inhibit shot speed by decreasing a shooter's ability to maximize the wind-up before a shot, thus shortening the lever arm needed to generate maximal velocity. Another example is the need for a defender to maintain a low center of gravity when engaged with an attacker. Increased hip and hamstring ROM enable this function.

The most common flexibility tests are the sit-and-reach test and the single-leg hamstring flexibility test.

Sit-and-Reach Test

Due to the nature of the sport and the demands placed on the musculature of the low back and trunk in shooting, passing, stick handling, and face-offs or draw control, low-back stress is rather common. The sit-and-reach test is a basic, easy-to-administer assessment tool that effectively measures low-back and hamstring flexibility. This test provides feedback about the athlete's current status and indicates whether that area should be of particular focus for more extensive flexibility work.

Purpose

This test measures hamstring and low-back flexibility.

Equipment

8- to 12-inch (20-30 cm) box, ruler

Setup

Attach the ruler to the top of the box with 6 inches (15 cm) extending past the edge of the box and 6 inches extending across the top of the box (the 6-inch mark is at the base of the box). The ruler is used to measure the distance of the reach.

Procedure

- Sit with the knees straight and the feet approximately three to four inches apart (figure 2.1*a*).
- Place one hand on top of the other.
- Reach as far as possible onto the box, extending the hands and holding for a brief moment (figure 2.1*b*). Two attempts may be given.

Results

The norms for the sit-and-reach test are provided in table 2.1. Measure from the edge of the box as the zero mark. A positive (+) score means that the athlete was able to reach beyond the end of the box (past the toes) and a negative score (-) means that the athlete was unable to reach the box.

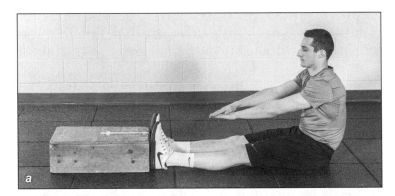

Figure 2.1   Sit-and-reach test.

Table 2.1 Sit-and-Reach Test Norms

	Male	Female
Excellent	>+6 in.	>+6 in.
Good	+3 in. to +6 in.	+3 in. to +6 in.
Average	0 in. to +3 in.	0 in. to +3 in.
Fair	-3 in. to 0 in.	-3 in. to 0 in.
Poor	<-3 in.	<-3 in.

Single-Leg Hamstring Flexibility Test

Hamstring flexibility is an area of concern for many lacrosse players. Given the amount of stress typically absorbed by this muscle group, it is crucial to have sufficient ROM. As in other field sports (e.g., soccer, field hockey) that require continuous movement up and down the field, hamstring strength, endurance, and flexibility play an important role. Another test of flexibility is the single-leg hamstring test. This test will help analyze hamstring flexibility without involvement of the low back. It can also be beneficial in the assessment of bilateral differences between the right and left legs. Such imbalances may contribute to the likelihood of injuries and can be corrected with additional flexibility training if necessary.

Purpose

This exercise measures unilateral hamstring ROM.

Equipment

Dowel or yardstick

Setup

The subject lies supine on a flat surface with the arms at the sides, both knees fully extended, and toes dorsiflexed, keeping the hips, shoulders, and head on the ground.

Procedure

- The subject slowly raises the test leg as high as possible while keeping the other leg fully extended, and the knee and heel in contact with the floor.
- The tester places one end of the dowel in the center of the hip joint and the other at the level of the center of the knee joint. The subject must keep the hips in contact with the floor at all times.
- The tester may allow for three attempts and accept the best result.
- The subject repeats the test with the opposite leg.

Results

The norms for the single-leg hamstring flexibility test are provided in table 2.2.

Table 2.2   Single-Leg Hamstring Flexibility Test Norms

	Male	Female
Excellent	>120°	>120°
Good	90°-120°	90°-120°
Average	90°	90°
Fair	70°-90°	70°-90°
Poor	<70°	<70°

Strength Assessments

Lacrosse players must be strong and able to exert force while executing the sometimes complex skills of the game. Strength is the maximum force a muscle or muscle group can generate at a specified velocity. It is the basis of all athletic development (e.g., speed, power, injury prevention) and is a contributing factor in most athletic skills. Although important to all athletes, hip strength relative to knee stability is particularly important for females with regard to preventing injury to the anterior cruciate ligament.

Upper-body strength is necessary for stick handling, shot and stick control, and body checking. Lower-body strength is required for rapid acceleration, deceleration, and maintaining position during physical engagements and serves as the base for explosive stick handling. Equally important is the role of strength in injury prevention. Strength provides joint stability during cuts and allows players to withstand the rigors of contact in order to protect themselves. Female athletes, who on average are more susceptible to knee injuries, must have substantial strength and joint integrity to prevent knee injuries.

The most common strength tests include the bench press test, the back squat test, the pull-up test, the sit-up test, the core hold test, and the push-up test.

DETERMINING YOUR ONE-REPETITION OR MULTIPLE-REPETITION MAXIMUM

When conducting free-weight, maximal-effort tests, it is important to know how these tests should be conducted. In the back squat test and bench press test, for example, a one-repetition maximum (1RM) or multiple-repetition maximum can be used. A 1RM tends to be most accurate but is not recommended for beginners, who are not prepared for handling maximal loads. A multiple-repetition maximum is appropriate for beginners as well as experienced lifters.

With the following simple calculation, a multiple-repetition maximum can be converted to a 1RM (Epley 1985):

$$\text{weight} \times \text{reps} \times .0333 + \text{weight} = \text{estimated 1RM}$$

This calculation is important when determining training intensity during the program design phase because percentages of 1RM will determine training weights. Without knowing the 1RM, either actual or estimated, this will not be possible.

When testing bodyweight events such as pull-ups, push-ups, sit-ups, and others, the focus is strength endurance so using a 1RM is unnecessary. When administering these tests, a multiple-repetition maximum (to muscular failure) is recommended.

For all assessment tools, a period of training acclimation should precede testing. For simple exercises such as pull-ups, sit-ups, and push-ups, a pretraining period of a week or two should be sufficient. For more complex movements such as the back squat, a longer period of acclimation (two to three weeks to two to three months, depending on technical adaptation) may be required. In all tests, the athlete's safety should be of primary concern. At no time should poorly executed technique be accepted. To protect the health and well-being of the athlete, the test administrator should be mindful of perfect execution and should not accept substandard test performance.

Bench Press Test

The bench press is a tool for measuring upper-body strength. Although the movement itself has limited application to lacrosse, it is often used as an indicator of shoulder, triceps, upper-back, and chest strength. Its importance should not be overestimated because many other tests (e.g., vertical jump, back squat, and 10-yard sprint) are more specific to lacrosse. However, the bench press is widely known to many coaches and the equipment is fairly accessible.

Purpose

This test measures shoulder, triceps, and upper-back strength.

Equipment

Bench, Olympic barbell, plates, collars

Setup

Lie faceup on a bench. A spotter should be on hand to assist. Before testing, perform 2 to 4 sets of 1 to 6 reps each as a warm-up.

Procedure

- Grasp the bar with a grip slightly wider than shoulder-width apart and remove the bar from the rack.
- Hold the bar with the arms in an extended position (figure 2.2a).
- Lower the bar to the chest (figure 2.2b).
- Touch the bar to the chest and return to the extended position in a controlled manner.
- A 1RM or multiple-repetition maximum may be used. For multiple-repetition maximums, a range of 2 to 10 reps is recommended.

Results

The norms for the bench press test are provided in table 2.3.

Figure 2.2   Bench press test.

Table 2.3 Bench Press Test Norms

	Male	Female
Excellent	120% body weight	Body weight+
Good	100%-120% body weight	85%-100% body weight
Average	Body weight	70%-85% body weight
Fair	80%-100% body weight	55%-70% body weight
Poor	<80% body weight	<55% body weight

Back Squat Test

One of the best indicators of lower-body and core strength is the back squat. This king of exercises is a great way to assess the strength and flexibility of all lacrosse players, regardless of position. A word of caution is necessary before moving forward: Technical precision must be employed when conducting this test. The positioning of the feet along with having the correct hip and knee angles is crucial. Maintaining a tight back and core is essential to maximizing the benefits of this movement. If any concern exists about an athlete's technique, consider postponing the test until the athlete demonstrates proficiency.

Purpose

This test measures hamstring, quad, glute, low-back, and core strength.

Equipment

Squat rack, Olympic barbell, plates, collars

Setup

Stand in front of a bar as it is secure in a squat rack. A spotter should be on hand to assist. Before testing, the athlete should perform 3 to 5 warm-up sets consisting of 1 to 6 reps each.

Procedure

- Using a grip that is slightly wider than shoulder width, place the bar behind the shoulders approximately 2 inches (5 cm) below the top of the trapezius muscle, and lift the bar off of the rack (figure 2.3a). The feet should be slightly wider than shoulder width and may be turned outward at a 30-degree angle.
- Lower the hips back, keeping the shins perpendicular to the floor and the back tight at all times. At no time should the knees turn inward toward the center of the body. In the bottom position, the hamstrings are at least parallel to the floor (figure 2.3b). Keep the chest up, back flat, and weight back on the heels.
- At the bottom of the movement (when the hamstrings are at least parallel to the floor), drive the bar upward, raising the hips and

Figure 2.3 Back squat test.

shoulders at the same rate of speed. If the hips accelerate faster than the shoulders, more stress will be placed on the low back and the athlete may lose proper positioning.

- The back should remain tight throughout the movement, with the head and eyes focused on a point straight in front of the lifter.
- Be sure to keep the knees aligned with the feet throughout the descent and ascent. The knees should never rotate inward at any time.
- The athlete should finish the movement by returning to the start (standing) position.
- A one-rep maximum or multiple-repetition maximum may be used. For multiple-rep maxes a 2- to 10-rep range is recommended.

Results

The norms for the back squat test are provided in table 2.4.

Table 2.4   Back Squat Test Norms

	Male	Female
Excellent	>150% body weight	>110% body weight
Good	100%-125% body weight	90%-110% body weight
Average	Body weight	70%-90% body weight
Fair	75%-100% body weight	50%-70% body weight
Poor	<75% body weight	<50% body weight

Pull-Up Test

The pull-up test is an excellent tool for identifying upper-body strength, particularly in the upper back, forearms, and hands. This rigorous event will identify the athlete's ability to handle his or her body weight for maximal reps. As a strength endurance assessment, it has a place in almost every lacrosse player's training and testing routine. This test may be particularly challenging for female athletes. In most cases, however, patient, consistent hard work will produce substantial improvement over time.

Purpose

This test measures shoulder, upper-back, forearm, and grip strength.

Equipment

Pull-up bar

Setup

Hold the bar with the palms facing up, down, or in and the arms in an extended position with the feet off the ground (figure 2.4a).

Figure 2.4 Pull-up test.

Procedure

- Keeping the body straight and avoiding any swinging motion, pull the body up and raise the chin above the bar (figure 2.4*b*).
- Return to the starting position and come to a complete stop.
- Pause at the bottom of the movement and repeat until failure.

Results

The norms for the pull-up test are provided in table 2.5.

Table 2.5　Pull-Up Test Norms

	Male	Female
Excellent	12+	5+
Good	8-12	4
Average	4-8	2
Fair	0-4	1
Poor	0	0

Sit-Up Test

Core strength is important in all facets of lacrosse performance. Contact, stick control, and linear and lateral movement all require stability of the core region to properly execute the skill. Without this stabilization, conduction of force through the supporting core musculature will be diminished. The sit-up test is a classic, easy-to-administer event that can be conducted with one participant or with an entire team.

Purpose

This test assesses core and hip flexor strength and endurance.

Equipment

Solid, comfortable floor area

Setup

Lie on the floor with the knees bent 90 degrees and the feet flat on the floor (figure 2.5*a*). The feet may be held down by a spotter. Place the hands either behind the head or crossed on the chest, and rest the shoulder blades on the floor.

Procedure

- Sit up until the elbows touch the knees (figure 2.5b). If the hands are behind the head, the hands should remain clasped throughout the test.
- Return to the starting position.
- Repeat for one minute and avoid bouncing on the floor. The tester (or spotter) should count all of the reps completed in the time interval allotted. Incomplete reps should be discounted.

Results

The norms for the sit-up test are provided in table 2.6.

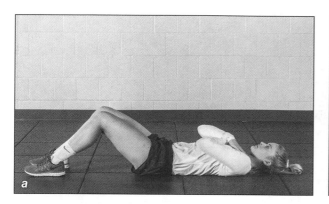 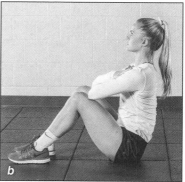

Figure 2.5   Sit-up test.

Table 2.6   Sit-Up Test Norms

	Male	Female
Excellent	60+	50+
Good	50-60	40-50
Average	40-50	30-40
Fair	30-40	20-30
Poor	<30	<20

Core Hold Test

Core strength and stability play a crucial role in many lacrosse skills. For many lacrosse players, the ability to stabilize the core for an extended period of time may be deficient. In the core hold test, the low back, abs, and shoulders are tested simultaneously. This test complements the training of core strength and stability which is a mainstay of many training programs.

Purpose

This test measures core strength and endurance and shoulder stability.

Equipment

Solid, comfortable floor area

Setup

Assume a plank position with the elbows under the shoulders, the feet extended, and the shoulders, hips, and ankles aligned. A position in which the elbows are bent at 90 degrees and the athlete is supported on his forearms is also acceptable.

Procedure

- Tighten the stomach muscles to help support the hips (figure 2.6).

- Maintain this position without lifting or lowering the hips until failure or a specified length of time. Generally, a one- or two-minute time period is recommended.

Figure 2.6   Core hold test.

- The test administrator should observe the athlete and check for skill deterioration. This includes an inability to maintain alignment or favoring one side over the other. The administrator may give one warning when skill begins to deteriorate; the test officially ends when the second warning is given.

Results

The norms for the two-minute core hold test are provided in table 2.7.

Table 2.7   Two-Minute Core Hold Test Norms

	Male	Female
Excellent	2:00	2:00
Good	1:30-2:00	1:30-2:00
Average	1:00-1:30	1:00-1:30
Fair	:30-1:00	:30-1:00
Poor	<:30	<:30

Push-Up Test

Upper-body strength is required in many lacrosse movements. The push-up test is a great way to assess the strength of the shoulders, chest, triceps, upper back, and core for all players, particularly beginners, younger athletes, or those lacking equipment. For intermediate or advanced athletes, this is a good way to evaluate upper-body strength endurance.

Purpose

This test measures shoulder, upper-back, core, and triceps strength and endurance.

Equipment

Solid, comfortable floor area

Setup

Assume a plank position with the hands slightly wider than shoulder width and the feet extended (figure 2.7a).

Procedure

- Lower the chest so that the bend of the elbows exceeds 45 degrees (figure 2.7b).
- A partner may hold a fist on the floor. The subject should lower the chin until it touches the top of the partner's fist.
- Press up and return to the fully extended position, pausing for one second at the top of the movement to ensure proper lockout of the elbows.

Figure 2.7 Push-up test.

- The test administrator should pay attention to skill technique to ensure validity. Reps in which the athlete does not extend the elbows or bend at the bottom below 90 degrees should be discounted.
- Repeat until failure or for a specified length of time.

Results

The norms for the push-up test are provided in table 2.8.

Table 2.8 Push-Up Test Norms

	Male	Female
Excellent	50+	25+
Good	40-50	20-25
Average	30-40	15-20
Fair	20-30	10-15
Poor	<20	<10

Power Assessments

Power is the ability to exert maximum muscular force in a brief period of time. The ability to accelerate, decelerate, change directions, shoot, and pass requires the expression of explosive power. Body movements in space, shots, transitions, and physical contact are all performed at maximum velocity. Players and teams that have the power advantage tend to be the most successful.

Because power is such an integral component of the game, testing and ultimately training for power are very important to a lacrosse player. The tests recommended are generally accepted as measurements of explosive potential. The most common power tests include the vertical jump test, the standing broad jump test, and the medicine ball toss.

Vertical Jump Test

Purpose

This test measures lower-body explosiveness in a vertical plane.

Equipment

Vertec testing device or wall, chalk, tape measure

Setup

Before testing the jump, the test administrator measures the athlete's reach capability. The athlete stands directly under the Vertec device with the ankles together, knees straight, and one arm fully extended overhead. At all times, the shoulder should be fully extended and the elbow straight. The administrator measures the distance from the floor to the top of the extended fingertips.

Procedure

- To measure the jump, the athlete stands close to a wall or Vertec device with the dominant hand closest to the wall or Vertec device.
- From a stationary position (feet cannot move or shift in the start position prior to take off) (figure 2.8a), the athlete jumps as high as possible and touches the wall or Vertec (figure 2.8b).

Figure 2.8 Vertical jump test.

- After three to five attempts, the administrator measures the distance between the floor and the Vertec or chalk mark on the wall. The vertical jump is the difference between the height of the jump and the height of the reach.

Results

The norms for the vertical jump test are provided in table 2.9.

Table 2.9 Vertical Jump Test Norms

	Male	Female
Excellent	26+ in. (60+ cm)	20+ in. (45+ cm)
Good	23-26 in. (55-60 cm)	18-20 in. (40-45 cm)
Average	20-23 in. (50-55 cm)	16-18 in. (35-40 cm)
Fair	17-20 in. (45-50 cm)	14-16 in. (30-35 cm)
Poor	<17 in. (<45 cm)	<14 in. (<30 cm)

Standing Broad Jump Test

The standing broad jump is an assessment of lower-body power. Although this test is used much like a vertical jump, the broad jump may be easier to administer because it requires less equipment.

Purpose

This test measures lower-body power in a horizontal plane.

Equipment

Tape measure, yardstick

Setup

Stand with the toes behind a line and the feet shoulder-width apart (figure 2.9a).

Procedure

- Jump as far as possible, landing with both feet and without any shuffling or falling forward or backward (figure 2.9b).
- Stand up without moving the feet.
- The test administrator should measure from the starting line to the back of the heels.

Results

The norms for the standing broad jump test are provided in table 2.10.

Figure 2.9　Standing broad jump test.

Table 2.10　Standing Broad Jump Test Norms

	Male	Female
Excellent	>96 in. (>245 cm)	>78 in. (>198 cm)
Good	90-96 in. (228-245 cm)	72-78 in. (182-198 cm)
Average	84-90 in. (213-228 cm)	66-72 in. (167-182 cm)
Fair	78-84 in. (198-213 cm)	60-66 in. (152-167 cm)
Poor	<78 in. (<198 cm)	<60 in. (<152 cm)

Medicine Ball Overhead Toss Test

The medicine ball overhead toss measures upper-body explosive power. In lacrosse, upper-body power is crucial for stick handling, shooting, and passing.

Purpose

This test measures upper-body power.

Equipment

Tape measure, 4- to 15-pound (2-7 kg) medicine ball (weight depends on test population)

Setup

Stand with toes behind a line with the feet shoulder-width apart. Hold the ball with the hands on the sides of the ball, just slightly behind the center of the ball.

Figure 2.10   Medicine ball overhead toss test.

Procedure

- Bring the ball behind the head (figure 2.10a).
- Throw the ball forward as far as possible (figure 2.10b). Do not step forward over the line after the ball is released.
- The test administrator measures the distance between the standing line and the point where the ball touches the floor.
- Two to three attempts are permitted.

Results

The norms for the medicine ball overhead toss test are provided in table 2.11. These numbers can vary depending on the size of the medicine ball.

Table 2.11   Medicine Ball Overhead Toss Test Norms

	Male	Female
Excellent	>30 ft.	>25 ft.
Good	26-30 ft.	21-25 ft.
Average	22-26 ft.	17-21 ft.
Fair	18-22 ft.	13-17 ft.
Poor	<18 ft.	<13 ft.

Speed Assessments

Speed is the ability to perform a movement in as short a time period as possible. Dodging, chasing ground balls, executing a clear, and playing effective defense are all expressions of speed. Lacrosse is a game of speed and, in particular, acceleration because most skills are executed within a limited (<30 yards or meters) area and players frequently change the direction of movement. The ability to start with a high velocity and maintain speed (either from a stationary position or in transition) is one of the most valued skills in the sport. In women's lacrosse, the free position shot relies on the shooter's ability to accelerate quickly and shoot before being covered by the defense.

When performing a movement analysis of lacrosse, it quickly becomes apparent that quickness in a confined area and proficiency in short bursts of speed are crucial. On both ends of the field, explosive, powerful movements define the game. When discussing speed assessment, two components must be distinguished. The first and most important requirement is acceleration—the ability to burst from either a stationary position or a slow tempo in just a few strides. The goal is to be as close to 100 percent of maximum speed capacity in as few strides as possible. An example of this is a defender using sudden, explosive acceleration to maintain position on an attacker in order to close the passing and shooting lanes in just a few steps. The second component of speed is top-end speed—the maximum velocity a runner can attain without regard for distance traveled. For example, a midfielder who has won a ground ball opportunity deep in the defensive end tries to push the ball upfield into the offensive zone. In that time, he has likely attained maximum-velocity speed in an attempt to move the ball without having to decelerate or redirect. Although not utilized as often during competition (most often during transition), top-end speed has an important role in the testing and training process.

The most common linear speed tests are the 10-yard sprint test and the 40-yard sprint test.

10-Yard Sprint Test

The 10-yard sprint test measures linear acceleration skills from a stationary start position. In lacrosse, the ability to accelerate from a stationary start in an area of short yardage is crucial for all positions.

Purpose

This test measures linear acceleration.

Equipment

Stopwatch, cones

Setup

The runner begins in a stationary position behind the starting line and holds the position for one second. The feet should be staggered, with one foot ahead of the other, and slightly less than shoulder-width apart.

Procedure

- On command, the runner takes off into a sprint and the timer starts the stopwatch.
- The timer stops the stopwatch when the runner's hips pass through the 10-yard mark. Allow 2 to 4 attempts to achieve the best score.

Results

The norms for the 10-yard sprint test are provided in table 2.12.

Table 2.12   '10-Yard Sprint Test Norms

	Male	Female
Excellent	<1.75 sec	<1.85 sec
Good	1.75-1.80 sec	1.85-1.90 sec
Average	1.80-1.85 sec	1.90-1.95 sec
Fair	1.85-1.90 sec	1.95-2.00 sec
Poor	>1.90 sec	>2.00 sec

40-Yard Sprint Test

The 40-yard sprint test is a great way to measure both acceleration and top-end speed. This distance is particularly relevant for midfielders because they must transition from one end of the field to the other throughout the game. In the United States, many athletes (regardless of sport) are familiar with this test and use it to compare themselves with other lacrosse players or athletes in other sports.

Purpose

This test measures acceleration and top-end speed.

Equipment

Stopwatch, cones

Setup

The runner begins in a stationary position behind the starting line and holds the position for one second. In the start position, the feet should be staggered with one foot ahead of the other and slightly closer than shoulder-width apart.

Procedure

- On command, the runner takes off into a sprint and the timer starts the stopwatch.
- The timer stops the stopwatch when the runner's hips pass the 40-yard mark.

Results

The norms for the 40-yard sprint test are provided in table 2.13.

Table 2.13 40-Yard Sprint Test Norms

	Male	Female
Excellent	<4.60 sec	<5.20 sec
Good	4.60-4.80 sec	5.20-5.40 sec
Average	4.80-5.0 sec	5.40-5.60 sec
Fair	5.0-5.20 sec	5.60-5.80 sec
Poor	>5.20 sec	>5.80 sec

Agility Assessments

Agility is the ability to perform multidirectional movement patterns without a decrease in speed and reactivity to external stimuli (either fixed or dynamic). This requires the synthesis of the neurological system and muscular system in a rapid manner to transition linear acceleration to multiplane movement patterns.

Lacrosse is a game of multidirectional movements that require significant speed, balance, and body control. For the skilled lacrosse player, the ability to decelerate rapidly is the most important factor in change-of-direction skill. Movement must be precise and fluid and performed at a consistently high rate of speed. The most successful players are those who can do so while maintaining offensive or defensive position, often through a congested area.

A well-prepared, organized system of training and testing will help prepare athletes for success. Although a number of drills and tests can be used to assess an athlete's ability to change direction, I focus on just a few. The most common agility tests are the Illinois agility test, the NFL agility test, and the 60-yard shuttle test.

Illinois Agility Test

The Illinois agility test measures acceleration, agility, and foot speed in a single drill. Although not as commonly used as other change-of-direction tests (e.g., the NFL agility drill), it is very applicable to lacrosse.

Purpose

This test measures acceleration, quickness, and agility.

Equipment

Cones, stopwatch, tape measure

Setup

The cones should be set up using the measurements provided in figure 2.11. Four cones are placed on the corners of a 5- × 10-meter rectangle. Four additional cones are placed in a straight line that runs through the center of the rectangle. Starting from the bottom/center, the four cones are placed 3.3 meters apart with one cone on the top line and another on the bottom line of the rectangle. The runner begins in a stationary position behind the starting mark and holds the position for one second. An additional element of specificity would be to have the athletes carry their lacrosse stick while performing this test.

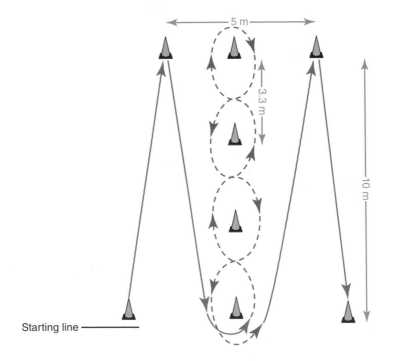

Figure 2.11   Illinois agility test.

Procedure

- On command, the runner takes off into a sprint and the timer starts the stopwatch.
- The runner sprints 10 meters, touches the line at the first cone with the left foot, sprints to the first of the middle four cones, and zigzags between them.
- Once the last cone has been circled, the runner runs to the top right corner of the box, touches the line at the first cone with the right foot, and sprints through the finish line.
- The timer stops the stopwatch when the runner's hips cross the finish line.

Results

The norms for the Illinois agility test are provided in table 2.14.

Table 2.14   Illinois Agility Test Norms

	Male	Female
Excellent	<11.90 sec	<12.50 sec
Good	11.90-12.20 sec	12.50-12.75 sec
Average	12.20-12.35 sec	12.75-13 sec
Fair	12.35-12.50 sec	13-13.25 sec
Poor	>12.50 sec	>13.25 sec

NFL Agility Test

The NFL agility test is a measurement of lateral speed. It requires sudden acceleration and rapid redirection. This test measures the athlete's ability to change direction pushing off with the right foot as well as the left foot.

Purpose

This test measures lateral speed and quickness.

Equipment

Cones, stopwatch, tape measure, athletic (or other clearly visible) tape if the field surface is not marked with lines that are 5 yards apart.

Setup

Three cones are placed in a straight line 5 yards apart from one another. The length of the course is 10 yards (figure 2.12). The runner begins by straddling the middle line with the feet shoulder-width apart and placing one hand on the center line. Hold the position for one second.

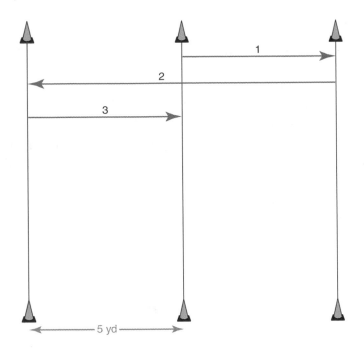

Figure 2.12 NFL agility test.

Procedure

- On command, the runner takes off into a sprint (either to the right or left) and the timer starts the stopwatch.
- The runner sprints 5 yards, touches the line with the outside hand, sprints across to the far line, touches with the opposite hand, and sprints through the start line, which becomes the finish line.
- The timer stops the stopwatch when the runner's hips cross the finish line. If the runner fails to touch any of the lines, the test is discounted. Two to three attempts may be given.

Results

The norms for the NFL agility test are provided in table 2.15.

Table 2.15   NFL Agility Test Norms

	Male	Female
Excellent	<4.40 sec	<4.75 sec
Good	4.40-4.60 sec	4.75-4.90 sec
Average	4.60-4.80 sec	4.90-5.05 sec
Fair	4.80-5.00 sec	5.05-5.20 sec
Poor	>5.00 sec	>5.20 sec

60-Yard Shuttle Test

The 60-yard shuttle test measures acceleration, deceleration, and agility. As the athlete builds speed with increasingly longer distances, rapidly decelerating and redirecting becomes more challenging.

Purpose

This test assesses acceleration, agility, balance, and body control.

Equipment

Cones, stopwatch, tape measure, athletic (or other clearly visible) tape if the field surface is not marked with lines that are 5 yards apart.

Setup

Four cones are placed in a straight line 5 yards apart. The total distance of the course is 15 yards (figure 2.13). The runner assumes a stationary position behind the starting line and holds it for one second.

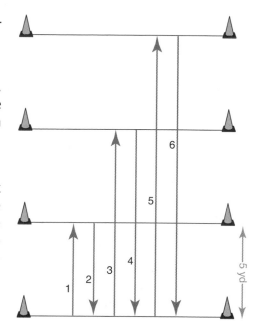

Figure 2.13   60-yard shuttle test.

Procedure

- On command, the runner takes off into a sprint and the timer starts the stopwatch.

- The runner sprints to the 5-yard line and touches a line that extends from the center of the cone with a hand (runner's choice). The runner then sprints back to the starting line and touches the start line with the opposite hand. The runner then repeats this movement pattern for 10 and 15 yards. The event ends when the runner has touched at the 15-yard mark and finishes through the start line.

- The timer stops the stopwatch when the runner's hips cross the finish line. If the runner does not touch any of the lines with the proper hand, the test is discounted. Two to three attempts may be given.

Results

The norms for the 60-yard shuttle test are provided in table 2.16.

Table 2.16   60-Yard Shuttle Test Norms

	Male	Female
Excellent	<11.80 sec	<13.50 sec
Good	11.80-12.00 sec	13.50-13.70 sec
Average	12.00-12.20 sec	13.70-13.90 sec
Fair	12.20-12.40 sec	13.90-14.10 sec
Poor	>12.40 sec	>14.10 sec

Conditioning Assessments

Conditioning is the ability to sustain speed and agility over the course of a game and season. Lacrosse is a sophisticated, multidimensional sport that requires the efficient integration of all three energy systems: the aerobic energy system (continuous activity lasting longer than 3 minutes), the ATP-PC system (events lasting less than 30 seconds) and the lactic acid energy system or LA (sustained activity lasting between 30 seconds and 3 minutes). The primary purpose of cardiovascular conditioning in lacrosse is to prevent skills from deteriorating throughout the course of a game. In addition, because fatigue is the number one cause of injury, a well-conditioned lacrosse player is less likely to be injured. Finally, a lacrosse player with a well-developed conditioning base can be mentally tough and work through difficult situations more easily. A well-planned, multiphased program enables the athlete to gradually adapt to conditioning stresses and be prepared for the challenges of the in-season.

One of the most valuable skills for a lacrosse player is the ability to maintain speed and agility throughout the course of a game. Given the intense tempo of the game, fatigue can set in rapidly and players may lose their concentration and focus. To combat this, players should follow a well-planned, comprehensive conditioning schedule that works all three energy systems: aerobic, ATP-PC, and LA. The primary focus should be on the ATP-PC system, particularly as the season nears and the energy demands become more specific. Although the ATP-PC system is the primary means of energy utilization on game day, the ideal lacrosse conditioning state is best acquired after a comprehensive preparation period that includes aerobic and LA training as well.

Speed endurance training involves developing a strong mental state along with a strong physiological state. A lacrosse player's fitness level stems not just from innate skill or talent but also from desire and hard work. Players and teams that commit to the highest level of physical conditioning tend to have a competitive edge in the latter stages of the game and can tolerate higher levels of lactic acid buildup for a longer period of time.

Some examples of lacrosse conditioning tests include the repeat shuttles test, the 3×300-yard sprint test, the 16×100-meter sprint test, and the 1-mile run test.

Repeat Shuttles Test

Repeat shuttles are a simple way to measure conditioning primarily in the ATP-PC and glycolytic energy systems. Although the test area remains fixed at 25-yard intervals, the distance for each repetition may be manipulated and typically ranges from 25 to 300 yards.

Purpose

This test measures speed endurance following conditioning sessions from the ATP-PC and LA energy systems.

Equipment

Cones, stopwatch, tape measure

Setup

Three or four cones should be placed along a line with another three to four cones placed on a parallel line 25 yards away (figure 2.14). The runner assumes a stationary position behind the starting line and holds the position for one second.

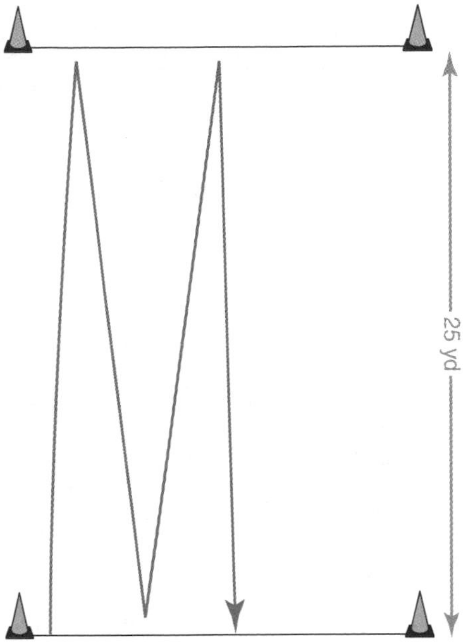

Procedure

- On command, the runner takes off into a sprint and the timer starts the stopwatch.

Figure 2.14 Repeat shuttles test.

- The runner sprints the prescribed distance, touches a second line with the foot, and returns to the starting line.
- Repeat each rep for the prescribed number of sets in the allotted time.
- This test is pass or fail based on whether the athlete makes it to the finish line before the prescribed time is up. If an athlete fails to touch a line, the rep is discounted and (if running with a team) the entire team should repeat the rep.

Results

The norms for the repeat shuttles test are provided in table 2.17.

The first column is the distance required for each rep. The second column is the number of reps performed at that distance. The third and fourth columns show the time to complete each rep for male and female athletes, respectively. Because it is difficult to time 25 yards, *full speed* means that the athlete should run as fast as possible for that interval (we sometimes tell athletes to run at game speed) with no definitive time limit.

Table 2.17   Repeat Shuttles Test Norms

Distance	Reps	Male	Female
25 yd	2	Full speed	Full speed
50 yd	2	<:10	<:11
100 yd	2	<:21	<:24
200 yd	1	<:45	<:51
100 yd	2	<:21	<:24
50 yd	2	<:10	<:11
25 yd	2	Full speed	Full speed

Coaches should be sure to address the recovery interval, which is typically a 1:3 work:rest ratio. This means that for every second of running, 3 seconds of recovery time is allowed. For example, if the run time is 10 seconds, the recovery interval between reps is 30 seconds.

3 × 300-Yard Sprint Test

The 3 × 300-yard sprint test assesses the athlete's glycolytic energy system. This test is particularly useful during the middle or late preseason as athletes begin final preparations for team practice.

Purpose

This test measures conditioning in the LA energy system.

Equipment

Cones, stopwatch, tape measure

Setup

Set up two lines with cones 50 yards apart (figure 2.15). The runner assumes a stationary position behind the starting line and holds it for one second.

Procedure

- On command, the runner takes off into a sprint and the timer starts the stopwatch.

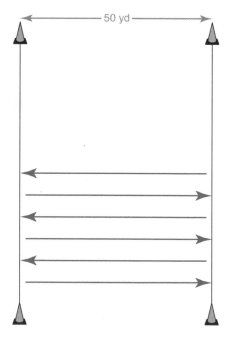

Figure 2.15   3 × 300-yard sprint test.

- The runner sprints a 50-yard distance, touches a second line with the foot, and returns to the starting line. The runner then repeats the sprint twice for a total of three lengths (300 yards).
- This test is pass or fail based on whether the athlete makes it to the finish line before the prescribed time is up. If the runner fails to touch any of the lines, the rep will be discounted. If running with a team, the team should be asked to repeat the rep for the offending individual.

Results

The norms for the 3 × 300-yard sprint test are less than 66 seconds for males and less than 72 seconds for females.

16 × 100-Meter Sprint Test

The 16 × 100-meter sprint test assesses speed endurance conditioning, particularly in the ATP-PC energy system. This test is a great way to get players on the field and build camaraderie before in-season practices begin.

Purpose

This test measures speed endurance, primarily in the ATP-PC energy system.

Equipment

Cones, stopwatch, tape measure

Setup

Three or four cones are placed along a line with another three to four cones placed along a parallel line 100 meters (110 yards) away. The runner assumes a stationary position behind the starting line and holds it for one second.

Procedure

- On command, the runner takes off into a sprint and the timer starts the stopwatch.
- The runner sprints a 100-meter distance in the prescribed time.
- The runner rests for 45 seconds and then repeats for the prescribed number of reps.

Results

The norms for the 16 × 100-meter sprint test are less than 17 seconds per 100 meters for males and less than 19 seconds per 100 meters for females.

Distance Run Test

The aim of this test is to complete a one-, 1.5-, or 2-mile course in the shortest possible time.

Purpose

This test measures the athlete's aerobic capacity or ability to resist high lactate levels.

Equipment

Cones, stopwatch, Olympic track

Setup

All participants line up behind the starting line.

Procedure

- On command, the runners take off and the timer starts the stopwatch.
- The athletes run at their own pace until they have completed the prescribed distance.
- This test is pass or fail based on whether the athlete makes it to the finish line before the prescribed time is up or shows improvement from a previous one-mile run test.

Results

The norms for the one-mile run test are less than 6 minutes 30 seconds for males and less than 7 minutes 15 seconds for females.

TEST ADMINISTRATION

Testing should be administered throughout the training cycle, especially during the off-season. If testing is administered infrequently, deficiencies in the workout plan may not be detected until it's too late. On the other hand, if testing is administered too frequently, significant results may not occur because the athlete is constantly preparing to test instead of taking time to train. The key is timing. Typically, in a 12-week cycle, testing would be conducted before the start (week 1), after week 6, and then again at the conclusion of the 12-week cycle. The timetable would look like this:

Before week 1: Pretest

Weeks 1 to 6: Training

After week 6: Testing (quiz)

Weeks 6 to 12: Training

After week 12: Testing (final exam)

Testing should include a wide range of categories (strength, speed, power, flexibility, agility, and conditioning) and involve some but not all of the tests mentioned. Testing too many events will detract from the actual program and may be too time consuming. Typically, one test is selected from each category and is used at the beginning, middle, and end of the cycle. Decide which tests are most appropriate and stick with them. The only exception might be conditioning. An emphasis on LA conditioning may be more appropriate at week 6 (e.g., 3 × 300-yard sprint test), when more LA development might be appropriate. As the season nears and the ATP-PC system becomes more of a priority in the training calendar, a more appropriate test might be a speed endurance test such as the repeat shuttles test.

Table 2.18 provides a sample test for a 14-year-old male with no training experience, and table 2.19 provides a sample test for a 17-year-old female with 2 to 3 years of training experience. Note that both tests include a wide range of events that encompass most of the test categories but that

Table 2.18 Sample Test for a 14-Year-Old Male With No Training Experience

Week 1	Flexibility	Sit-and-reach test
	Upper-body strength	Pull-up test
	Power	Standing broad jump test
	Speed	10-yard sprint test
	Agility	NFL Agility test
	Core strength	Sit-up test
Week 6	Flexibility	Sit-and-reach test
	Upper-body strength	Pull-up test
	Power	Standing broad jump test
	Speed	10-yard sprint test
	Agility	NFL Agility test
	Core strength	Sit-up test
	Conditioning	1-mile run test
Week 12	Flexibility	Sit-and-reach test
	Upper-body strength	Pull-up test
	Power	Standing broad jump test
	Speed	10-yard sprint test
	Agility	NFL Agility test
	Core strength	Sit-up test
	Conditioning	Repeat shuttles test

Table 2.19 Sample Test for a 17-Year-Old Female With 2 to 3 Years of Training Experience

Week 1	Flexibility	Sit-and-reach test
	Lower-body strength	Back squat test 3-6 RM
	Upper-body strength	Bench press test 3-6 RM
	Power	Vertical jump test
	Speed	40-yard sprint test
	Agility	Illinois agility test
	Core strength	Core hold test
Week 6	Flexibility	Sit-and-reach test
	Lower-body strength	Back squat test 3-6 RM
	Upper-body strength	Bench press test 3-6 RM
	Power	Vertical jump test
	Speed	40-yard sprint test
	Agility	Illinois agility test
	Core strength	Core hold test
	Conditioning	3 × 300-yard sprint test
Week 12	Flexibility	Sit-and-reach test
	Lower-body strength	Back squat test 3-6 RM
	Upper-body strength	Bench press test 3-6 RM
	Power	Vertical jump test
	Speed	40-yard sprint test
	Agility	Illinois agility test
	Core strength	Core hold test
	Conditioning	Repeat shuttles test

the tests differ based on age and experience. The tests for the athlete with less experience are less complicated, especially in the resistance-training events, compared with the tests for the athlete with more experience.

Tracking test results through the 12-week model is a means of gauging progress. Gains should be realized in most events at weeks 6 and 12. The amount of progress depends on a number of factors. Work ethic (those who work hard tend to make greater gains), genetics (some are blessed with more innate talent), training experience (beginners tend to make large gains early on), and recovery (proper diet and rest will result in better performance) may influence the outcome. If any of these are deficient, gains may not be as substantial and adjustments (e.g., better nutritional practices) should be made during the subsequent phase. In most cases, any type of gain should be considered progress. Although they may not meet expectations, even slight improvements in performance should be appreciated. In many cases, continued hard work in both the training and recovery portions of the workout between weeks 6 and 12 will produce the breakthrough most athletes are working toward. Don't allow temporary setbacks to ruin goals and expectations!

Overall, testing is an important aspect of training and can be an effective tool in the athletic-development plan. For athletes, testing and evaluation are a means of tracking progress. Is the program producing the right results? Are any changes necessary? Empirical results in test events are motivating and can push an athlete to work even harder to break through larger barriers.

Coaches may use testing to evaluate and rank athletes during the off-season. Testing outcomes can help a coach monitor progress to gauge athletes' work ethic and commitment. Athletes who work hard and produce results are more likely to earn the respect and trust of teammates and coaches. An athlete who may not have the most talent on game day but who possesses an iron will to succeed can be the engine behind a successful program. Coaches appreciate these individuals because they tend to make everyone around them better. In the long run, a consistent, well-planned testing and evaluation program that complements training can have a major positive effect on performance, attitude, and team dynamics.

Chapter **3**

Warm-Up and Flexibility

An effective warm-up is crucial in preparing for competition (preevent) and beginning the recovery process afterward (postevent). Muscle activation during lacrosse training and competition is intense, and athletes must be proactive in order to perform at their highest capability. Failing to warm up properly may result in a higher susceptibility to injury. Athletes can best achieve an active state of readiness by performing a series of dynamic movements that prepare the body and mind for the rigors of intense activity. At the conclusion of an event, the recovery process must begin immediately. The most effective way to begin recovery is to engage in static stretches.

PREWORKOUT DYNAMIC WARM-UP

For many younger athletes, one of the most neglected areas of the workout is the preactivity routine. Some athletes feel as though such a routine is unimportant and either fail to perform any type of warm-up activity or greatly reduce the amount of time spent preparing the neuromuscular system for more intense activity. Before performing any type of physical activity, including workouts, practice, or competition, lacrosse players should engage in a total-body warm-up. Such a warm-up allows for a gradual increase in the body's core temperature, enabling the joints and muscles to function at their full capacity when called upon in maximal-effort events. In addition, the warm-up helps the neurological system gradually awaken from daily, mundane activities and prepare for ballistic, intense activity.

Athletes often come to practice or games from more sedentary activities, such as class or meetings, and fail to prepare their bodies and minds for a physically demanding series of events. Players who do not perform some type of warm-up activity are more susceptible to injury and may not perform at their best. A sufficient warm-up also has a positive effect on power, strength, reaction time, and rate-of-force production—all crucial for success in lacrosse.

Each preparation activity is a crucial ingredient in the overall training regimen. The warm-up should begin with a simple, low-intensity activity (e.g., a slow jog or bike ride) for two to three minutes to gradually elevate the heart rate. As the body adapts to this more intense state, the warm-up routine should progress to more complex in-place movements such as jumping jacks, body-weight lunges, or squats for a total of 3 to 5 minutes. The athlete should then progress to dynamic movement patterns that increase joint mobility and allow for another gradual increase in heart rate and joint range of motion. After four or five simple movements such as tin soldier or walking lunges, the speed and complexity of the warm-up should increase. Single-joint movements should transition to multi-joint, ballistic movement patterns such as skipping with high knees and backpedaling. After four or five activities of this type, the athlete should be ready for three or four reps of all-out explosive movements (e.g., 10- to 20-yard linear sprint) just before the workout, practice, or game.

Players can use the warm-up time to engage the mind as well as the body. This is an excellent opportunity to focus on the task at hand and tune out the day's activities, concerns, and distractions. Numerous events and situations compete for a player's attention. Athletes can use these few moments to bring individual and team responsibilities to mind and get emotions fine-tuned and ready for competition. If done properly, the dynamic warm-up allows for physical, emotional, and mental engagement and concludes with the athlete being fully prepared to meet and overcome the challenges of the day.

Preworkout Flexibility

Some lacrosse players may feel better prepared for activity by incorporating static, or in-place, stretches into the dynamic routine. By performing a combination of dynamic and static movements, the athlete can tailor the routine to suit individual preferences. For example, a dynamic backpedal (intended to warm up the hip flexors) may be followed with a kneeling hip flexor static stretch. Including light static stretching allows the athlete to benefit from multiple types of flexibility enhancement and, in some cases, enables the athlete to address specific weaknesses. For some athletes, static stretching is part of their individual preworkout routine and should not be discouraged. If an athlete chooses to perform static stretches during this time, the intervals should be relatively brief (5-15 seconds) and should stretch the larger muscle groups, such as the hamstrings, calves, shoulders, and back.

A well-executed warm-up before a workout, practice, or game elevates the body's core temperature (the athlete should show signs of perspiration), activates the muscles, helps lubricate the joints, and focuses the mind on the demands of the training session. Depending on the nature of those demands (which are slightly different for a resistance-training session, speed and agility workout, practice, or game) and the amount of space available, the athlete can select which dynamic routine is most appropriate. For example, if the athlete is performing strength training only on that particular day, he or she may want to engage in in-place dynamic and static movements. If space is limited, an in-place warm-up would be the most appropriate. In many cases, most commercial or school weight rooms don't have open space to perform a longer-distance dynamic warm up. If space is unlimited, such as in a field or other open area used for training, a movement-oriented warm-up can be used. For example, before a speed training session or practice when a considerable amount of running will be performed, longer-range dynamic warm-ups that include running, skipping, or carioca, for example. would best prepare the athlete for the physiological demands of that particular training session.

In-Place Dynamic Flexibility Exercises

When space is limited, muscular and neural activation can take place in a confined area (e.g., a hallway or locker room). In-place dynamic warm-ups produce results similar to those elicited from movement-oriented warm-ups.

Bodyweight Squat

Purpose

This exercise activates the hip, knee, and ankle joints as well as the quads, hamstrings, and low back—most of the joints and muscle groups involved in lacrosse performance training.

Setup

Stand with the feet slightly wider than shoulder-width apart and the hands either in front of the body or behind the head (figure 3.1a). The toes may be turned out 30 degrees.

Procedure

- Initiate the movement by bending at the knee and hip joints, sitting with the weight back until the hamstrings are parallel to the floor. Keep the chest upright (figure 3.1b).
- Keep the shins perpendicular to the floor. Maintain balance and control so that the body weight remains on the heels.
- Perform 10 to 20 reps.

Figure 3.1   Bodyweight squat.

Lateral Squat

Purpose

This exercise addresses the core, groin, and low-back muscle groups and allows for a greater degree of lateral flexibility. It is especially important to perform this exercise before doing any type of cutting or lateral movements.

Setup

Stand with the feet slightly closer than shoulder-width apart (figure 3.2a).

Procedure

- Keeping one foot stationary, step to the side with the opposite foot. Keep the toes slightly pointed outward, the chest up, and the foot flat, with weight concentrated on the heel (figure 3.2b). The knee should bend as far as hip mobility allows.
- Return to the starting position and repeat with the opposite foot in the opposite direction, gradually increasing the length of the stride as mobility increases.
- Perform 5 to 10 reps in each direction.

Figure 3.2   Lateral squat.

Push-Up

Purpose

This easy-to-perform exercise is an efficient way to activate the joints and muscle groups of the upper body. It loosens the shoulders, chest, upper back, and triceps and is beneficial for most activities, not just upper-body strength training.

Setup

Assume a plank position with the feet approximately 6 inches (15 cm) apart and the hands slightly wider than shoulder-width apart. Extend the arms, keeping the torso straight (figure 3.3*a*).

Procedure

- Bend the elbows and lower the torso toward the floor, keeping the shoulder joint at approximately 45 degrees and the torso straight (figure 3.3*b*).
- When the chin is approximately 3 inches (7 cm) from the floor, extend the elbows and return to the starting position.
- Perform 10 to 20 reps.

Figure 3.3   Push-up.

Twisting Push-Up

Purpose

This exercise engages the shoulders, chest, upper back, and triceps. A more in-depth version of the push-up, it provides an upper-body dynamic warm-up along with shoulder and core stabilization and trunk rotation.

Setup

Assume a plank position with the feet approximately 6 inches (15 cm) apart and the hands slightly wider than shoulder-width apart. Extend the arms, keeping the torso straight (figure 3.4a).

Procedure

- Bend the elbows and lower the torso toward the floor, keeping the shoulder joint at approximately 45 degrees and the torso straight (figure 3.4b). Be sure to avoid rotating the elbows outward thus placing undue stress on the shoulder joint. This is a common mistake with younger athletes.

- When the chin is approximately 3 inches (7 cm) from the floor, extend the elbows. Keep one hand on the floor and extend the other arm up toward the ceiling, turning the torso in the same direction (figure 3.4c).

- Rotate back to the neutral position and return both hands to the floor during the lowering phase. Repeat the movement to the opposite side.

- Perform 5 to 10 reps to each side.

Figure 3.4 Twisting push-up.

Spider Lunge

Purpose

This exercise increases range of motion in the glutes, groin, hip flexors, and hamstrings and is an efficient way to address several crucial muscle groups simultaneously. The movement patterns used in this exercise are similar to many movements used on the field.

Setup

Assume a plank position with the feet approximately 6 inches (15 cm) apart and the hands slightly wider than shoulder-width apart. Extend the arms, keeping the torso straight (figure 3.5a).

Procedure

- Keeping the hands on the floor, step with one foot to a point just beyond one of the stationary hands. Sink the hips as far as mobility allows (figure 3.5b). Keep the head and chest up throughout.
- Pause for 3 to 5 seconds.
- Return the forward foot to the starting position and repeat with the opposite foot.
- Perform 5 to 10 reps on each side.

Figure 3.5   Spider lunge.

Rotation Stretch

Purpose

This exercise activates the muscle structure of the rotator cuff. It prepares the shoulder for more intense rotational activities and increases range of motion in the shoulder joint.

Setup

Stand tall with the elbows raised to shoulder height, and elbows bent to 90 degrees (figure 3.6a)

Procedure

- Imagine a straight line running from elbow to elbow. Rotate the hands without raising or lowering the elbows beyond the straight line (figure 3.6b).
- When full range of motion is attained, pull the hands backward as far as possible, rotating on the same axis.
- Keep the elbows at a 90-degree angle throughout.
- Perform 10 to 12 reps.

Figure 3.6   Rotation stretch.

Arm Circle

Purpose

This exercise increases activity in and lubricates the shoulder joints, pectorals, lats, and deltoids. It prepares the athlete for resistance training, stick-handling drills, and physical contact.

Setup

Stand with the arms at the sides of the hips (figure 3.7a).

Procedure

- Rotate the shoulders forward and backward, keeping the elbows slightly bent (figure 3.7b).
- Gradually increase the circumference of the circles as shoulder mobility increases.
- Perform 5 to 10 reps forward and 5 to 10 reps backward.

Figure 3.7   Arm circle.

Trunk Twist

Purpose

This exercise increases blood flow and engages the obliques and shoulders. It also activates the low back, which can easily be irritated in lacrosse players. This region is vital because it connects upper- and lower-body activity.

Setup

Stand with the arms extended outward and bent at 90 degrees.

Procedure

- Slowly rotate the torso from side to side (figure 3.8, *a* and *b*).
- Gradually increase the range of motion as mobility increases.
- Perform 5 to 10 reps to each side.

Figure 3.8   Trunk twist.

Forward and Backward Leg Swing

Purpose

This exercise engages the hip flexors, extensors, and core. Warming up the muscles in this region helps reduce the chance of hamstring strains and pulls. This simple movement can be done along a wall or fence.

Setup

Stand with the shoulders perpendicular to a wall, railing, or partner and the chest upright (figure 3.9*a*).

Procedure

- Swing one leg forward and backward, keeping the opposite foot stationary (figure 3.9, *b* and *c*). The chest should remain upright and stationary.
- Gradually increase the range of motion (both forward and backward) as hip mobility allows.
- Perform 10 to 20 reps on each leg.

Figure 3.9   Forward and backward leg swing.

Lateral Leg Swing

Purpose

This exercise loosens the abductor and adductor muscles, which is important before performing any lateral movements on the field or in the weight room.

Setup

Stand with the shoulders parallel to a wall, railing, or partner and the chest upright (figure 3.10a).

Procedure

- Swing one leg inside and outside, keeping the opposite foot stationary (figures 3.10, b and c). The working foot should move across the stationary leg and as high up to the side as possible. Keep the chest and torso upright and stationary throughout.
- Gradually increase the range of motion as hip mobility allows.
- Perform 10 to 20 reps on each leg.

Figure 3.10   Lateral leg swing.

Scorpion

Purpose

This exercise initiates trunk rotation and hip mobility. It is a great way to prepare the back and hips for the rigors of lacrosse-training motions.

Setup

Lie facedown on the floor with the arms out to the sides (figure 3.11a).

Procedure

- Keeping the hips low to the ground, extend the foot on one side back over your body to a point just beyond the opposite hip, touching the floor at waist level (figure 3.11b).
- The torso should remain relatively stationary, and the arms should remain at the sides to counterbalance the leg swing.
- Return to the starting position and repeat with the opposite leg.
- Perform 5 to 10 reps on each side.

Figure 3.11   Scorpion.

Iron Cross

Purpose

This exercise activates the hamstrings, glutes, low back, and groin—many of the muscle groups crucial in lower-body training and movement-skill training and on game day.

Setup

Lie faceup on the floor and extend the arms out to the sides approximately 90 degrees at the shoulder joint (figure 3.12a).

Procedure

- Keeping the shoulder blades in contact with the floor, cross one leg over the body and touch the foot to the opposite hand (figure 3.12b).
- During each kick, keep the torso stationary and turn the head away from the working leg.
- Return to the starting position and repeat with the opposite foot.
- Perform 5 to 10 reps on each side.

Figure 3.12   Iron cross.

Single-Leg Kick

Purpose

This exercise isolates the hamstrings, glutes, and low-back muscles one leg at a time. It is a great way to loosen the lower body for practice, speed training, or resistance training.

Setup

Lie faceup on the floor with one leg bent, and rest arms at the sides close to the torso (figure 3.13*a*).

Procedure

- Kick one foot up over the torso, trying to get the hip joint to at least 90 degrees (figure 3.13*b*).
- The down leg can be either straight or slightly bent. Keep the hips in contact with the floor during the kick phase.
- Return to the starting position and repeat with the opposite foot.
- Perform 10 to 20 kicks on each side.

Figure 3.13 Single-leg kick.

Movement-Oriented Dynamic Flexibility Exercises

Select from the following exercises if the athlete has sufficient space to engage in a movement-oriented warm-up. Make sure to address all of the joints and muscles that will be activated during that particular session. These exercises enable the athlete to progress from inactivity to more intense activity (e.g., speed and agility sessions, practice, or games) in a gradual, controlled manner.

Walking Lunge

Purpose

This exercise activates the hamstrings, hips, and low back and prepares the lower body for more strenuous activity. It is a basic way to elongate the hamstrings and warm up the hip flexors and knee joints.

Setup

Stand with hands on the hips, behind the head, or at the sides (figure 3.14a).

Procedure

- Step forward with one foot until the knee is bent approximately 90 degrees. Keep the toes of that foot in front of the bent knee and the chest and torso upright (figure 3.14b).
- Step through with the opposite foot, taking care not to drag that foot on the floor.
- Continuously repeat for 10 to 25 yards, gradually increasing the length of the stride.

Figure 3.14   Walking lunge.

Lunge With Twist

Purpose

This exercise activates the hamstrings, hips, and low back and prepares the lower body for more strenuous activity. It adds a rotation to the walking lunge to engage the core muscles as well.

Setup

Stand with the feet approximately 6 inches apart.

Procedure

- Step out with one foot until the knee is bent approximately 90 degrees. Keep the toes of that foot in front of the bent knee.
- At the end of the movement, rotate the upper body, turning the trunk toward the front leg (figure 3.15*a*).
- Step through with the opposite foot and rotate trunk toward the front leg, taking care not to drag that foot on the floor (figure 3.15*b*).
- Continuously repeat for 10 to 25 yards, gradually increasing the length of the stride.

Figure 3.15   Lunge with twist.

Tin Soldier

Purpose

This exercise loosens the hamstrings, glutes, and calves and prepares the lower-body musculature to move beyond the typical range of motion used in daily activities.

Setup

Stand upright with the arms at the sides.

Procedure

- Kick one foot up as high as hip mobility allows and touch the foot to the opposite hand. Strive to kick the toes up to eye level (figure 3.16).
- Return the foot to the ground, step, and repeat with the opposite foot.
- Repeat for 10 to 25 yards, gradually increasing the height of the kicks. This movement can be performed as a walk or as a skip.

Figure 3.16   Tin soldier.

Carioca

Purpose

This exercise activates the hips, low back, and groin and allows the athlete to incorporate more demanding movement patterns into the warm-up routine.

Setup

Stand with the arms at the sides as the athlete faces sideways, perpendicular to the starting line (figure 3.17a). The foot closest to the start line is the front foot.

Procedure

- Move sideways at a slow to moderate pace by striding with the back foot across the torso with slight hip rotation (figure 3.17b).
- Upon contacting the ground, immediately stride with the front foot across and behind the trunk (figure 3.17c).
- Keep the shoulders parallel to the sideline throughout the movement.
- Repeat for a distance of 10 to 25 yards in each direction.

Figure 3.17   Carioca.

Shuffle

Purpose

This exercise loosens the groin and low back and helps the athlete transition from in-place dynamic movements to active, movement-oriented drills. This is especially important when doing agility drills.

Setup

Stand with the arms at the sides.

Procedure

- Moving sideways, stride laterally with the front foot. Bring the back leg toward the front foot and make contact with the ground, but never cross the feet (figure 3.18, *a-c*).
- Start slowly and gradually increase the speed.
- Repeat for 10 to 25 yards.

Figure 3.18   Shuffle.

Step, Shift, and Pivot

Purpose

This exercise activates the groin, hamstrings, and low back and helps the athlete transition from in-place dynamic movements to active, movement-oriented drills. It helps defensive players in particular get into the flexed position required for defensive play.

Setup

Stand with the arms at the sides standing perpendicular to the start line.

Procedure

- Step forward with the front foot using a long stride. Keep the chest upright and the heel of the front foot in contact with the ground (figure 3.19*a*).
- Shift the center of gravity and slide horizontally over the back foot, stretching the groin.
- Bring the feet together, pivot on the front foot (so that you rotate your body 180 degrees) take another long stride with the front foot, shift and pivot facing the opposite direction (figures 3.19, *b* and *c*).
- Repeat for the prescribed distance, alternating the positioning of your body throughout.

  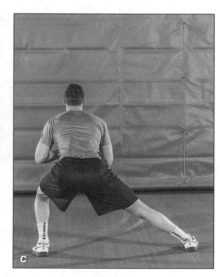

Figure 3.19   Step, shift, and pivot.

Run With High Knees

Purpose

This exercise activates the hip flexors and extensors and begins to intensify foot speed. It incorporates running movements that go beyond the joints' typical range of motion to help athletes prepare for more ballistic activity.

Setup

Stand with the arms at the sides.

Procedure

- Run at 75 percent of maximum speed with an exaggerated knee lift, maintaining a smooth, controlled motion (figure 3.20, *a* and *b*).
- The elbows should remain fixed at a 90-degree angle, and the shoulders should move forward and backward (i.e., avoid crossover).
- Perform the movement for 10 to 25 yards.

Figure 3.20 Run with high knees.

Skip With High Knees

Purpose

This exercise engages the hips, knees, ankles, and core. It allows for greater range of motion in the hip flexors, which is crucial before performing any type of all-out linear movement.

Setup

Stand with the arms at the sides.

Procedure

- At a moderate (75 percent) pace, skip forward and bend the knee of the front leg approximately 90 degrees (figure 3.21).
- Repeat with the opposite knee.
- Continuously repeat for 10 to 25 yards.

Figure 3.21   Skip with high knees.

Backpedal With Reach

Purpose

This exercise uses backward movement to engage the hip flexors and quads, which are necessary in any situation that requires acceleration or deceleration. It is also crucial for defensive players who must be able to shuffle, slide, and retreat at an angle.

Setup

Stand with the arms at the sides, facing away from the starting line.

Procedure

- Keeping the chest upright, run backward. Kick the heel of the back foot through the glutes and back, reaching back as far as possible with each stride (figure 3.22, *a* and *b*).
- Gradually lengthen the stride and cover more ground with each step.
- Continuously repeat for 10 to 25 yards.

Figure 3.22   Backpedal with reach.

Backward Skip With Open Hips

Purpose

This exercise opens the hip joint and prepares it for multidirectional movement patterns. This is important given the amount of trauma the hip joint absorbs during lacrosse play particularly for defensive players who must retreat at an angle.

Setup

Stand behind the start line, facing away from the finish line (figure 3.23a).

Procedure

- Skip in a backward motion, lifting one knee up and rotating it away from the midline at waist height (figure 3.23b).
- Return the foot to the starting position.
- Upon ground contact, repeat with the opposite foot (figure 3.23c). Throughout the movement, keep the shoulders facing straight ahead with minimal side-side rotation. The emphasis is on opening the angle of the hip joint.
- Continuously repeat for 10 to 25 yards.

Figure 3.23 Backward skip with open hips.

Power Skip for Height

Purpose

This exercise loosens the hip flexors and hip extensors and helps activate the knee joint. It exaggerates the running motion and can serve as a bridge between slower runs and all-out bursts of speed.

Setup

Stand behind the starting line with the arms at the sides.

Procedure

- Move forward at a moderate (75 percent) pace, skipping as high as possible and raising the front knee toward the chest as far as hip mobility allows (figure 3.24).
- The objective is to skip for height rather than distance.
- Continuously repeat for 10 to 25 yards.

Figure 3.24   Power skip for height.

Cobra

Purpose

This exercise stretches the upper and lower abs as well as the hip flexors and provides substantial activation of the core and trunk muscles. It is a great way to keep the vertebrae in alignment and is often recommended by athletic trainers as a way to promote a healthy low back.

Setup

Lie facedown with the hands slightly wider than shoulder-width apart (figure 3.25*a*).

Procedure

- Keeping the hips, knees, and feet in contact with the ground, extend the upper body by locking the elbows (figure 3.25*b*).
- Stretch upward until you feel a mild stretch in the low back and abs.
- Hold for 10 to 30 seconds.

Figure 3.25   Cobra.

Cat

Purpose

This exercise lengthens the spinal erectors and upper back muscles and helps reduce tension in the low back.

Setup

Assume a prone six-point stance with both hands, both knees, and both feet on the ground and the hands slightly wider than shoulder-width apart.

Procedure

- Arch the low back upward toward the ceiling and round the spine.
- Hold for 10 to 30 seconds.

Figure 3.26   Cat.

Sample Dynamic Total-Body Warm-Ups

Before beginning any workout or other activity, the athlete should identify which muscle groups the workout targets. Are specific muscle groups being worked (e.g., in an upper-body strength-training session), or does the activity work the whole body? Does the athlete need to address any limitations or weaknesses? For example, if the athlete is particularly inflexible in the hamstrings, he or she should be sure to perform extra dynamic movements to address the hamstrings during the warm-up. In addition, the athlete must determine how much space is available for performing the warm-up. When plenty of field space can be used before a practice or game, a movement-oriented dynamic warm-up can be performed (see table 3.1). On the other hand, if the athlete is doing a weight-training session in a small weight room or commercial gym, an in-place warm-up would be the most appropriate (see table 3.2).

Table 3.1 Sample Prepractice or Pregame Dynamic Total-Body Warm-Up

Exercise	Page	Duration
1. Jog		2-3 min
2. Walking lunge	62	25 yd
3. Bodyweight squat	49	10 reps
4. Lateral squat	50	5 reps each side
5. Push-up	51	10 reps
6. Tin soldier	64	25 yd
7. Spider lunge	53	5 reps each side
8. Cobra	73	10 sec
9. Arm circle	55	5 reps forward, 5 reps backward
10. Trunk twist	56	5 reps each side
11. Run with high knees	68	25 yd
12. Backward skip with open hips	71	25 yd
13. Carioca	65	25 yd each direction
14. Power skip for height	72	25 yd
15. 90% sprint		25 yd
16. 100% sprint		25 yd

Table 3.2   Sample Dynamic Total-Body Warm-Up for a Strength-Training Session

Exercise	Page	Duration
1. Stationary bike	232	3 min
2. Forward and backward leg swing	57	10 reps each direction
3. Lateral leg swing	58	10 reps each direction
4. Bodyweight squat	49	10 reps
5. Lateral squat	50	5 reps each side
6. Twisting push-up	52	5 reps each side
7. Scorpion	59	5 reps each side
8. Cobra	73	30 sec
9. Cat	74	30 sec
10. Single-leg kick	61	10 reps each side
11. Iron cross	60	5 reps each side
12. Rotation stretch	54	5 reps each side
13. Trunk twist	56	5 reps each side
14. Vertical jump	27	5 reps each side

POSTWORKOUT STATIC FLEXIBILITY

At the end of any training session, it is critical to address muscle flexibility with static, or in-place, stretching. Performing longer static stretches at the conclusion of workouts improves joint range of motion and begins the recovery process. Several theories about the ideal stretch program exist, but most researchers and practitioners agree that it is best to perform passive stretches that address the major muscle groups for lacrosse players (hamstrings, groin, quads, hip flexors, low back, torso, and shoulders), either with a partner or individually, for 10 to 15 minutes at the end of the workout. Athletes should perform these types of stretches to mild discomfort (rather than moderate to extreme pain) and hold them for 15 to 30 seconds.

Contrary to popular belief, it is not the intensity of stretching but rather the frequency of flexibility training that results in the best improvements in long-term performance. A stretching program performed consistently— every day, even on off days—will enable the athlete to make greater strides in flexibility improvement compared with infrequent stretching at a higher intensity. In recent years, some programs have added formal flexibility routines such as yoga to the training routine, resulting in substantially improved range of motion and enhanced muscle recovery. Whatever the strategy used, increased flexibility can only benefit lacrosse skill enhancement.

Static Flexibility Exercises Without a Partner

Athletes can perform static stretches in a number of ways. One convenient option is using one's body weight and gravity for resistance. This option is simple and reliable, especially when working alone.

Feet-Apart Hamstring Stretch

Purpose

This exercise stretches the low back, hamstrings, and groin, which are used constantly in lacrosse. Athletes must take special care to ensure they have full range of motion and can resist injury while in training or on game day.

Setup

Sit with the feet slightly wider than shoulder-width apart and the toes slightly pointed outward (figure 3.27a).

Procedure

- Hinge at the hip joint with a flat back and slowly lower the chest toward the right knee (figure 3.27b).
- Allow gravity to pull the chest down toward the floor.
- After completing the stretch to the right leg, slowly transition the stretch to the left leg. When the stretch is completed to that side, lower to the left and then to the middle.
- Hold each stretch for 15 to 30 seconds.

Figure 3.27   Feet-apart hamstring stretch.

Sumo Squat

Purpose

This exercise improves motion in the hips, groin, and ankles, which are involved in lateral movement during games and practices.

Setup

Stand with the feet slightly wider than shoulder-width apart and the toes pointed out at 45 degrees (figure 3.28*a*).

Procedure

- Lower the hips while keeping the chest upright and body weight concentrated on the heels (figure 3.28*b*). If you are unable to keep the heels in contact with the ground, widen the base.
- Gently push outward on the knees, stretching the groin.
- Hold for 15 to 30 seconds.

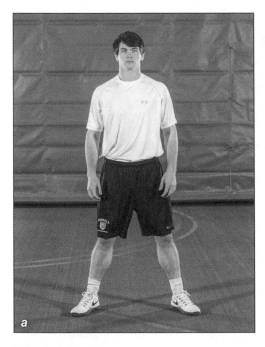 

Figure 3.28   Sumo squat.

Lying Quad Stretch

Purpose

This exercise stretches the quads and hip flexors. It is important to address these muscle groups after performing significant lacrosse movement (especially deceleration) to ensure regeneration and range of motion maintenance.

Setup

Lie on one side with the legs together and fully extended. The down arm should be in front of the shoulder at 90 degrees (figure 3.29a).

Procedure

- Gradually lift the heel of the top foot toward the hamstrings, keeping the knee bent.
- Grab the shin or foot and, in a controlled manner, slowly bring the heel closer to the hamstrings (figure 3.29b). The knee and foot should remain aligned throughout.
- Repeat on the opposite side.
- Hold the stretch for 15 to 30 seconds.

Figure 3.29   Lying quad stretch.

Iliotibial Band Stretch

Purpose

This exercise stretches the iliotibial (IT) band and glutes. Through proper stretching, athletes can maintain range of motion and help prevent breakdown.

Setup

Assume a six-point position with both hands, both knees, and both feet on the ground and the hands slightly wider than shoulder-width apart (figure 3.30a).

Procedure

- Bend one knee and bring it under the sternum while keeping it and the ankle in contact with the floor (figure 3.30b).
- Press the shoulders forward, keeping the shoulders square, the back flat, and the torso upright.
- Repeat on both sides.
- Hold each stretch for 15 to 30 seconds.

Figure 3.30   Iliotibial band stretch.

Kneeling Hip Flexor Stretch

Purpose

This exercise lengthens the hip flexors and stretches the trunk muscles during rotation. Mobility in the hip flexors may help to lengthen an athlete's stride during running and lessen the likelihood of injury during change of direction.

Setup

Assume a kneeling position with one knee down on a comfortable surface.

Procedure

- Extend the hips forward, keeping the shoulders back and the chest upright (figure 3.31)
- Keep the front foot out so that the knee remains behind the toes.
- Perform on both sides.
- Hold each stretch for 15 to 30 seconds.

Figure 3.31   Kneeling hip flexor stretch.

Shoulder Stretch

Purpose

This exercise stretches the medial and posterior deltoids, which are required for stability and control during upper-body activation (e.g., ball handling, body contact). Having greater mobility in these areas is essential.

Setup

Stand with the feet shoulder-width apart.

Procedure

- Bend one arm and place the hand on the opposite shoulder without allowing the elbow to drop. Reach across with the opposite hand and hold the elbow (figure 3.32).
- Push the elbow in and back toward the outside of the shoulder.
- Repeat on both sides.
- Hold each stretch for 15 to 30 seconds.

Figure 3.32   Shoulder stretch.

Static Flexibility Exercises With a Partner

In order to increase the intensity of stretches, a partner can provide bio-mechanical leverage that is difficult to replicate when stretching alone. A word of caution is in order here. A partner should reinforce the same principle that is applied during individual stretches: slow, steady resistance that does not exceed mild discomfort and that does not include jerking or bouncing. Communication between partners is a must, and individuals should conduct themselves in a safe, helpful manner.

Partner-Assisted Feet-Apart Hamstring Stretch

Purpose

This exercise stretches the hamstrings, low back, and groin. Because the hamstrings are so important for lacrosse players, maintaining strength, stability, and flexibility are essential.

Setup

The working partner sits with the feet wider than shoulder-width apart, and the assisting partner stands behind. The working partner should be sure to keep the toes up and knees extended.

Procedure

- The assisting partner pushes the working partner's torso toward the right knee and provides light resistance to the middle of the back (figure 3.33). The working partner should maintain a flat back.
- The stretch is repeated to the left and toward the middle.
- The working partner should communicate with the assisting partner regarding resistance levels.
- Hold each stretch for 15 to 30 seconds.

Figure 3.33　Partner-assisted feet-apart hamstring stretch.

Single-Leg Hamstring Stretch

Purpose

This exercise stretches the hamstrings and glutes. By isolating each leg the athlete can perceive differences in range of motion, which can be addressed through exercises and stretches that will help correct the imbalance.

Setup

The working partner lies on the back with one heel on the floor and the opposite leg up in the air with the knee slightly bent (figure 3.34a). The assisting partner kneels near the working partner's leg.

Procedure

- The assisting partner holds the working partner's heel and knee, providing mild resistance (figure 3.34b).
- The assisting partner attempts to move the working partner's leg beyond 90 degrees or until mild discomfort is achieved.
- Repeat on the opposite side.
- Hold each stretch for 15 to 30 seconds.

Figure 3.34   Single-leg hamstring stretch.

Glute Stretch

Purpose

This exercise stretches the glutes and hip abductors. It will help alleviate stress and promote quicker recovery when muscle soreness and fatigue occur in this region of the body.

Setup

The working partner lies on the back with one heel on the floor and the opposite leg up in the air with the knee bent. The assisting partner kneels near the working partner's leg.

Procedure

- The working partner rotates the lower leg across the torso, bringing the ankle toward the opposite shoulder (figure 3.35).
- At the same time, the assisting partner gently pushes the ankle and knee straight back toward the shoulders.
- Repeat on the opposite side.
- Hold each stretch for 15 to 30 seconds.

Figure 3.35   Glute stretch.

Shoulder–Pectoral Stretch

Purpose

This exercise increases mobility in the pectorals and deltoids. Working on flexibility in the shoulder and upper-torso regions is especially beneficial when engaging in resistance training, practice, or game.

Setup

The working partner sits and places the hands together at the back of the head. The assisting partner stands with one knee between the working partner's shoulder blades for support.

Procedure

- The assisting partner gently pulls the working partner's elbows back to allow for increased range of motion in the pectorals and shoulders (figure 3.36).
- Hold for 15 to 30 seconds.

Figure 3.36 Shoulder–pectoral stretch.

Static Flexibility Exercises With Equipment

For many lacrosse players, the difference between stretching with and without a partner is substantial. Many prefer the added resistance of a partner and realize the benefits from this form of recovery. When a partner is unavailable, the athlete may use a band or towel to provide the needed resistance. As with any means of flexibility training, athletes should perform each stretch to mild discomfort and recognize that long-term benefits come more from frequency than from added intensity.

Resisted Single-Leg Hamstring Stretch

Purpose

This exercise stretches the hamstrings and glutes. Hip mobility is essential for engaging in lacrosse-specific movement patterns.

Setup

Lie faceup and place a band, strap, or towel under the sole of the working foot. Slightly bend the working knee. Straighten or slightly flex the opposite knee.

Procedure

- Pull the foot back toward the torso, allowing the hip joint to reach 90 degrees (figure 3.37). Repeat on the opposite side.
- Hold each stretch for 15 to 30 seconds.

Figure 3.37 Resisted single-leg hamstring stretch.

Resisted Groin Stretch

Purpose

This exercise isolates mobility in the hips while maintaining core stability. It also improves range of motion in the groin, which is important for all lacrosse players, especially in defensive shuffles and slides.

Setup

Lie on the back and place a band, strap, or towel under the sole of the working foot. Bring the foot out to the side just past the shoulder. Flex the opposite knee 90 degrees and place the shoulder blades flat on the floor.

Procedure

- With the hand on the side of the working leg, pull the band or strap up over the shoulder, stretching the groin (figure 3.38).
- Repeat on the opposite side.
- Hold each stretch for 15 to 30 seconds.

Figure 3.38   Resisted groin stretch.

Figure Four

Purpose

This exercise stretches the posterior leg muscles and promotes greater mobility in the iliotibial band, glutes, and hamstrings.

Setup

Lie on the back with one leg bent 90 degrees and the opposite ankle crossed over it, resting the outside of the ankle on the knee. Wrap a resistance band, strap or towel around the working foot.

Procedure

- With the hand closest to the working knee, gently pull the outside of the knee toward the shoulder.
- With the opposite hand, grasp the band and pull it toward the shoulder until the stretch is felt in the glutes and hips (figure 3.39).
- Repeat on both sides.
- Hold each stretch for 15 to 30 seconds.

Figure 3.39   Figure four.

Resisted Hip Stretch

Purpose

This exercise lengthens the abductor muscles and stretches the low back. For hip and back health, lacrosse players must include movements that address these muscle groups after every workout, practice, or game.

Setup

Lie flat on the back and hold a band, strap, or towel under the working foot. Keep the opposite leg as straight as possible.

Procedure

- Holding the band, strap, or towel in the hand opposite the working leg, cross the foot over the torso, pulling the foot as close to shoulder height as possible (figure 3.40).
- If possible, keep the shoulder blades in contact with the floor.
- Repeat on both sides.
- Hold each stretch for 15 to 30 seconds.

Figure 3.40   Resisted hip stretch.

Resisted Lying Quad Stretch

Purpose

This exercise adds range of motion to the hip flexors and lower abs. After an intense game or workout, the quads and hip flexors may be especially tight. This movement will help release the tightness and soreness and prepare the athlete for the next event.

Setup

Lying facedown or on the side, place a band or strap on top of the foot (like shoelaces) and bring the strap over the shoulder.

Procedure

- Gently pull the strap upward so that the working knee and thigh slightly lift off the floor (figure 3.41).
- Maintain knee and foot alignment at all times and, if possible, keep the opposite knee on the floor.
- Repeat on the opposite side.
- Hold each stretch for 15 to 30 seconds.

Figure 3.41   Resisted lying quad stretch.

Resisted Shoulder Stretch

Purpose

This exercise stretches the deltoids as well as the triceps. Greater shoulder flexibility helps improve mobility during stick handling.

Setup

Stand with the feet shoulder-width apart.

Procedure

- Hold a band, strap, or towel with one hand. Bring the arm behind the head and bend the elbow.
- With the opposite hand, reach behind the waist and grab the band, strap, or towel. Pull it downward until the top shoulder is flexed (figure 3.42).
- Repeat on the opposite side.
- Hold each stretch for 15 to 30 seconds.

Figure 3.42   Resisted shoulder stretch.

The human body consists of more than 600 muscles and 200 bones. These individual components are connected by the neurological system, which originates in the brain and sends commands to the extremities. The lacrosse player must make time to gradually prepare to integrate these sophisticated systems before maximal exertion takes place. The entire system—muscles, joints, and connective tissues—must be aroused in stages in order to ensure a healthy, productive performance and to avoid injury.

A thorough, well-designed flexibility program should be part of every lacrosse player's routine. A movement-oriented warm-up should precede everything else when an athlete arrives at the field or gym. When the day's work is completed, players must take the time to do static stretches, which yield substantial long-term benefits. Great players know how to manage their bodies and do what is necessary to ensure peak performance every day!

Chapter 4

Strength and Power

It happens in every game. The offense begins to set up while the defense settles into position, trying to find the right match-ups. Looking for a clear shooting lane, a midfielder cradles the ball as he backs away from the box to create space between himself and the closest defender. He moves forward and looks for an open teammate as he tries to sense hesitation on the part of the defender covering him. The defender shuffles under control at an angle, trying to steer the midfielder toward his weaker hand. Suddenly, a burst of speed toward the edge of the defense unleashes a flurry of offensive screens and defensive responses. What at first appears to be chaos is actually a sophisticated chess match between the teams, with adjustments and counteradjustments being made as play unfolds. Seemingly out of nowhere, an attackman breaks free for a split second, receives a quick pass, and sends a wrist shot to the corner of the cage just past the goalie's stick.

This well-coordinated offensive assault is the result of a number of athletic, powerful moves. Ball movement, screens, and cuts characterize offensive play in front of the crease. The defense, hoping to disrupt the offensive flow, must be equally strong and powerful in their execution. Maintaining a low defensive posture in coverage and performing aggressive stick and body checks require great strength, balance, and lateral speed. Whatever the positional requirements on game day, lacrosse players must be strong, powerful, and versatile.

STRENGTH DEVELOPMENT FOR LACROSSE

During the heat of battle in a game situation, lacrosse players must execute a wide variety of skills while focusing on game strategy, team communication, and technical execution. Dodging a defender, stick handling through heavy traffic, making a quick shot after a pass, transitioning from one end of the field to another, and playing solid defense all require a high degree of strength and power. These actions, repeated continuously throughout the course of a game, ultimately determine success.

In lacrosse, strength is crucial for both injury prevention and skill enhancement. Athletes who are stronger tend to be more resistant to injury and can better withstand the stress of intense competition over the course of a game and, ultimately, a season. In addition, stronger, more explosive athletes are generally more successful. Maximum productivity in the areas of acceleration, agility, stick handling, and physical contact all require a comprehensive, foundational level of strength.

Much like any skill, strength can be improved regardless of current status. With hard work, consistency, and a commitment to long-term, gradual gains, any athlete can make significant upgrades in strength that lead to improved performance. With regard to lacrosse-specific training, it is important to create muscle balance in all of the joints and planes in order to avoid injury and increase overall effectiveness. Many younger athletes tend to focus on one element of strength and exclude other equally important areas. For example, working on upper-body movements (e.g., bench press) several times a week and ignoring other crucial muscle groups tends to create an imbalanced, less effective player. Striving to achieve balance in all areas of the body (upper and lower, anterior and posterior, left and right) will enable the athlete to be more effective when playing the game and better able to withstand the effects of stress on muscles and joints.

In addition, all of the links in the kinetic chain should be addressed in the training cycle. For example, the force generated in a shot is initiated in the hips, but in order to accelerate and control the ball, the force must pass from the hips into the torso, through the arms and wrists, and, ultimately, into the stick, which propels the ball to its destination. All of the muscles and joints involved in the final skill (hamstrings, calves, glutes, core, shoulders, forearms, and wrists) can be strengthened in the training process. Unnecessary emphasis on one area in the training program may result in neglect of another area.

Functional strength is strength that can be applied effectively on the field and transferred to practical, game-day skills. The ultimate goal of any successful training program should be to enhance lacrosse skill. The truly successful program integrates weight room gains into an effective, comprehensive system of strength, power, speed, agility, and conditioning development that results in the improvement of practical lacrosse skills. If a player can't harness training gains and transition them into game-day skills, workout time is wasted and alternative training strategies should be considered. This crucial concept distinguishes sport-specific development from bodybuilding or powerlifting, which are ends in themselves.

Strength-Training Fundamentals

Before creating a workout plan, the athlete must think through some of the following fundamental issues. Taking the time to learn *how* to train must precede determining *what* to train.

Safety Considerations

Workouts are most productive when they are conducted in a safe, healthy environment. Given that one of the fundamental goals of training is to avoid injury during competition, similar care must be taken during the preparation phase. Training injuries can be frustrating, and the time lost during recovery may result in devastating setbacks in performance. By using safe equipment and practicing proper technique, the athlete will have a healthy, productive experience.

Train with proper technique. Athletes should strive for perfect technique at all times regardless of the training activity (e.g., resistance training, speed, agility, flexibility). During strength training, the athlete should always have the ability to control the resistance throughout the entire range of motion. Regardless of what the external resistance might be: Olympic barbell, dumbbells, bands, etc., the athlete should concentrate on perfect execution of every rep with maximum mental concentration. If the objective is to get stronger and not just to impress peers, technical precision must take precedence over the amount of weight used (i.e., intensity). Adaptation to higher stress follows technique!

Use a spotter. When training with free weights such as dumbbells and barbells, athletes should be sure to have a spotter available to assist if needed. The spotter can stabilize the weight as the lifter gets into a proper position, such as on a barbell or dumbbell press, or help if the lifter is unable to complete the movement, such as on a back squat. Athletes who are training alone should avoid complex movements that may end in technical failure.

Ensure that equipment functions properly. A coach, parent, or teacher should check that all Olympic bars, dumbbells, bands, as well as kettlebells and selectorized machines are working properly before starting a program. If repairs are needed, the equipment should be serviced by a professional. Faulty equipment can hinder progress and possibly lead to serious injury.

Perform a needs analysis. Before a training program is developed, the athlete must conduct a detailed self-analysis and comprehensive testing. This objective view of performance strengths and weaknesses will help formulate the specifics of subsequent programming. Which skills did the athlete perform well? Which skills need improvement? In addition, having an honest conversation with a coach will help the athlete discover which areas of performance are lacking and need to be addressed before the start of the next season. The needs analysis should address the following questions.

- *What is the athlete's experience level?* Each athlete should be classified as being a beginner, intermediate, or advanced. Most high-school lacrosse players are generally considered beginners or intermediate. Generally, an athlete with fewer than five years of year-round, comprehensive training falls into either of these categories. Only after significant development would an athlete be classified as advanced. The scope of the athlete's training experience should also be taken into account. For example, some younger athletes may have experience with upper-body exercises (e.g., bench press, biceps curls) and relatively little experience working the core or lower body. In this case, the athlete should be considered a beginner due to a lack of comprehensive experience.

- *What is the athlete's injury history?* Does the athlete have a history of significant injuries? If so, training should be adjusted to accommodate the injured joint or muscle. For example, a program for an athlete with a history of knee-related injuries should include a focus on lower-body strengthening movements in the weight room along with an on-field program of progressive acceleration, deceleration, and change of direction to allow for adaptation before the start of competition. Addressing injuries in advance allows for the development of sufficient strength and technique and reduces the possibility that the injury will recur.

- *What equipment is available?* A program's level of sophistication depends to a certain extent on the type of equipment that is available. Positive results, however, do not depend on highly technical equipment! Improvement in strength and power is the result of hard work and consistency rather than a specific program or modality. Gains are possible regardless of the type of equipment athletes have at their disposal. The athlete should take inventory of the equipment available at home, school, or a professional training facility and design the program accordingly.

- *How much time is available?* Each athlete's time availability is unique due to academic commitments, practice schedules, family obligations, and other considerations. The athlete must decide how much time he or she is willing to devote to training. Often, athletes overestimate the amount of time they have and, after only a few weeks of training, become frustrated and quit. At first, the athlete should be conservative in the estimation of daily training time available; training for 30 minutes 3 times a week is a reasonable starting point. Daily training time or number of training days per week can always be increased but rarely decreased without some level of frustration.

Selection and Order

The exercises that an athlete chooses should meet the total physiological needs of a lacrosse player. Limiting the training protocol to just a few muscle groups may not be as effective for skill development and injury prevention. For example, if the athlete selects a total-body workout, lower- and upper-body pushing and pulling movements, grip, core, and (in some cases) neck-stability movements should be included. In addition, medical history and specific fitness goals should play a role in exercise selection. More time can be spent in areas of concern. For example, if speed is a focus, lower-body strength training, power development, and technical running skills should be the focus. Skill deficiencies can be transitioned into strengths if the athlete is willing to address them in a safe, honest manner.

For most workout sessions, the athlete should perform complex, multi-joint exercises first and then progress to simple, single-joint exercises. For example, free-weight squats should be performed before hamstring isolation exercises (e.g., glute-ham raise). This enables the athlete to perform the more complex movements when the physiological and neurological systems are fresh. More technically advanced movements (typically multi-joint movements) should always be completed before the athlete becomes fatigued and the stabilizing muscles are compromised. In addition, performing explosive exercises such as plyometrics earlier in the session is generally recommended.

Phases of Training

In each phase, the training emphasis shifts as the athlete moves closer to the season. For example, early in the program, higher volume (total sets and reps) and lower weights are used during weight training. As the program progresses, the volume of work decreases and the amount of weight used increases. This system of progressive overload allows the body to gradually adapt to the stress of training and builds toward a peak in strength and power levels as the season nears.

Table 4.1 shows a sample basic training progression for an intermediate athlete in an 8- to 12-week off-season training cycle with 2- to 3-week intervals.

Table 4.1 Off-Season Training Phases

	General preparation phase	Hypertrophy phase	Strength phase	Power phase
Number of weeks	2 or 3	2 or 3	2 or 3	2 or 3
Sets	2 or 3	3 or 4	3 or 4	3 or 4
Reps	15-20	8-12	3-6	1-5
Intensity	Low	Moderate	High	High
Volume	High	High	Moderate	Low

Intensity

How much resistance should an athlete use? Depending on the athlete's starting strength, age, and experience, the answer may vary greatly. For beginners, body weight, bands, and light resistance are recommended. After several weeks of basic instructional training, during which the muscles, joints, and connective tissue have adapted to training, the athlete can progress to a more advanced routine. Once the athlete has learned proper technique and sufficiently adapted, additional means of resistance (e.g., dumbbells, barbells) may then be integrated into the regimen. At no time should the athlete progress beyond the body's ability to adapt physiologically. The athlete should strive for perfect technique and form at all times and refuse to compromise for the sake of using heavier weight. Hard work with perfect technique should always be the goal!

Recovery

Recovery is crucial for all athletes regardless of developmental state. Resting between workouts and practices, maintaining proper nutritional habits, and consistently hydrating are the keys to producing positive training results. Consuming the appropriate amount of calories, protein, and complex carbohydrate will result in strength and power gains and supercompensation, which is the desired outcome of training. Gains are achieved when the system is stressed properly and breakdown occurs, followed by adequate recovery and consumption of calories. This enables muscle tissue to adapt and prepare for even greater levels of stress.

Strength-Development Exercises

Total-body strength is a must for lacrosse players. The upper body, core, lower body, forearms, and hands are all crucial links in the kinetic chain of performance. Strengthening some but not all areas will result in less-effective performance and may lead to injury. Although all joints and muscles work together on game day, resistance training typically involves some degree of muscle isolation. As long as all muscle groups are addressed at some point during the course of a training week, a composite training effect will be realized. Whether the athlete engages in a total-body workout (i.e., all muscle groups are addressed in a single workout session) or a split routine (i.e., the upper-body and lower-body muscle groups are worked in isolation), the outcome will be effective gains in strength and power.

Lower-Body Strength Exercises

Without a strength base, most lacrosse skills cannot be executed with maximum productivity. A strong foundation allows players to better exhibit balance and body control and produce force at a high level of proficiency. These skills are crucial for dodging, shooting, ball protection, ground ball recovery, and defensive maneuvering (e.g., sliding, body checking).

Lower-body strength is particularly important. Almost every skill used in lacrosse requires engaging the lower body, which makes lower-body strength one of the most—if not *the* most—important considerations when designing a training program.

Back Squat

The back squat is the king of all exercises in that it addresses the major joints and muscle groups used in lacrosse performance. This lift, more than any other, will help develop the strength and power necessary for success on the field. Great track athletes (who are most concerned with speed development) tend to be very good squatters. As lacrosse players who are interested in both linear and lateral speed, the squat should be a part of every healthy, experienced player's routine. Squatting is challenging, both physically and mentally, and some players choose to skip this exercise in favor of other movements. In my professional experience, the most dedicated, hardcore lacrosse players I've been around have loved to squat!

Purpose

This exercise strengthens the hamstrings, quads, glutes, groin, low back, and core.

Equipment

Squat rack, Olympic barbell, plates, collars

Setup

Stand in front of the barbell as it is securely placed in the squat rack. A spotter should be on hand to assist. Be sure that the weights are secured with a collar and that the safety catches are set at an appropriate height. The lifter must be able to set the bar on the safety catches if unable to compete the rep.

Procedure

- With feet slightly wider than shoulder width, using a grip that is slightly wider than shoulder width, place the bar behind the shoulders approximately two inches below the top of the trapezius muscle and lift the bar off of the rack (figure 4.1*a*).
- Lower the hips back, keeping the shins perpendicular to the floor and back tight at all times. The knees should never slide forward in front of the knees. In the bottom position, the hamstrings should be at least parallel to the floor. Keep the chest up, back flat, and weight back on the heels (figure 4.1*b*).
- Ascend with the chest up, moving the hips and shoulders upward at the same rate of speed to ensure proper positioning throughout.
- Perform the movement in a controlled manner, keeping the knees forward and the hips and shoulders lowering and raising at the same rate of speed.

Figure 4.1   Back squat.

Front Squat

The front squat is a great total-body development exercise that can be particularly valuable in helping to train for Olympic lifts such as the power clean. This exercise may be used instead of a back squat (e.g., for a three-week cycle) or may be performed in addition to back squats on a different day. This exercise is one of the best ways to develop core strength and stability.

Purpose

This exercise strengthens the hamstrings, glutes, groin, low back, and core.

Equipment

Squat rack, Olympic barbell, plates and collars.

Setup

Stand in front of the bar as it is positioned in a squat rack. A spotter should be on hand to assist if necessary. Position the bar on the front of the torso near the tops of the shoulders. The hands may be positioned in a power clean position (palms up) or crossed over the shoulder (palms down); either way, the elbows remain pointing forward (figure 4.2a). Position the feet no wider than the inside of the shoes to the outside of the shoulders. Keep the back flat and the chest up.

Procedure

- Start the descent by moving the hips back (never slide the knees in front of the toes) and keeping the weight on the heels throughout the movement.
- Descend as far as hamstring and ankle flexibility allow, ideally to when the hamstrings are at or just below parallel to the floor (figure 4.2*b*).
- Ascend with the chest and elbows up, moving the hips and shoulders up at the same rate of speed.
- Be sure to keep the knees and feet aligned without allowing the knees to rotate inward toward the center of the body.

Figure 4.2   Front squat.

Goblet Squat

For experienced athletes, goblet squats may be used for supplemental work on a high-repetition day. For beginners, the goblet squat is a way to introduce and learn the fundamental principles of squat technique in a short period of time. For some athletes, this movement is a great way to master proper back squat depth. In addition, for some injured athletes who may not be able to perform a back or front squat, the goblet squat may be a great alternative.

Purpose

This exercise strengthens the hamstrings, glutes, groin, low back, and core.

Equipment

Dumbbell

Setup

Hold a dumbbell under the top head with both hands, keeping the elbows high. Place the feet no wider than the inside of the shoes to the outside of the shoulders (figure 4.3a). The athlete may turn the toes out to 30 degrees. Keep the back flat and the chest up.

Procedure

- Start the descent by moving the hips back (never slide the knees in front of the toes), keeping the weight on the heels throughout the movement.
- Descend as far as hamstring and ankle flexibility allow, ideally to when the top of the thigh is at or below parallel to the floor (figure 4.3b).
- Ascend with the chest up, moving the hips and shoulders up at the same rate of speed.

Figure 4.3   Goblet squat.

Romanian Deadlift

The Romanian deadlift can complement squatting movements in that it provides additional support for strengthening the hamstrings, low back, and glutes. It is also a component of the power clean and can be used to improve technique in that lift.

Purpose

This exercise isolates the joints and muscle groups of the posterior chain (glutes, hamstrings, and low back).

Equipment

Olympic barbell, plates, and collars. Substituting dumbbells (one in each hand) for a barbell is a great alternative.

Setup

Hold a barbell with the hands slightly wider than shoulder-width apart (i.e., with a power clean grip). Place the feet at or slightly closer than shoulder-width apart and bend the knees slightly (figure 4.4*a*).

Procedure

- While maintaining a flat back, hinge at the hip joint and lower the bar to approximately midshin or lower, depending on hamstring flexibility (figure 4.4*b*).
- Keep the weight back on the heels at all times and keep the bar over the shoelaces. In some cases, curling the toes upward can help keep the center of gravity in the proper position.
- Raise the bar by driving the hips back to a position of full hip extension. The hips should move on a horizontal plane.

Figure 4.4   Romanian deadlift.

Single-Leg Romanian Deadlift

The single-leg Romanian deadlift is a great unilateral movement that addresses posterior-chain strength in the hamstrings, glutes, and low back as well as balance and body control. This is particularly important for injury prevention in that it helps to stabilize the hip and knee joints and lessens the likelihood of knee-related injuries.

Purpose

This exercise isolates the joints and muscle groups of the posterior chain (glutes, hamstrings, and low back).

Equipment

Dumbbells (optional)

Setup

Stand upright on two legs with the feet six to eight inches apart. Dumbbells may be held in each hand, although the exercise should first be attempted with body weight only. Progress to holding dumbbells after a time of acclimation to this exercise (figure 4.5a).

Procedure

- Bend the knee of the post (planted) leg slightly and hinge at the hip joint, raising the heel of the opposite leg toward the ceiling to counter-balance the torso (figure 4.5b).
- Keep the back flat at all times and the hands (or dumbbells) over the shoelaces of the working foot. Allowing the dumbbells to move beyond the foot may put excess stress on the low back. The weight should be concentrated on the heel of the post foot.
- Hinging on the post knee, drive the torso back up to the start position.

Figure 4.5 Single-leg Romanian deadlift.

Hex Bar Deadlift

The hex bar, which is sometimes referred to as a trap bar, can be used to perform deadlift movements from the floor. For some, the hex bar (as opposed to an Olympic bar) reduces stress on the low back by distributing the load more evenly and placing more stress on the glutes and hamstrings. The hex bar can make teaching and learning deadlift technique less complicated.

Purpose

This exercise strengthens the hamstrings, glutes, groin, low back, and core.

Equipment

Hex bar, plates, collars

Setup

Hold the handles of the hex bar and stand with the feet no wider than the inside of the shoes at the outside of the shoulders (figure 4.6a).

Procedure

- Drive the hips forward and extend at the hip joint, maintaining a flat back and keeping the weight on the heels and the head aligned with the spine (figure 4.6b).
- Lower the bar under control, never bouncing the weights off the floor.

Figure 4.6   Hex bar deadlift.

Leg Press

This multijoint lower-body movement can be used as an alternative to the squat for those with injuries. More experienced athletes can incorporate this exercise into high-rep routines, sometimes to muscular failure. The leg press is a good way to teach beginner athletes to maintain knee and toe alignment in preparation for squatting.

Purpose

This exercise strengthens the quads, hamstrings, and calves.

Equipment

Leg press machine

Setup

Sit in a leg press machine with the back flat against the back pad. Extend the knees (although do not completely straighten them) with the feet flat and the weight concentrated on the heels. It is at this point that many leg press machines require the release of a safety mechanism to allow for full range of motion. The feet should be positioned on the foot plate at approximately shoulder width at an angle that allows the knee to remain behind the toes in the flexed position (figure 4.7a).

Procedure

- Lower the carriage until the knee joint is at or just below 90 degrees (figure 4.7b).
- Extend the legs back to the starting position. Drive through the heels evenly rather than through the balls of the feet.
- During extension, the knees should never be fully extended.
- Keep the back flat and always maintain control of the machine during the lowering and raising phases.

Figure 4.7   Leg press.

Glute-Ham Raise

In lacrosse, the ability to move quickly and powerfully on the field requires strong hamstrings and glute muscles. Successful sprinting, cutting, shuffling, and even shooting is the result of a solid power zone, which the glute-ham raise helps develop.

Purpose

This exercise strengthens the hamstrings, glutes, and low back.

Equipment

Glute-ham bench

Setup

Lie facedown on a glute-ham bench with the shins locked securely into the machine. Position the feet shoulder-width apart and rest the quads toward the back of the pads so that you are in an upright, kneeling position (figure 4.8a).

Procedure

- Maintaining a flat back and keeping the hips extended, bend at the knee joint until the torso is parallel to the floor (figure 4.8b).
- Drive the torso back to the upright starting position in a smooth, controlled manner.
- If additional resistance is needed, either hold a weight or use a rubber mini band.
- The angle of the hip joint should not change; the pivot point is at the knee joint.

Figure 4.8   Glute-ham raise.

Dumbbell Lunge

Single-leg, lower-body movements, such as those performed in this exercise, are a vital aspect of lacrosse development. Many movements of the game, such as running and cutting, are performed on one foot. Unilateral exercises address the joints and muscle groups involved in executing those skills on the field.

Purpose

This exercise strengthens the muscles of the posterior chain and provides stability to the knee and hip joints and the core.

Equipment

Dumbbells

Setup

Stand upright with a dumbbell in each hand (figure 4.9*a*).

Procedure

- Keeping the torso upright, stride forward with one foot, allowing for full range of motion (approximately 90 degrees) in the front knee joint (figure 4.9*b*).
- The toes of the front foot should point forward and be positioned in front of the knee joint. Be careful not to allow the knee to collapse inward.
- Stride back to the starting position, driving primarily with the front foot, keeping the core tight.
- Repeat with the opposite foot.

Figure 4.9   Dumbbell lunge.

Dumbbell Step-Up

The dumbbell step-up is a great way to develop unilateral strength in the lower body.

Purpose

This exercise strengthens the muscles of the posterior chain and provides stability to the knee and hip joints.

Equipment

Dumbbells, a 12- to 18-inch (30-45 cm) box

Setup

Stand in front of the box with a dumbbell in each hand.

Procedure

- With the torso upright, place one foot on the box and bend the knee joint of that leg approximately 90 degrees (figure 4.10*a*). The size of the box will depend on the height of the athlete. With the foot on top of the box, the front knee should be bent to 90 degrees.
- Keeping the majority of the body weight on the front leg, fully extend the knee of the front leg and bring the back foot to the top of the box (figure 4.10*b*). The working knee should always remain behind the toes of the front foot and should never rotate inward.
- Lower the back leg to the starting position.
- Repeat for the prescribed number of reps and then switch legs.

Figure 4.10   Dumbbell step-up.

Dumbbell Elevated Split Squat

One of the more advanced lower body unilateral exercises is the elevated split squat. This movement requires balance, core control, and strength. As a compliment to the back (or front) squat, this exercise should be a part of every healthy lacrosse player's leg-training routine. It is a great way to stabilize the knee and hip joints.

Purpose

This exercise strengthens the muscles of the posterior chain, hip flexors, and core and provides stability to the knee and hip joints.

Equipment

Dumbbells, a 6- to 12-inch (15-30 cm) box

Setup

Stand upright facing away from the box, holding a dumbbell in each hand at the sides.

Procedure

- Place the toes of the back foot on the box and place the front foot forward in a lunge position (figure 4.11*a*). The toes of the front foot should point forward and remain behind the front knee.
- Keeping the chest upright, lower the center of gravity until the front knee is at or below 90 degrees (figure 4.11*b*). Do not allow the front knee to rotate inward.
- Drive the center of gravity straight up until the front knee is almost fully extended.
- Repeat for the prescribed number of reps and then repeat with the opposite leg.

Figure 4.11   Dumbbell elevated split squat.

Calf Raise

The calves and ankles are crucial in the drive phase of linear and lateral speed. Given the amount of contact and movement in traffic, ankle injuries are fairly common in lacrosse. Calf raises provide extra support to that joint.

Purpose

This exercise strengthens the calves and ankle joint.

Equipment

2-inch × 4-inch (5 cm × 10 cm) board or calf raise machine; dumbbells or plates (optional)

Setup

Stand upright on the board or calf raise machine (figure 4.12*a*) (also can stand with the heels off the edge of the support mechanism). Weight can be added by holding dumbbells or plates or by using the resistance of a calf raise machine.

Procedure

- Elevate the body, extending through the balls of the feet, keeping the knees straight and the torso upright (figure 4.12*b*).
- Return the ankles to the starting position.

Figure 4.12   Calf raise.

Nordic Curl

In many athletes the quads tend to be much stronger than the hamstrings. This imbalance may result in injuries. That is why hamstring isolation movements, such as those performed in this exercise, should be in every athlete's protocol.

Purpose

This exercise isolates the muscle groups of the posterior chain (glutes, hamstrings, and low back).

Setup

Start in a kneeling position with heels secured (figure 4.13a).

Procedure

- Slowly lean forward, hinging at the knee joint and not the hip joint. The hamstrings and glutes should engage during the downward phase.

- As the working athlete slowly falls forward (figure 4.13b), put hands in front to catch body as it nears the floor (figure 4.13c).

- Push back slightly with the hands to start the upward movement. Attempt to regain control of the torso with the glutes and hamstrings.

Figure 4.13   Nordic curl.

Swiss Ball Hamstring Curl

Hamstring isolation is a key part of overall lacrosse training. Improved hamstring strength will allow for more power production and help to resist injuries during practice and competition. In many school and commercial facilities, Swiss balls have become a common piece of equipment.

Purpose

This exercise isolates the hamstrings and engages the core muscles.

Equipment

Swiss ball

Setup

Lying faceup, place the heels on top of a Swiss ball with the feet 6 inches (15 cm) apart and the toes pointed up.

Procedure

- Fully extend the hips toward the ceiling, holding the arms at the sides of the torso with the palms facing down (figure 4.14*a*).
- Bend at the knee joint and roll the ball underneath the hips until the knee joint is bent at least 90 degrees (figure 4.14*b*).
- Slowly extend the knees and return to the starting position, keeping the hips off the ground at all times.

Figure 4.14   Swiss ball hamstring curl.

Dumbbell Lateral Squat

Lateral speed and mobility are crucial skills in lacrosse. The dumbbell lateral squat focuses on strength, flexibility, and knee stability to increase the power of lateral movements and help prevent knee and ankle injury.

Purpose

This exercise strengthens the groin and glutes and helps stabilize the knee joint.

Equipment

Dumbbell

Setup

Stand with the feet wider than shoulder-width apart and hold the top head of one dumbbell with both hands in front of the body (figure 4.15a).

Procedure

- With the chest upright, slowly shift the center of gravity to one foot, keeping the weight concentrated on the heel.
- Keeping the back flat, bend the knee and lower the center of gravity as far as flexibility allows (figure 4.15b), touching the dumbbell to the floor if possible.
- Return to the starting position and repeat to the other side, alternating sides with each repetition.
- Keep the dumbbell between the feet throughout the movement.

Figure 4.15   Dumbbell lateral squat.

Barbell Lateral Slide

Another great movement to address lateral movement is the barbell lateral slide. This movement stresses not only strength in the adductors and abductors but also hip flexibility.

Purpose

This exercise strengthens the groin and glutes and helps stabilize the knee joint.

Equipment

Barbell

Setup

Stand with the feet wider than shoulder-width apart and hold the barbell behind the head with the bar placed 2 inches (5 cm) below the top of the trapezius (figure 4.16a).

Procedure

- With the chest upright, slowly shift the center of gravity to one foot, keeping the weight concentrated on the heel.
- Lower as far as flexibility allows and shift the center of gravity toward the other foot, sliding the hips on a horizontal plane (figure 4.16b).
- Perform the prescribed number of repetitions.

Figure 4.16   Barbell lateral slide.

Band Slide

Lateral speed and mobility are crucial skills in lacrosse. The band slide focuses on strength, flexibility, and knee stability to increase the power of lateral movements and help prevent knee and ankle injury.

Purpose

This exercise strengthens the groin and glutes and helps stabilize the knee joint.

Equipment

Mini band

Setup

Stand upright with a mini band just below the knees.

Procedure

- Flex slightly at the knee and hip joints in an athletic position (figure 4.17a).
- Keeping the chest upright, step as far as possible with the lead foot. When the lead foot has achieved full range of motion, the trail foot should then be moved toward the lead foot but be placed no closer than 12 to 16 inches from the lead foot (the feet should never be brought together) and repeat in a shuffling manner (figure 4.17, b and c).
- Perform the prescribed number of repetitions and then repeat in the opposite direction.

Figure 4.17   Band slide.

Upper-Body Strength Exercises

Although lower-body strength provides the primary base of support for most lacrosse movements and skills, upper-body strength is also a critical component for a lacrosse player. Finely tuned stick control, the ability to finish a shot with sufficient velocity, having adequate body armor to withstand body checks, and passing strength and accuracy all require upper-body strength. Shoulder, back, and forearm strength contribute to stick control; back, shoulder, and core strength are used to defend against (or deliver!) body checks; and shoulder, trapezius, and neck strength stabilize the head during contact. A well-designed, thorough strength program should address all of these components, which are crucial for executing lacrosse-specific skills.

Barbell Bench Press

In many programs, the bench press is a popular measurement of upper-body strength. Although not specific to lacrosse (lacrosse players should never be on their backs looking up!), this exercise is a good general indicator of shoulder and triceps strength and is used in both training and testing.

Purpose

This exercise strengthens the chest, shoulders, upper back, and triceps.

Equipment

Bench rack, Olympic barbell, plates, collars

Setup

Lie faceup on a bench with the hips and shoulder blades in contact with the bench and the feet flat on the floor. Place the hands slightly wider than shoulder-width apart on the bar with thumbs wrapped around the bar (figure 4.18a).

Procedure

- With the aid of a spotter, remove the bar from the rack and pause to stabilize shoulders.
- Lower bar until it touches the base of the sternum (figure 4.18b). Elbows should rotate inward, not flare outward.
- Avoid excessive arching of the back and bouncing the bar off of the chest after the descent.
- In a controlled manner, push the bar back up along a consistent path and return to the starting position
- Perform the prescribed number of reps and then return the bar to the rack.

Figure 4.18   Barbell bench press.

Dumbbell Bench Press

The dumbbell variation of the bench press requires each arm to work independently, which is similar to the way the upper body operates on the lacrosse field. The dumbbell bench press can be used as either a supplement or an alternative to the barbell bench press.

Purpose

This exercise strengthens the chest, shoulders, and triceps.

Equipment

Dumbbells, bench

Setup

Lie faceup on a bench holding a dumbbell in each hand with the arms straight toward the ceiling (figure 4.19a). The hands may be turned in slightly (45 degrees) to avoid excessive joint stress. Place the feet flat on the floor.

Procedure

- Keeping the shoulder joint at approximately 45 degrees, lower the dumbbells until the upper arms are at least parallel to the floor (figure 4.19b).
- Avoid jerking or bouncing at the bottom of the movement.
- Raise the dumbbells and return to the starting position.

Figure 4.19   Dumbbell bench press.

Dumbbell Alternating Incline Press

This unilateral movement addresses the musculature of the upper chest. It also requires shoulder stability in that while one arm is pressing, the other is stabilizing at the top of the movement. This is important in injury prevention.

Purpose

This exercise strengthens the chest, shoulders, upper back, and triceps.

Equipment

Dumbbells, a 30- to 45-degree incline bench

Setup

Lie faceup on the incline bench with the arms extended, holding a dumbbell in each hand. The hands may be turned in slightly to avoid excessive joint stress. Place the feet flat on the floor (figure 4.20a).

Procedure

- Keeping one arm extended, lower the opposite dumbbell until the upper arm is at least parallel to the floor (figure 4.20b).
- Raise the dumbbell and return to the starting position.
- Perform the same movement with the opposite hand, alternating dumbbells each time.

Figure 4.20 Dumbbell alternating incline press.

Dumbbell Shoulder Press

The dumbbell shoulder press is a great way to build shoulder, core, and triceps strength and develop shoulder flexibility.

Purpose

This exercise strengthens the deltoids, upper back, and triceps.

Equipment

Dumbbells, weight bench with back

Setup

Sit upright on weight bench with the back flat against the backrest and the feet shoulder-width apart. Hold a dumbbell in each hand at approximately the width of the shoulder joint with the hands facing forward (figure 4.21a).

Procedure

- Keeping the muscles of the torso tightened, press up and extend the arms until the elbows are locked with the dumbbells overhead (figure 4.21b).
- Push in a vertical plane to alleviate stress on the low back. Moving the dumbbells too far in front of the shoulders may place excessive stress on the supporting structures of the low back.

Figure 4.21   Seated dumbbell shoulder press.

Barbell Military Press

For athletes who do not have shoulder impingement or low-back restrictions, the barbell military press is a great way to build shoulder, core, and triceps strength and develop shoulder flexibility.

Purpose

This exercise strengthens the deltoids, upper back, and triceps.

Equipment

Olympic barbell, plates, collars, rack

Setup

Stand upright with the feet shoulder-width apart. Hold a barbell at the level of the shoulders with the hands approximately shoulder-width apart (figure 4.22a).

Procedure

- Keeping the back flat and the core tight throughout, press the bar up and extend the arms until the elbows are locked (figure 4.22b).
- Once the bar clears the head, push backward and then up in a vertical plane and extend the bar directly overhead to alleviate stress on the low back.
- Lower the bar to the start position.

Figure 4.22　Barbell military press.

Chin-Up

This multijoint movement addresses several muscle groups simultaneously and is therefore a very efficient addition to any program. It can also be used for training or testing upper-back and grip endurance.

Purpose

This exercise strengthens the upper back, shoulders, biceps, forearms, and hands.

Equipment

Chin-up bar

Setup

Hold a chin-up bar with the palms facing up and the arms and body fully extended (figure 4.23*a*).

Procedure

- Without swinging the legs or torso, pull the chin to a point just above the bar (figure 4.23*b*).
- Lower the torso until the arms are fully extended and the shoulders are depressed.

Figure 4.23   Chin-up.

Towel Pull-Up

By holding a towel or rope, the same muscle groups are being worked as in the traditional chin-up with an added challenge to the hands and forearms.

Purpose

This exercise strengthens the upper back, shoulders, biceps, forearms, and hands.

Equipment

Two towels or ropes, chin-up bar

Setup

Wrap a towel or rope around a chin-up bar. (Make sure that the towel or rope is strong enough to withstand the force of the movement.) Hold the towel or rope with the palms facing each other (see figure 4.24a).

Procedure

- Without swinging the legs or torso, pull the chin to a point just above the bar (figure 4.24b).
- Lower the torso until the arms are fully extended and the shoulders are depressed.

Figure 4.24　Towel pull-up.

Dumbbell Shrug

Stabilizing the upper back and neck is essential in contact sports such as lacrosse. Given the amount of contact (stick–stick, stick–body, and body–body) involved in lacrosse, the shoulders, neck, and trapezius region must be strong to withstand (and deliver) repeated upper-body blows and prevent injury.

Purpose

This exercise isolates the trapezius and helps to stabilize the head and neck.

Equipment

Dumbbells

Setup

Stand upright with the feet shoulder-width apart. Hold a dumbbell in each hand with the palms facing in (figure 4.25a).

Procedure

- Elevate the traps and hold at the top of the movement for one second (figure 4.25b).
- Lower to the starting position.

Figure 4.25 Dumbbell shrug.

Upright Row

The upright row is a beneficial supplement to pressing and pulling movements because it reinforces the strength in the shoulders and upper-back region. Much like the shoulder shrug, it helps develop some of the musculature used to stabilize the shoulder and neck region.

Purpose

This exercise addresses the trapezius, shoulders, and upper back.

Equipment

Olympic barbell, plates (optional), collars

Setup

Stand upright with the feet shoulder-width apart. Hold a bar with the hands 6 to 8 inches (15-20 cm) apart and the palms facing down in an overhand grip (figure 4.26a).

Procedure

- Keeping the core muscles tight, raise the bar toward the chin, leading with the elbows (figure 4.26b).
- Keep the elbows higher than the bar throughout the range of motion.
- Once the bar is just below the chin, lower to the starting position.

Figure 4.26   Upright row.

Single-Arm Dumbbell Row

The movements in this exercise help develop upper-back and shoulder strength. Rowing or pulling help to create balance and stability in the shoulder joint because many athletes tend to overemphasize pushing movements (e.g., bench press) and often neglect the countermovement (i.e., pulling). If the anterior and posterior muscle groups are not adequately balanced, the shoulder joint may be more susceptible to injury.

Purpose

This exercise strengthens the upper back, shoulders, biceps, forearms, and hands.

Equipment

Dumbbell, weight bench

Setup

Stand with one foot positioned on the floor next to the bench and the other knee bent and placed on the top of the bench. Hold a dumbbell in the hand of the foot that is on the floor and place the hand on the side with the bent knee on the bench (figure 4.27a). This hand should be positioned slightly ahead of the shoulders so that the back remains parallel to the floor.

Procedure

- Keep the back flat and drive the elbow of the working arm toward the ceiling, maintaining control of the dumbbell throughout the range of motion (figure 4.27b).
- When the dumbbell reaches torso height, lower it in a controlled manner back to the starting position.

Figure 4.27   Single-arm dumbbell row.

Lat Pulldown

Another way to train the upper back and biceps is the lat pulldown. It can be used by athletes who are unable to perform pull-ups or as a supplemental movement in addition to other upper-back exercises such as seated rows or chin-ups.

Purpose

This exercise strengthens the upper back and biceps.

Equipment

Lat pulldown machine

Setup

Begin by sitting on the seat of a lat pulldown machine. Grip the handles either with a wide grip (figure 4.28a) or with a narrow-grip handle or "V" attachment.

Procedure

- Maintaining a flat back, pull the bar in a controlled, smooth motion to the chin (figure 4.28b). Pause for one second.
- Slowly raise the bar to the start position with a one-second pause at the top.

Figure 4.28   Lat pulldown.

Machine Low Row

Much like the single-arm dumbbell row, the seated row develops strength and stability in the upper back and posterior deltoid region. If a low row machine is available, this exercise will be beneficial in helping to compliment other horizontal pushing movements.

Purpose

This exercise strengthens the upper back, shoulders, biceps, forearms, and hands.

Equipment

Low row machine

Setup

Begin in a seated position on a low row machine. Hold the handles with both hands approximately 6 to 8 inches (15-20 cm) apart and the arms fully extended (figure 4.29a). The back should be flat and the torso upright (90 degrees from the floor).

Procedure

- Maintaining a flat back for support throughout the movement, pull the hands toward the sternum, driving the elbows back as far as shoulder flexibility will allow (figure 4.29b).

- Lower the handles toward the starting position, extend the arms forward, and return to the start position. During both the start and fully extended positions, the angle of the torso may extend beyond 90 degrees (approximately 20 degrees in either direction) but the spine should remain erect throughout. Those with greater hip mobility may be able to achieve slightly more range of motion than those who are more inflexible.

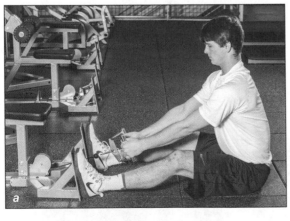 

Figure 4.29   Machine low row.

Reverse Pull-Up

For those who may be unable to perform a body-weight pull-up, the reverse-pull up is a way to perform a similar movement without having to support the entire weight of the body. In addition, those with mobility restrictions or injury can find this exercise very beneficial.

Purpose

This exercise strengthens the upper back, shoulders, biceps, forearms, and hands.

Equipment

Power rack, Olympic barbell

Setup

Place a bar in a power rack approximately three to four feet (1-1.2 m) above the floor. Begin in a faceup position and grip the bar with the hands slightly wider than shoulder-width apart.

Procedure

- With the hips fully extended, lower the torso toward the floor (figure 4.30a).
- Once the arms are fully extended, pull the torso toward the bar. Touch the chest to the bar if flexibility and strength allow (figure 4.30b).
- Keep the back and core flat throughout.

Figure 4.30   Reverse pull-up.

Suspension Row

This exercise helps lacrosse players develop strength and stability in the shoulders and upper back. This is crucial for stick control and injury prevention.

Purpose

This exercise strengthens the upper back and posterior deltoids.

Equipment

Suspension device, cross bar or hook

Setup

Stand upright with the hips and knees extended. Hold the handles of a suspension device with both hands in front of the chest. Place the feet together and position them underneath the shoulders.

Procedure

- While extending the arms, lean back until the body is at a 45-degree angle with the heels planted firmly on the ground (figure 4.31a).
- Separating the hands slightly, pull the body back to the upright starting position, pulling the elbows past the level of the spine (figure 4.31b).
- Keep the back flat throughout the movement.
- To increase resistance, move the feet forward, ahead of the hips.

Figure 4.31 Suspension row.

Suspension Reverse Fly

The suspension reverse fly isolates the posterior deltoid muscles. This muscle plays a major role in stabilizing the shoulder joint. Due to limited strength, many athletes find this exercise very challenging.

Purpose

This exercise isolates the posterior deltoids.

Equipment

Suspension device, cross bar or hook

Setup

Stand upright with the hips and knees extended. Hold the handles of a suspension device with both hands in front of the chest, arms extended and locked (figure 4.32a). Place the feet together and position them slightly ahead of the shoulders.

Procedure

- Keeping the elbows bent just a few degrees throughout the movement, pull the arms apart so that the shoulder is at a 90-degree angle with the palms facing in. Drive the torso and hips forward, making a T shape at the top of the movement (figure 4.32b).
- Lower the body back to the starting position, keeping the hips extended throughout the movement.
- To increase resistance, move the feet forward, ahead of the hips.

Figure 4.32 Suspension reverse fly.

Suspension Push-Up

Upper-body strength is crucial for stick handling, ball control, checking, and maintaining balance when changing directions.

Purpose

This exercise strengthens the core, chest, shoulders, and triceps.

Equipment

Suspension device, cross bar or hook

Setup

Face away from the Suspension and place the hands in the handles with the palms facing down. Walk the feet back until the body is approximately 45 degrees to the floor (figure 4.33a).

Procedure

- Keeping the hips extended, lower the chest toward the floor (figure 4.33b).
- Perform a push up, extending the arms at the top of the movement.
- To increase resistance, move the feet back away from the suspension device handles so that the body is more parallel to the floor. To decrease resistance, move the feet forward so that the body is more upright.

Figure 4.33   Suspension push-up.

Lateral Raise

Fending off a stick check, stick handling, passing, shooting, and body contact all require strong deltoids and stability in the shoulder joint. Because contact is often initiated with the shoulders, having sufficient body armor to protect the joint is important.

Purpose

This exercise isolates the medial deltoid muscles.

Equipment

Dumbbells

Setup

Stand upright with the feet shoulder-width apart. Hold a dumbbell in each hand with the arms at the sides and the elbows slightly bent (figure 4.34a).

Procedure

- Raise the arms to the sides until the dumbbells are at shoulder height (figure 4.34b).
- Throughout the movement, the palms should be facing down (or turned out at the top) and not turned forward.
- Lower the dumbbells back to the starting position in a slow, controlled manner.

Figure 4.34   Lateral raise.

Dumbbell Lying Triceps Extension

Triceps-isolation movements help improve triceps strength, which is necessary for other pushing movements such as the bench press and the shoulder press.

Purpose

This exercise strengthens the triceps.

Equipment

Weight bench, dumbbells

Setup

Lie flat on a bench with a dumbbell in each hand.

Procedure

- Raise the tip of the elbows up toward the ceiling and keep the palms facing the midline (figure 4.35a).
- Extend the arms up toward the ceiling until the elbows are fully extended (figure 4.35b).
- Lower the dumbbells toward the tops of the shoulders in a smooth, controlled manner.

Figure 4.35   Dumbbell lying triceps extension.

Triceps Dip

Dips with body weight or added weight improve triceps strength and endurance, which can bolster other pressing movements such as the bench press and the shoulder press.

Purpose

This exercise strengthens the upper back, shoulders, and triceps.

Equipment

Dip bar

Setup

Step up to a dip bar with the arms fully extended. Place the hands below the shoulders (figure 4.36a).

Procedure

- Bend the elbows and lower the torso toward the floor or the top of the dip stand, trying to achieve a 90-degree angle at the elbow joint (figure 4.36b).
- When 90 degrees or lower is attained, extend the arms back up to a locked position.
- Add weight by using a weighted vest or holding a dumbbell between the calves of crossed ankles.

Figure 4.36 Triceps dip.

Reverse Dip

Some athletes may be unable to perform a standard triceps dip on a dip stand. An alternative is the reverse dip, which elicits similar results.

Purpose

This exercise strengthens the upper back, shoulders, and triceps.

Equipment

Two weight benches

Setup

Place the hands, palms facing back, on the front edge of the back bench. Place the feet on the top of the opposite bench with the knees slightly bent (figure 4.37a).

Procedure

- Bend the elbows and lower the hips toward the floor, trying to achieve a 90-degree angle at the elbow joint (figure 4.37b).
- When 90 degrees or lower is attained, extend the arms back up to a locked position.
- Add weight by having a partner place weight plates on the lap.

Figure 4.37   Reverse dip.

Dumbbell Alternating Biceps Curl

The biceps play a role in lacrosse performance, primarily in stick control. Being able to activate the biceps during a stick check will help the athlete maintain control of the ball.

Purpose

This exercise strengthens the biceps.

Equipment

Dumbbells

Setup

Stand upright with the feet shoulder-width apart. Hold a dumbbell in each hand with the arms at the sides, palms facing in.

Procedure

- Curl one dumbbell upward until full range of motion is attained (figure 4.38a). Keep the other hand down at the side.
- Slowly rotate the dumbbell from a palms-in position to a palms-up position at the top of the movement (figure 4.38b).
- Lower the dumbbell to the starting position and repeat with the other hand.

Figure 4.38 Dumbbell alternating biceps curl.

Dumbbell Hold

Ball-handling skills, such as passing, shooting, and checking, require strong hands and forearms. These vital links in the kinetic chain connect the stick to the hips and core.

Purpose

This exercise strengthens the forearms and hands.

Setup

Stand upright with the feet shoulder-width apart.

Equipment

Dumbbells

Procedure

- Hold the outside edge of the top head of a dumbbell in each hand (figure 4.39).
- Hold for as long as finger and grip strength allow—ideally 30 seconds or longer.

Figure 4.39   Dumbbell hold.

Plate Hold

A strong grip is necessary for stick handling and maneuvering. Hand and finger strength should be addressed throughout the year, even in-season.

Purpose

This exercise strengthens the forearms and hands.

Equipment

Weight plates

Procedure

- Hold the outside edge of a 25- to 45-pound (12-20 kg) weight plate in each hand (figure 4.40).
- Hold for as long as finger and grip strength allow—ideally 30 seconds or longer.

Figure 4.40   Plate hold.

Reverse Curl

Forearm strength is essential for a lacrosse player. The reverse curl is a great way to strengthen this muscle group.

Purpose

This exercise strengthens the forearms and hands.

Equipment

Olympic barbell with or without added weight, EZ-Curl bar with or without added weight, light bar (usually 10 kg), or dumbbells

Setup

Stand holding a bar with the hands shoulder-width apart and the palms facing down (figure 4.41a).

Procedure

- Keeping the elbows tucked in to the torso, curl the bar upward toward the top of the chest (figure 4.41b).
- Lower in a smooth, controlled manner.
- Keep the hand and the forearm aligned and minimize flexion of the wrist joint.

Figure 4.41   Reverse curl.

Core-Strength Exercises

One of the most underdeveloped muscle groups in younger athletes is the core. The core muscles stabilize and support the torso and provide adequate stability in most sport movements. Core-strengthening exercises generally fall into the following categories: stabilization, rotation, extension, and flexion. Maintaining body position, shooting, passing, changing direction, and checking all require a substantial level of core development. In each of these skills, the power and strength generated by the major musculature of the lower body must be transferred, via the core, to the upper body and ultimately to the stick. The core is recognized as a vital link in the kinetic chain connecting the working muscles together to generate movement. Every lacrosse training program should include elements of core training regardless of the time of year.

Front Plank

Lacrosse players must have great core strength to execute on the field. A strong core provides body control and stability during movement. The plank is a simple, easy-to-perform exercise that can be done year round, either in a weight room or on the field.

Purpose

This exercise promotes core strength and endurance.

Setup

Lie facedown on the floor.

Procedure

- Bend the elbows 90 degrees and position them under the shoulders. Hold the torso straight at all times in a push-up position (figure 4.42).
- Maintain a flat back for the prescribed time, usually 30 seconds or longer.

Figure 4.42   Front plank.

Resisted Crunch

Resisted crunches allow a lacrosse player to perform a core flexion movement against resistance (e.g., a medicine ball or plate). A stronger core adds power to shots and helps the athlete avoid back pain due to the constant torso rotation involved in lacrosse.

Purpose

This exercise strengthens the upper and lower abs.

Equipment

Swiss ball and dumbbell or medicine ball

Setup

Lie faceup on a Swiss ball. Hold a dumbbell or medicine ball in the air with the elbows slightly bent (figure 4.43a).

Procedure

- Keeping the lower back positioned on the ball, raise the chest up and forward. Keep the elbows fixed in order to isolate the core muscles (figure 4.43b).

- Return to the starting position. Try to use the abdominal muscles instead of the shoulders to elevate the dumbbell or medicine ball. A controlled tempo will yield better results.

Figure 4.43 Resisted crunch.

Sit-Up

The sit-up is a core-flexion movement that can be used in both training and testing.

Purpose

This exercise strengthens the upper and lower abs.

Setup

Lie faceup with the knees at 90 degrees and the feet either unsupported or supported by a partner or hooked under a machine or rack (figure 4.44a).

Procedure

- With the arms folded across the chest, raise the torso up toward the knees and bring the hip joint beyond 90 degrees (figure 4.44b).
- Maintain a flat back throughout the entire range of motion. Avoid jerking and bouncing during both the up and downward phases. Always maintain proper technique.

Figure 4.44   Sit-up.

Band Torso Rotation

Lacrosse movements require a great deal of torso rotation. If the torso muscles are not strengthened during preparation, the athlete may not have sufficient power for shooting and passing. In addition, stronger oblique muscles will help the athlete avoid excessive fatigue and thus avoid low-back pain and soreness.

Purpose

This exercise strengthens the trunk and core (obliques).

Equipment

Resistance band, support post such as a power rack

Setup

Stand upright with the feet slightly wider than shoulder-width apart. Securely fix the band to a rack support or other upright column. Hold the band with the hands interlocked in front of the torso with the elbows slightly bent (figure 4.45a).

Procedure

- Rotate in one direction against the resistance of the band, rotating the back hip 90 degrees (figure 4.45b). The band should remain horizontal throughout.
- Rotate the head, shoulders, hands, and hips as a single component.

Figure 4.45 Band torso rotation.

Barbell Rotation

Much like the band torso rotation exercise, the barbell rotation improves core rotation strength and power.

Purpose

This exercise strengthens the trunk and core (obliques).

Equipment

Olympic barbell, land mine device

Setup

Stand upright with the feet slightly wider than shoulder-width apart. Hold both hands together on the end of an Olympic bar that is placed in a corner of the room or in a land mine device (figure 4.46a). Hold the arms out in front of the torso with the elbows slightly bent.

Procedure

- Rotate in one direction against the resistance of the bar, rotating the back hip and bringing the hands lower than the hip (figure 4.46b).
- Rotate the head, shoulders, hands, and hips as a single component.
- Rotate the bar back to the start position and continue to the other side of the body.
- Always control the speed of the bar, making sure that the core muscles are worked rather than just the shoulders.

Figure 4.46   Barbell rotation.

Medicine Ball Torso Toss

Explosive power generated by the core is also a major area of development for lacrosse players. Torso tosses with a medicine ball help to develop core stability and power.

Purpose

This exercise strengthens the trunk and core (obliques).

Equipment

Medicine ball

Setup

Stand upright beside a partner or wall with the feet slightly wider than shoulder-width apart. Hold a medicine ball in front of the chest.

Procedure

- Bend slightly at the hip joint and assume an athletic position, with the elbows bent slightly and out in front of the body.
- Holding the ball, rotate the hips in one direction and bring the head, eyes, and hands toward one hip (figure 4.47a).
- Rotate the hips back toward the center point and release the ball toward the wall or partner (figure 4.47b).
- Repeat on the opposite side.

Figure 4.47   Medicine ball torso toss.

Swiss Ball Stabilization

Lacrosse players must have great core strength to execute on the field. This stabilization movement is similar to a plank but adds the instability of a Swiss ball for more intensity.

Purpose

This exercise promotes strength and endurance in the core and shoulder joints.

Equipment

Swiss ball

Setup

With locked elbows, palms facing the midline and the fingertips pointing out, place the hands shoulder-width apart on either edge of a Swiss ball.

Procedure

- Maintain a push-up position with the legs extended and the hips straight (figure 4.48).
- Try to minimize lateral or rotational movement and keep the shoulders squared at all times.
- Hold the position for the prescribed amount of time, usually 30 seconds or longer.

Figure 4.48　Swiss ball stabilization.

Swiss Ball Rollout

Another exercise that features the Swiss ball is the rollout. This movement stresses the core and low-back muscles and requires the athlete to maintain hip extension. Perfect form is required!

Purpose

This exercise elongates the abs and creates vertical stress on the trunk musculature.

Equipment

Swiss ball

Setup

Kneel on the floor in front of a Swiss ball.

Procedure

- Place the hands on top of the Swiss ball and fully extend the hips in an upright, kneeling position (figure 4.49a).
- Slowly roll the ball away from the knees and hinge at the knee joint—not the hips—until full range of motion is achieved (figure 4.49b). Stabilize the trunk by rolling the forearms along the top of the ball.
- Once fully extended, slowly roll back and bring the torso into an upright position. On the way up, do not flex at the hip joint but rather keep the shoulders upright and bend at the knee joint.

Figure 4.49 Swiss ball rollout.

Neck-Strength Exercises

Neck strength is a critical component for lacrosse players due to the amount of physical contact involved in the sport. As lacrosse players continue to develop strength, power, speed, and size, the collisions grow in magnitude. Incidences of head trauma, concussions, and other contact-related injuries to the head and neck necessitate the regular inclusion of neck-strengthening movements in the training routine. Stabilization of the head and neck is often ignored by younger athletes but may be one of the most important elements of the training program from the standpoint of injury prevention.

Four-Way Neck Strengthening

For athletes involved in contact sports such as lacrosse, neck stability is essential to preventing neck and head injuries. No exercise can guarantee injury-free performance. However, stronger neck stabilizers allow the athlete to better withstand checks and other hits and may reduce the number and severity of head and neck injuries. A special thank you to Coach Mike Gittleson (a legend in the strength & conditioning profession) for his tips on this neck training section.

Purpose

This exercise stabilizes the neck muscles.

Equipment

Bench, towel or T-shirt

Setup

One athlete lies on a bench with the head extended over the edge. The spotter stands next to the bench and provides manual resistance. The spotter can use a towel or T-shirt to keep the hands from slipping.

Procedure

- The athlete performs each repetition with slow, steady movement with a goal of six to eight reps in each direction. The positions are as follows:
  - Lying faceup with the spotter's hands on the forehead (figure 4.50a)
  - Lying facedown with the spotter's hands on the back of the head (figure 4.50b)
  - Lying on the right side with the spotter's hands on the side of the head (figure 4.50c)
  - Lying on the left side with the spotter's hands on the side of the head (figure 4.50d)

Figure 4.50   Four-way neck strengthening.

- The athlete activates the muscles of the neck and attempts to deactivate the shoulders during the movement. This allows for isolation of the neck muscles during the movement.
- The spotter allows the athlete to perform each repetition at the same pace and accommodates the athlete's range of motion and leverage, while providing consistent resistance. The spotter should set the tempo of raising in 1 to 2 seconds and lowering in 4 to 5 seconds.
- The reps should initially be performed with mild resistance and should gradually increase to all-out effort on the final repetition.
- There should be no jerking or bouncing, and the lifter should pause with pressure against the spotter's resistance at the top of the movement.
- The lifter must provide feedback to the spotter to ensure the move is done safely.

Shoulder Shrug

For prevention of head and neck injuries, shoulder shrugs should complement neck-isolation movements. The neck, trapezius, and upper back are all interconnected and support and reinforce one another. Some variation of the shoulder shrug, with either dumbbells or a barbell, is important for maintaining a strong, healthy neck and upper-back region.

Purpose

This exercise isolates the upper back and trapezius.

Equipment

Dumbbells or barbell

Setup

Stand upright with a dumbbell in each hand or a barbell. Hold with arms extended and palms down (figure 4.51a).

Procedure

- Elevate the traps and hold at the top of the movement for one second (figure 4.51b).
- Lower the shoulders to the starting position.
- Be sure to use appropriate resistance.

Figure 4.51   Shoulder shrug.

POWER DEVELOPMENT FOR LACROSSE

Power is the product of force and velocity. In other words, it can be described as "the ability to produce force in as short a time period as possible" (Baechle and Earle 2008). In a sport in which few differences often exist between teams, the ability to execute lacrosse skills in a limited amount of time may be the difference in making a play and not or winning a game and losing. Accelerating from a stationary position, repetitive lateral defensive movement, dodging an opponent, and releasing a shot before a defender has time to react all require the generation of explosive force. The better an athlete can decelerate and transfer the momentum in another plane, the better he or she will be able to withstand the stress of high-velocity redirection. In addition, using proper technique and mastering the fundamental mechanics of jump training and landing reduce the likelihood of injury. Incorporating this type of training into the routine will better prepare the joints and connective tissue for more dynamic, high-speed activity such as practice and games. Power should be trained along with strength, speed, and conditioning to produce the most effective long-term gains.

Power-Training Fundamentals

Lacrosse is essentially a fast-moving expression of speed and power. Making decisions rapidly as play unfolds, accelerating, cutting, shooting, passing, and blocking shots all require the combination of physical and mental strength and speed. Power training enables the athlete to transfer the strength earned through many hours of resistance training to powerful, quick movements on the field.

Technique

Power training must be performed properly in order to fully realize the benefits. By concentrating on the speed and technical specifics of each movement, the athlete will have a more beneficial and safer experience. Having a sense of which muscle groups are being activated and feeling the body's muscular and neurological systems interact should be a part of power development. This kinesthetic awareness should transfer to the field in the execution of lacrosse-specific skills.

- When starting a plyometric movement, athletes should maintain a flat back and a tight core.
- When starting and landing in any jump exercise, the athlete should keep the ankle and knee joints in alignment. This means that during the takeoff and landing stages, the hips, knees, and feet are in line with one another. Without emphasizing alignment, poor technique will be reinforced and injuries may occur. Younger athletes often initiate jumping movement or land with the knees bowed inward.

This is generally a signal that the hip and knee joints are not strong and may need extra strength development.

- The objective in any plyometric exercise is to move the center of gravity as far as possible. In a box jump, for example, the hips should be elevated as high as possible. Many younger athletes are impressed with the movement of the feet. To truly gauge the success of a movement, the hips (i.e., center of gravity) should be the focus.
- When finishing a jump, athletes should land with a flat back with the knees slightly bent and the hips, knees, and ankles aligned. The body should be under control during the landing phase, much like a gymnast sticks the landing after performing a routine.

Progression

Athletes should start with bilateral (i.e., two leg) jumps and progress to unilateral (i.e., one leg) jumps only after significant experience. To allow for a gradual adaptation the stress imposed by this type of training, inexperienced athletes should begin with a relatively low volume and progress to a higher volume over time (Chu and Faigenbaum 2002). For an adult beginner, 80 to 120 contacts (the number of times a foot contacts a surface) are recommended and should progress gradually to no more than 200 total contacts per session (Chu and Faigenbaum 2002). For youth and adolescent athletes, begin plyometric training with 1 to 3 sets of 6 to10 reps for the lower and upper body (Chu and Myer 2013).

Safety

The jumping surface must be dry and free of hazards (e.g., dumbbells, boxes) to allow for a clear landing. Athletes should wear soft-soled shoes or cross-training shoes, to help absorb the impact and should wear clothes that allow for full range of motion. Finally, athletes should focus the mind on the event at hand and eliminate possible distractions.

Power-Development Exercises

Explosive power is a major key to success for a lacrosse player. Plyometric training is a way for the athlete to become more explosive and react faster. Band-resisted movements and Olympic variations can also improve power.

The athlete goes through three stages while performing a plyometric movement, and each stage must be executed carefully. The first is the eccentric, or muscle-lengthening, phase, during which energy is generated. The next stage is a slight pause known as the amortization phase. When performing plyometric movements, the athlete should try to shorten this phase as much as possible by minimizing contact time on the ground or between movements. The third phase is the concentric, or muscle-shortening, phase, which is the actual jump or rebound portion of the movement.

Box Jump

The box jump is a great tool for working on double-leg explosiveness. Training with box jumps improves the vertical and broad jumps and helps improve on-field speed by simulating the sudden burst of speed from a stationary position.

Purpose

This exercise develops lower-body explosiveness.

Equipment

12- to 32-inch (30-80 cm) box

Setup

Stand with the feet approximately shoulder-width apart in front of a box.

Procedure

- Shift the weight back to the heels, flexing at the knee and hip joints slightly. Bring the hands back through the hips (figure 4.52a).
- Keep the back flat and core muscles tightened at all times.
- Drive the hands forward and jump (figure 4.52b), extending the knee and hip joints rapidly.
- Land on box with both feet flat, the knees and hips slightly flexed, and the chest up (figure 4.52c). The objective is to land without a heavy impact.
- Step off the box and repeat.

Figure 4.52   Box jump.

Single-Leg Power Hop

Single-leg power hops are a great way to train the initial push phase of linear running motion. The athlete can maximize leg power and work on getting full extension of the top leg while maintaining great upper-body running form.

Purpose

This exercise promotes single-leg explosiveness, balance, and body control.

Equipment

12- to 18-inch (30-45 cm) box

Setup

Stand with one foot on the edge of a box and the opposite foot on the floor (figure 4.53a). Focus the body weight primarily on the front foot. The toes of the front foot should be in front of the knee in the start position and the elbows should be fixed at 90 degrees.

Procedure

- With the chest upright, drive off of the top foot into the air and extend the top knee to full capacity, lifting the foot off of the box if possible (figure 4.53b).
- The elbows should remain fixed at 90-degree angles, with rotation occurring at the shoulder joint and the hands driving down through the hips, much like when running forward.
- Lower to the starting position until balance is achieved and repeat for the prescribed number of reps.
- Repeat with the opposite foot.

Figure 4.53 Single-leg power hop.

Split Jump

Many of the skills required for success in lacrosse are performed on one foot. The split jump is a means of training single-leg power while reinforcing upper-body sprint mechanics.

Purpose

This exercise promotes single-leg explosiveness, balance, and body control.

Setup

Stand upright with the arms at the sides and the feet shoulder-width apart.

Procedure

- Stride forward with one foot into a lunge position until the knee is bent approximately 90 degrees (figure 4.54a). When this position is achieved, the arms should separate (one forward and one back) and remain fixed at 90-degree angles at the elbow joints.
- From this lunge position, jump into the air, driving primarily with the front foot. Exchange the feet in midair and switch the arms to simulate proper upper-body running mechanics (figure 4.54b). Land in a lunge position (figure 4.54c).
- The elbows should remain fixed at 90-degree angles, with rotation occurring at the shoulder joint and the hands driving down through the hips, much like when running forward.
- Always return to a fully balanced position between reps.

Figure 4.54   Split jump.

Ice Skater

Lateral speed must be executed forcefully and with as little wasted motion as possible. This exercise can reinforce initial movement while helping the athlete work on stopping, keeping the core under control, and maintaining a low profile throughout.

Purpose

This exercise develops lateral power.

Setup

Stand upright with the back flat and the knees slightly bent.

Procedure

- Drive the body weight laterally, landing on the outside foot and gaining balance (figure 4.55a).
- Flex the front knee to absorb the force and drive toward the opposite direction (figure 4.55b). The side-to-side motion should resemble ice-skating (figure 4.55c).
- The hips should move primarily in a horizontal plane.

Figure 4.55   Ice skater.

Double-Leg Lateral Hurdle Hop

Reactivity is the ability to land under control and rapidly explode off the ground to another point. This drill requires the athlete to rebound off the floor as fast as possible and get the feet across a barrier quickly.

Purpose

This exercise promotes explosiveness, balance, body control, and foot speed.

Equipment

Cones, low hurdles, foam rollers, or other 6- to 8-inch barriers can be used.

Setup

Prepare to jump, keeping the back flat and the knees slightly bent (figure 4.56a).

Procedure

- With the feet shoulder-width apart, jump and drive the body weight laterally over the hurdle (figure 4.56b) landing on both feet on the other side of the hurdle.
- Quickly land, flexing the knees and hips to absorb the force (figure 4.56c), and drive the body weight upward and back over the hurdle to the starting position.
- The idea is to get off the floor and back to the other side as fast as possible.
- The side-to-side action should take place as quickly as possible for the prescribed number of reps.

Figure 4.56 Double-leg lateral hurdle hop.

Single-Leg Lateral Hurdle Hop

Lateral power on one foot is the key to success in changing direction. This drill reinforces the skills necessary for cutting and braking. It can also help strengthen and stabilize the ankle joint.

Purpose

This exercise promotes explosiveness, balance, body control, and foot speed while on one foot.

Equipment

Cones or mini hurdle

Setup

Stand upright with the back flat and the knees slightly bent.

Procedure

- With one foot only, drive the body weight laterally over the hurdle (figure 4.57a).
- Quickly land flat-footed, flexing the knees and hips to absorb the force, and drive the body weight upward and back over the hurdle (figure 4.57b) to the starting position.
- Repeat for the prescribed number of reps on one foot and then repeat with the other foot (figure 4.57c).

Figure 4.57   Single-leg lateral hurdle hop.

Band Snap-Down

The band snap-down reinforces proper lower-body linear running technique and strengthens the muscles required in the drive phase of linear speed training. This exercise is a great way to work unilateral power and technique simultaneously.

Purpose

This exercise develops hamstring and glute activation and power.

Equipment

Flex band

Setup

Attach the band to a bar or rack. Stand upright with one foot inside a flex band, knee pointed forward and the toes up (figure 4.58a).

Procedure

- Extend the band foot down and back until full hip extension (similar to the drive phase of the running motion) is achieved (figure 4.58b).
- Keep the opposite foot stationary and the chest upright and tall.
- The working leg should be the only element moving in the exercise.

Figure 4.58   Band snap-down.

Medicine Ball Overhead Toss

Upper-body strength and power are essential for ball control, stick handling, and contact.

Purpose

This exercise develops explosive power in the upper body as well as shoulder strength and mobility.

Equipment

3- to 16-pound (1.5-7 kg) medicine ball

Setup

Stand 12 to 15 feet (3.5-4.5 m) away from a partner or wall, holding a medicine ball with both hands.

Procedure

- Holding the ball, extend the ball overhead, reaching back as far as shoulder flexibility allows (figure 4.59a).
- Drive the arms forward and throw the ball at the partner or wall, following through with the upper body (figure 4.59b). As the ball is released, step forward with one foot and complete the movement in a split position.
- Keep the core muscles engaged and tight throughout.
- With each throw, alternate steps and perform for the prescribed number of reps.

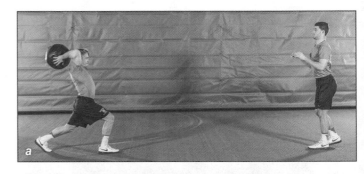

Figure 4.59   Medicine ball overhead toss.

Medicine Ball Squat Throw

Most lacrosse movements require all of the muscles and joints to work together in a powerful manner. In order to throw the medicine ball, the athlete must initiate power in the hips and conduct the force through the core and out through the upper body.

Purpose

This exercise develops total-body power.

Equipment

Medicine ball

Setup

Stand with the feet shoulder-width apart and hold a medicine ball with both hands.

Procedure

- Holding the ball in both hands, squat into a slightly flexed position at the knee and hip joints (figure 4.60*a*). The back should remain flat throughout.
- Drive the body upward, exploding with the hips and extending the hands upward, and release the ball as it clears the upper body (figure 4.60*b*).
- Keep the core muscles engaged and tight throughout.

Figure 4.60   Medicine ball squat throw.

Medicine Ball Chest Pass

The chest pass will complement the overhead pass as a means of developing strength and power in the upper body. Although beneficial for all athletes, the medicine ball drills may be especially helpful (and fun!) for younger athletes and beginners.

Purpose

This exercise develops explosive power in the upper body.

Equipment

3- to 16-pound (1.5-7 kg) medicine ball

Setup

Stand 12 to 15 feet (3.5-4.5 m) away from a partner or wall, holding a medicine ball with both hands (figure 4.61*a*).

Procedure

- Holding the ball in both hands in front of the chest, drive the hands forward similar to a chest pass in basketball.
- Follow through with full extension of the arms without falling forward and stride through with one leg as the ball is released (figure 4.61*b*).
- Keep the core muscles engaged and tight throughout.
- With each throw alternate steps and perform the prescribed number of reps.

Figure 4.61   Medicine ball chest pass.

Hang Clean

For athletes with access to a coach who can teach and monitor proper technique, the hang clean is a great way to work on hip, core, and upper-body power. It works the muscles of the entire body in a coordinated manner and can be instrumental in improving overall strength, flexibility, and explosiveness.

Purpose

This exercise develops total-body power, speed, and flexibility.

Equipment

Olympic barbell, plates, collars

Setup

Start by holding a barbell with the hands slightly wider than shoulder width and stand with the feet a little closer than shoulder width in a power-producing position.

Procedure

- With a flat back, drop the bar to a point just below the knees with the shoulders in front of the bar and the bar close to the shins (figure 4.62a).
- Using the lower body initially, raise the hips and shoulders at the same rate of speed until the bar passes the knees.

Figure 4.62   Hang clean.

- Once the bar crosses the knees, extend the hips into the bar and drive the traps upward in a shrugging motion. At the top of this pull, the athlete should achieve triple extension of the ankle, knee, and hip joints (figure 4.62b).

- When the body is fully extended and the shoulders have shrugged the bar, elevate the feet off the ground, shifting them from the initial foot position to a wider stance (feet slightly wider than the shoulders). On ground contact the feet should be flat. At the same time, bend the elbows slightly at the top of the shrug, rotate the elbows under the bar in a scooping manner, and place the bar on the frontal deltoids with the palms facing up in a front squat position (figure 4.62c).

- Stabilize the body in the bent position and finish by standing up (figure 4.62d).

- Lower the bar to the knees and begin the next rep.

Dumbbell Hang Snatch

The dumbbell hang snatch works the joints and muscles of the entire body and is a way to work explosively with some added resistance. It requires strength, explosiveness, and flexibility.

Purpose

This exercise develops total-body power and flexibility.

Equipment

Dumbbell

Setup

Stand upright with the feet approximately shoulder-width apart. Hold a dumbbell in one hand directly under the center of gravity and between the knees (figure 4.63a). The non-working arm can be placed behind the back, on the hips, or off to the side.

Procedure

- Bend the knees and rotate the hips back, maintaining a flat back at all times.

- Initiate movement by driving the hips upward into a fully extended position. Drive primarily with the lower body during this phase (figure 4.63b).

Figure 4.63   Dumbbell hang snatch.

- At the top of the extension, shift from a narrow stance to a wider stance and extend the dumbbell overhead in one motion (figure 4.63c). The athlete should achieve a quick lock-out of the elbow. If the extension of the elbow and shoulder is too slow, the weight may be too heavy.
- During the catch phase, the feet should land flat with the knees slightly bent.
- At the catch phase, hold the dumbbell in place overhead for one to two seconds and then return the dumbbell to the starting position.
- Repeat for the prescribed number of reps with one hand and then switch to the opposite hand.

Developing strength and power during the off-season will result in improved performance, enhanced skill, and a lower susceptibility to injuries. Careful, consistent hard work and dedication will pay dividends over time, but the athlete must stay the course, especially when circumstances are most challenging. Every athlete wants to be successful on game day and attain individual and teams goals. There is great satisfaction in working hard as a cohesive unit and seeing that hard work pay off. Not every athlete, however, is committed to training toward those goals during the off-season. Many lose focus and get distracted easily. Great lacrosse players have the ability to see the big picture and appreciate the commitment necessary for becoming a champion when others may not have the courage to do so. Take advantage of every moment of training and prepare for opportunities before they arise.

Chapter 5

Speed and Agility

The sheer excitement generated for lacrosse can be traced to one primary element: speed! Sudden changes of possession, skillful offensive maneuvering, and defensive teamwork that can lock down and frustrate an offense all require the application of some element of speed and agility. Players who can explode into a full sprint, redirect with little apparent effort, and stick handle through a defense with the finesse of a magician are thrilling to watch! Speed and agility skills are the keys to success in lacrosse.

In order to be successful, every lacrosse player must have the movement fundamentals that enable him or her to execute the skills of the game with precision, quickness, and fluidity. Regardless of the position played on the field, all lacrosse players need to be fast, well-coordinated, and able to rapidly change direction and adapt to continuously changing circumstances. All training programs should include every facet of speed and athletic development in order to improve lacrosse movement skills. These include foot speed, acceleration, top-end speed, deceleration and lateral speed (agility) movements. These are all crucial elements of successful lacrosse training.

- *Foot speed* is the ability to maintain balance and body control, move the feet rapidly and skillfully in a restricted area, and move in the chosen direction quickly and with as little wasted motion as possible.

- *Acceleration* is the ability to transition to a sprint from either a stationary position or a slower tempo.

- *Top-end speed* is the ability to run at full speed. Although rarely achieved in most game situations, top-end speed is essential for midfielders during transition situations in which a 50- to 75-yard sprint is required into the offensive or defensive zones. When ball possession changes and play moves to the opposite end of the field, players must quickly re-direct and sprint at full speed in order to get into position on the opposite end of the field.

- *Deceleration* is the ability to slow down or stop in as short a space as possible without compromising balance and body control.
- *Agility,* or change of direction, is the ability to put all movement skills together in a cohesive, well-coordinated manner. The ultimate goal of the training program is to transfer strength, power, balance, and flexibility to functional, useful game skills.

FOOT SPEED DEVELOPMENT

Leverage, balance, and maximum body control are important for effectively controlling body movements during game situations. The process of improving these skills begins with coordinated footwork. Lacrosse players should utilize foot speed drills both to engage the neurological system after a dynamic warm-up (before more intense activity) and to improve balance and movement control. The following are some common foot speed drills.

Ladder Drills

Traditional ladder drills are an excellent way to train foot speed. Use either a commercial ladder or a homemade device. Athletes should typically perform 8 to 20 reps, depending on the overall volume of training planned for that day.

Run Through

Purpose

This exercise develops foot strike frequency in a pattern similar to the linear running motion.

Setup

Begin behind the ladder with both feet outside the first square.

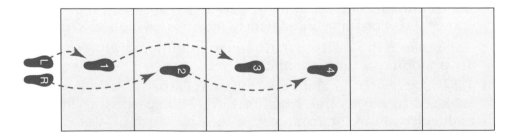

Figure 5.1   Run through.

Procedure

- Run through the ladder, performing one foot strike per square (figure 5.1). Touch each square in the ladder before finishing through the final square.
- During each step, the body weight should be concentrated on the ball of the foot.
- The same upper-body technique used in linear speed drills should be employed during all foot speed drills. These will allow for efficient movement with as little wasted motion as possible.

Hop Through

Purpose

This exercise develops power and speed while keeping the feet underneath the hips to maintain body control.

Setup

Begin behind the ladder with both feet together outside the first square (figure 5.2).

Procedure

- Keeping the feet together, hop forward, touching each square one time.
- Focus on spending as little time as possible in each square and proceeding to the next square quickly.

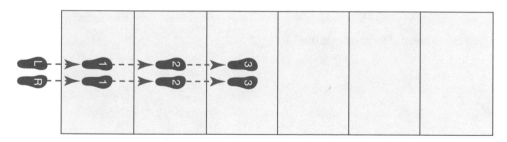

Figure 5.2   Hop through.

Lateral Step and Gather

Purpose

This exercise addresses lateral quickness and foot speed, which is beneficial for defensive players.

Setup

Stand sideways to the ladder with both feet outside the first square.

Procedure

- Step into the first square with the lead (front) foot and then step into the first square with the trail (back) foot (figure 5.3).
- Step into the second square with the lead foot and then step into the second square with the trail foot.
- Continue with this foot-strike pattern through the final square.
- Keep the knees slightly flexed and the shoulders squared throughout.
- Keep the center of gravity moving in a horizontal plane and minimize vertical hip movement.

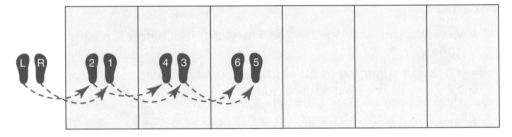

Figure 5.3   Lateral step and gather.

Icky Shuffle

Purpose

This exercise develops foot speed, lateral movement, and balance in a more challenging movement pattern.

Setup

Begin beside the ladder with both feet outside the first square.

Procedure

- Step into the ladder with the lead (inside) foot. Bring the trail (outside) foot into the ladder alongside the lead foot. Both feet are now in (figure 5.4).
- Step outside the opposite edge of the ladder with the lead foot only. That foot is now out. The trail foot is now the lead foot.
- Step into the second square with the new lead foot followed by the new trail foot (in, in).
- Step outside of the opposite edge of the ladder with the lead foot only (out).
- Repeat in a continuous in-in-out pattern through the final square.
- The feet should never cross one another.

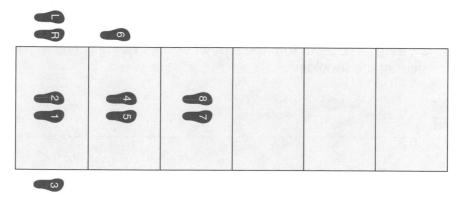

Figure 5.4   Icky shuffle.

Crossover Step and Shuffle

Purpose

This exercise develops crossover foot skills while turning the hips and keeping the shoulders square to the end of the ladder. This is especially important for offensive players.

Setup

Begin to the side of the ladder with both feet outside the first square.

Procedure

- Cross over the body with the lead (outside) foot and step in the first square (figure 5.5).
- Bring the trail (inside) foot across the first square and step just outside the edge of the first square. Then, bring the lead foot outside the first square and place it between the edge of the square and the trail foot. The feet are now out, out.
- The foot on the outside is now the lead foot. Cross the lead foot over into the second square (in).
- Bring the trail foot across the second square and step just outside the edge of the second square. Then, bring the lead foot outside the second square and place it between the edge of the square and the trail foot (out, out).
- Repeat in a continuous in-out-out pattern through the final square.
- On each step, try to turn the hips while minimizing lateral movement of the shoulders.

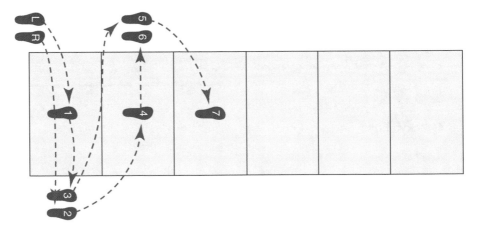

Figure 5.5   Crossover step and shuffle.

Backward Icky Shuffle

Purpose

This exercise improves backward and lateral movement. This is especially important for defenders, who sometimes must retreat quickly at an angle.

Setup

Begin at the side of the ladder. Face away from the ladder with the shoulders perpendicular to the long side of the ladder.

Procedure

- Step at a 45-degree angle backward into the ladder with the lead (inside) foot. Bring the trail (outside) foot into the ladder alongside the lead foot. Both feet are now in, in (figure 5.6).
- Step at a 45-degree angle backward outside the opposite edge of the ladder with the lead foot only. That foot is now out. The trail foot is now the lead foot.
- Step into the second square with the new lead foot followed by the new trail foot (in, in).
- Step outside of the opposite edge of the ladder with the lead foot only (out).
- Repeat in a continuous backward in-in-out pattern through the final square.
- Keep the shoulders steady and squared. The center of gravity may be shifted backward slightly to help counterbalance the upper body.

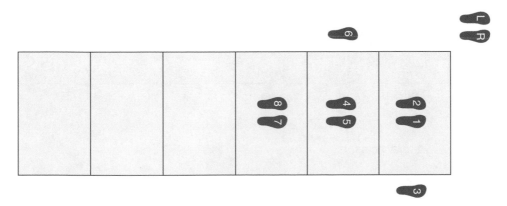

Figure 5.6 Backward icky shuffle.

Lateral Scissors

Purpose

This exercise improves unilateral foot speed, coordination, and balance.

Setup

Stand outside of the ladder with the shoulders parallel to the long side of the ladder.

Procedure

- Facing sideways, step into the first square with the lead foot. Move the trail foot to just behind the first square (figure 5.7).
- Hop so that both feet are in the air at the same time. Switch the feet in midair so that the trail foot is now in the second square and the lead foot is now out.
- Hop again and switch the feet again so that the lead foot is in the third square and the trail foot is out.
- Hop and switch the feet again so that the trail foot is now in the second square.
- Continue this in-out scissor motion for the entire length of the ladder.
- Never have two feet in the same square at the same time.

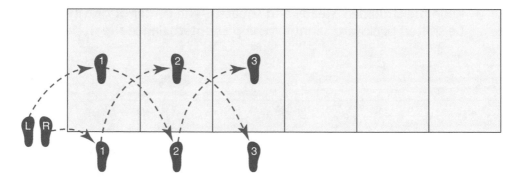

Figure 5.7 Lateral scissors.

Lateral Jab Step

Purpose

This exercise addresses lateral movement, foot speed, and body control.

Setup

Stand outside of the ladder with the shoulders parallel to the long side of the ladder.

Procedure

- Facing sideways, step into the first square with the lead foot. Then step into the first square with the trail foot (in, in) (figure 5.8).
- Step back just outside of the second square with the lead foot. Then step back just outside of the second square with the trail foot (out, out).
- Step into the second square with the lead foot. Then step into the second square with the trail foot (in, in).
- Repeat this in-in-out-out pattern for the entire length of the ladder.
- Keep upper-body movement controlled and fluid.

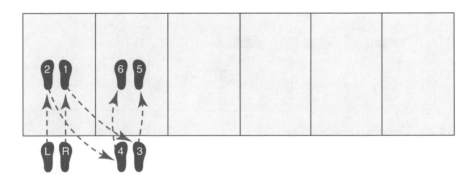

Figure 5.8   Lateral jab step.

Single-Leg Hop Through

Purpose

This exercise develops ankle strength, unilateral quickness and balance, and body control.

Setup

Stand behind the ladder facing forward (figure 5.9).

Procedure

- With one foot, hop into the first square.
- With the same foot, hop into the second square.
- Repeat the single-leg hop for the entire length of the ladder. At the end of the ladder, turn and repeat with the opposite foot.
- Do not let the center of gravity (hips) gain momentum faster than the foot can follow. This will cause the athlete's hips to move faster than the rest of the body resulting in a loss of balance and body control.

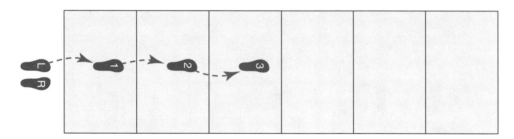

Figure 5.9   Single-leg hop through.

Two-Cone Drills

These drills, which use two 6-inch (15 cm) cones or other low barriers, are an excellent way to work on foot speed, balance, and body control. In addition, these drills are simple to administer in a team setting with limited space. One coach can monitor multiple athletes working at the same time. Athletes should perform these drills for 8 to 15 seconds each. A total of 6 to 12 reps is recommended.

Double-Leg Lateral Hop

Purpose

This exercise develops foot speed, balance, and body control.

Setup

Place two cones approximately three feet (1 m) apart. Stand next to the cones with the shoulders facing sideways, knees bent slightly, and the chest up.

Procedure

- Keeping the feet together, hop laterally over the top of the first cone. Immediately hop laterally over the second (far) cone (figure 5.10a).
- As quickly as possible, jump back over the second cone and then over the first cone, returning to the starting position (figure 5.10b).
- Perform this movement pattern for the designated time period.
- Spend as little time as possible on the ground between cones.
- Keep the shoulders, hips, and torso aligned throughout the drill. The body should remain centered, with the torso, hips, and feet moving together as a cohesive unit.

Figure 5.10 Double-leg lateral hop.

Single-Leg Lateral Hop

Purpose

This exercise addresses single-leg speed and power. It also strengthens the ankle, knee, and hip joints, which is necessary for injury prevention.

Setup

Place two cones approximately three feet (1 m) apart. Stand next to the cones with the shoulders facing sideways, knees bent slightly, and the chest up.

Procedure

- Staying on one foot throughout the drill, hop laterally over the top of the first cone (figure 5.11a). Immediately hop laterally over the second (far) cone.
- As quickly as possible, jump back over the second cone (figure 5.11b) and then over the first cone, returning to the starting position.
- Perform this movement pattern for the designated time period.
- Repeat on the opposite foot.
- Spend as little time as possible on the ground between cones.
- Keep the shoulders, hips, and torso aligned throughout the drill. The body should remain centered, with the torso, hips, and foot moving together as a cohesive unit.

Figure 5.11 Single-leg lateral hop.

Step and Gather

Purpose

This exercise focuses on lateral foot speed, coordination, and timing.

Setup

Place two cones approximately three feet (1 m) apart. Stand next to the cones with the shoulders facing sideways, knees bent slightly, and the chest up.

Procedure

- Moving laterally, step over the top of the first cone with the lead (front) foot and then step over the top of the first cone with the trail (back) foot. Both feet are then together between the two cones (figure 5.12a).

- Step over the top of the second cone with the lead foot and then step over the top of the second cone with the trail foot. Both feet are then outside of the second cone.

- As soon as the trail foot touches the ground, it becomes the lead foot. Immediately step back over the top of the second cone with the lead foot (figure 5.12b) and then step over the top of the second cone with the trail foot. Both feet are then together between the cones.

- Step over the top of the first cone with the lead foot and then step over the top of the first cone with the trail foot. The feet are back at the starting position.

- Perform this movement pattern for the designated time period.

- The body should remain centered, with the torso, hips, and feet moving together as a cohesive unit.

Figure 5.12 Step and gather.

Hockey Stop

Purpose

This exercise improves foot speed, coordination, and timing. It simulates the rapid redirection patterns used in lateral movement.

Setup

Place two cones approximately three feet (1 m) apart. Stand next to the cones with the shoulders facing sideways, knees bent slightly, and the chest up.

Procedure

- Moving laterally, step over the top of the first cone with the lead (front) foot (figure 5.13*a*) and then step over the top of the first cone with the trail (back) foot. Both feet are now together between the two cones (figure 5.13*b*).
- Step over the top of the second cone with the lead foot, shifting the center of gravity slightly over the top of the second cone. The trail foot does not touch the ground outside of the second cone but rather becomes the lead (front) foot as the athlete redirects in the opposite direction, moving toward the middle of the cones. Both feet are again together between the cones.
- Step with the new lead foot over the top of the first cone, again shifting the center of gravity slightly over the first cone.
- Perform this movement pattern for the designated time period.
- Keep the body centered, with the torso, hips, and feet moving together as a cohesive unit.

 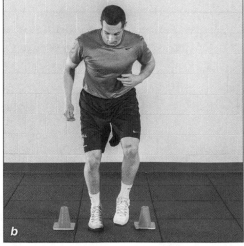

Figure 5.13   Hockey stop.

Lateral Figure 8

Purpose

This exercise improves body control and foot speed and is especially useful for defenders.

Setup

Place two cones approximately three feet (1 m) apart. Stand next to the cones with the shoulders facing sideways, knees bent slightly, and the chest up.

Procedure

- Moving the feet rapidly, step behind the first cone (figure 5.14a). Continue in a figure-8 pattern around the first cone, in front of the second cone, and outside and around the second cone (figure 5.14b).
- Continue by moving in front of and around the first cone.
- Repeat this pattern for the designated time period.
- Move the feet quickly, stay low with the knees flexed, and maintain proper body mechanics and control throughout the drill.
- Keep the body centered, with the torso, hips, and feet moving together as a cohesive unit.

Figure 5.14   Lateral figure 8.

Forward and Backward Figure 8

Purpose

This exercise focuses on rapid foot movement in a nonlinear pattern and on keeping the center of gravity low for an extended period of time.

Setup

Place two cones approximately three feet (1 m) apart. Stand behind the cones with the shoulders facing the cones, knees bent slightly, and the chest up.

Procedure

- Moving the feet rapidly, step to one side of the first cone. Continue forward in a figure 8 pattern around the first cone, in front of the second cone, and outside and around the second cone (figure 5.15, a and b).
- Once around the second cone, continue with the figure-8 pattern around both cones.
- Repeat this pattern for the designated time period.
- Move the feet quickly, stay low with the knees flexed, and maintain proper body mechanics and control throughout the drill.
- Keep the body centered, with the torso, hips, and feet moving together as a cohesive unit.

Figure 5.15   Forward and backward figure 8.

Reactive Cone Drill

Purpose

This drill works to improve coordination, foot speed, reactivity, and the ability to respond to an external cue, which can be especially helpful for goalies.

Setup

Place two cones 6 to 10 feet (2-3 m) apart. The working athlete stands between the cones with the partner standing in front. One partner responds to the other partner's verbal and/or visual cues.

Procedure

One partner gives verbal and visual commands, and the other partner must respond to the commands within the allotted time (usually 10-15 seconds) and space. Partners can make up their own cues or use some of the following.

- *Foot fire:* The athlete moves the feet in place while maintaining a flat back and bent knees in a good athletic position.
- *Shuffle:* The partner points left or right and calls out "shuffle". The athlete shuffles laterally with rapid foot speed in that direction.
- *90-degree hip turns:* The partner calls out "turn" and points left or right, and the athlete turns the hips 90 degrees and then back to the original position with rapid foot fire, keeping the hips squared to the partner.
- *Knee touch:* The partner calls out "drop" and points left or right, and the athlete rapidly touches that knee to the ground, returns to a standing position, and then performs rapid foot fire.
- *Jump:* The partner calls out "jump". The athlete jumps in place, lands with the chest up and knees bent, and then performs rapid foot fire.

Low-Hurdle Drills

Using hurdles, the athlete can work on foot speed, balance, agility, and acceleration in a single drill. After an initial teaching phase (usually two to three weeks) in which technique is emphasized, the athletes should progress from performing the drills at 50 percent of maximum speed to 75 percent of maximum speed and eventually at 100 percent of maximum speed. Coaches can use these drills to teach practical skills. Athletes can carry their lacrosse sticks when performing the drills.

In addition, a team can break into smaller groups and compete against each other. Each subgroup can race through its own row of hurdles to a cone at the end of the line, or players can have a relay race in which they go through the row of hurdles, return to the starting line, and tag the next person in line. If a member of the group knocks over a hurdle, the next person in line must fix the hurdle before starting. This creates a penalty situation that helps teach discipline and attention to detail in addition to foot speed. Competition will encourage excellence in any drill!

Forward Speed Hop

Purpose

This exercise improves foot speed, power, and body control while minimizing ground contact time.

Setup

Set up several 6- to 10-inch (15-25 cm) hurdles approximately 3 feet (1 m) apart. Start with the feet together behind the first hurdle.

Procedure

- Keeping the feet together throughout the drill, hop over the first hurdle.
- Continue hopping over each hurdle until all have been cleared (figure 5.16, a and b).
- Between hurdles, spend as little time as possible on the ground and rebound quickly.

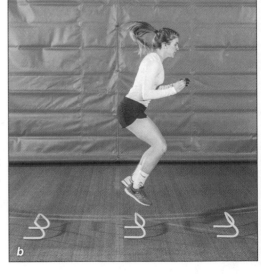

Figure 5.16   Forward speed hop.

Forward Power Hop

Purpose

This exercise focuses on explosive power and body control.

Setup

Set up several 6- to 10-inch (15-25 cm) hurdles approximately 3 feet (1 m) apart. Start with the feet together behind the first hurdle.

Procedure

- Keeping the feet underneath the shoulders, jump as high as possible over the first hurdle (figure 5.17*a*) and land with the knees slightly flexed and the feet flat. Gather the feet together and prepare for the next jump.
- Repeat over each hurdle until the final one is cleared (figure 5.17*b*).
- Try to maximize the height of each jump.

Figure 5.17   Forward power hop.

Single-Leg Speed Hop

Purpose

This exercise promotes unilateral speed, hip and ankle strength, balance, and body control.

Setup

Set up several 6- to 10-inch (15-25 cm) hurdles approximately 3 feet (1 m) apart. Start with the feet together behind the first hurdle (figure 5.18a).

Procedure

- Jump with one foot over the top of the first hurdle, driving the knee of the jumping foot up as high as possible.
- Land and immediately repeat over each hurdle, spending as little time as possible on the ground between jumps (figure 5.18b).
- Attempt to maintain control of the body throughout.
- Point the toes forward upon landing to avoid any type of internal rotation of the knee joint.

Figure 5.18   Single-leg speed hop.

Double Clutch Speed Hop

Purpose

This exercise addresses rapid foot strike, body control, and balance.

Setup

Set up several 6- to 10-inch (15-25 cm) hurdles approximately 3 feet (1 m) apart. Start with the feet together behind the first hurdle.

Procedure

- Keeping the feet together throughout the drill, hop over the first hurdle.
- After clearing the first hurdle, perform an in-place hop with as little ground contact as possible and then hop over the second hurdle.
- Repeat this pattern until all hurdles have been cleared (figure 5.19, *a* and *b*).
- Keep the feet under the center of gravity and be sure not to lean the torso too far forward near the end.

Figure 5.19   Double clutch speed hop.

Hurdle Run Through

Purpose

This exercise focuses on running technique, stride frequency, and upper-body linear speed mechanics.

Setup

Set up several 6- to 10-inch (15-25 cm) hurdles approximately 3 feet (1 m) apart. Start with the feet together behind the first hurdle.

Procedure

- Run down the line of hurdles, using one foot strike between each hurdle.
- Alternate steps between each hurdle (figure 5.20, *a* and *b*).
- Attempt to minimize ground contact time.

Figure 5.20   Hurdle run through.

Lateral Hurdle Step and Gather

Purpose

This exercise improves lateral foot speed and power.

Setup

Set up several 6- to 10-inch (15-25 cm) hurdles approximately 3 feet (1 m) apart. Start with the feet together behind the side of the first hurdle.

Procedure

- Step over the top of a hurdle with the front foot (figure 5.21*a*). Then step over with the back foot.
- Repeat this sequence (step with the front foot and gather with the back foot) over the tops of the remaining hurdles (figure 5.21*b*).
- The center of gravity should move in a horizontal plane. Keep the shoulders at 90 degrees to the hurdles throughout the drill.
- Keep the knees slightly bent and stay on the balls of the feet while moving laterally.

Figure 5.21   Lateral Hurdle step and gather.

Lateral Weave

Purpose

This exercise addresses lateral movement and foot speed.

Setup

Set up several 6- to 10-inch (15-25 cm) hurdles approximately 3 feet (1 m) apart. Start with the feet together behind the side of the first hurdle.

Procedure

- With rapid foot strikes and keeping the shoulders squared throughout the drill, move forward and go in front of and around the first hurdle.
- Once the first hurdle is cleared, backpedal between the first and second hurdles and go around the back of the second hurdle (figure 5.22a).
- Once the second hurdle is cleared, sprint forward between the second and third hurdles and go around the front of the third hurdle (figure 5.22b).
- Continue the pattern of sprinting and backpedaling through the hurdles until all hurdles have been cleared.
- Stay low and keep the feet moving and underneath the hips. Do not overextend so that the feet cannot stay under the hips.

Figure 5.22   Lateral weave.

Forward Weave

Purpose

This exercise focuses on foot speed, balance, and quickness while moving through traffic.

Setup

Set up several 6- to 10-inch (15-25 cm) hurdles approximately 3 feet (1 m) apart. Start with the feet together behind the first hurdle.

Procedure

- Keeping the shoulders squared throughout the drill, move forward and go around the right side of the first hurdle.
- Once the first hurdle is cleared, shuffle at a 45-degree angle between the first and second hurdles and go around the left side of the second hurdle.
- Once the second hurdle is cleared, shuffle at a 45-degree angle between the second and third hurdles and go around the right side of the third hurdle (figure 5.23).
- Continue in this pattern until all hurdles have been cleared.
- Stay low and keep the feet moving and underneath the hips. Do not overextend the upper body so that the feet cannot stay under the hips.

Figure 5.23   Forward weave.

Backward Weave

Purpose

This exercise addresses backward movement, which is important especially for defensive players.

Setup

Set up several 6- to 10-inch (15-25 cm) hurdles approximately 3 feet (1 m) apart. Start with the feet together behind the first hurdle, facing away from the hurdles (figure 5.24a).

Procedure

- Backpedal to the right around the outside of the first hurdle.
- Once the hurdle is cleared, shuffle at a 45-degree angle backward between the first and second hurdles and go around the left side of the second hurdle (figure 5.24b).
- Once the second hurdle is cleared, shuffle at a 45-degree angle backward between the second and third hurdles and go around the right side of the third hurdle.
- Continue in this pattern until all hurdles have been cleared.
- Stay low and keep the feet moving and underneath the hips. Do not overextend so that the feet cannot stay under the hips. Try to keep the shoulders squared to the first hurdle while slightly turning the hips.

Figure 5.24   Backward weave.

LINEAR AND TOP-END SPEED DEVELOPMENT

One of the most essential skills in lacrosse is the ability to accelerate in a linear (i.e., straight ahead) plane. The explosive bursts involved in face-off support, initial movement toward a dodge, racing for a ground ball, and switching defensive responsibilities require the ability to move from either a stationary position or a slow-tempo start. These skills make lacrosse such a fast-paced, exciting sport!

Much like any skill, acceleration components can be learned and improved, but doing so involves a great deal of hard work. In some cases, younger athletes want to be fast but make the mistake of bypassing linear speed training and immediately move into change-of-direction skills. Learning how to run straight ahead (and stop!) will lay the foundation needed for all agility skills. Without this initial learning process, the athlete may not fully understand and appreciate agility fundamentals. Continuous strength development, power improvement, and joint stabilization in the weight room should accompany technical skill mastery to make the necessary improvement in movement-skill development.

When training for acceleration, lacrosse players should master the mechanics of running without a stick. It is easier to learn to run like an Olympic sprinter first and then make adjustments to sport-specific mechanics. Once the athlete understands the upper- and lower-body mechanics of running and makes progress toward achieving fundamental linear mechanics, he or she may progress to speed training while holding a lacrosse stick.

The objective of linear speed is to move the center of gravity toward a specific target as quickly and efficiently as possible. That target can be anything from a specific location on the field or (in training) a finish line. The runner should strive to maximize force production down and back under the hip (away from the target). Any type of foot strike in front of the hip will put a braking force between the runner and the objective and decelerate the center of gravity. Accelerating from a stationary or slow start requires the athlete to extend the ankle, knee, and hip joints to maximize force production and to gradually raise the center of gravity. Decelerating requires the athlete to bend the ankle, knee, and hip joints. The upper- and lower-body components must work together in a cohesive manner. Movement in one extremity (upper or lower body) will affect the center of gravity and, ultimately, influence the outcome of movement in another extremity and possibly disrupt the entire mechanism. Upper-body control is typically one of the first skills taught in that many athletes do not appreciate the impact that the upper body has on lower-body movement. Excessive movement or wasted motion with the upper body (horizontal rotation of the shoulders, limited forward-backward range of motion at the shoulder joint, etc.) will result in unwanted lower-body movement. In order to maintain balance, the action of one part of the body must be countered with an equal and opposite reaction in another part of the body.

Max Seibald is one of the greatest players in the history of Cornell lacrosse. Although he had strong ball-handling and scoring skills, his top-end speed capabilities really set him apart from other players. His ability to accelerate and seemingly gain speed in open-field situations became legendary. Whether carrying the ball through traffic and outrunning well-positioned defenders or chasing down a ball carrier to make a remarkable stick check from behind, Max used his top-end speed to make big plays in big games! Developing top-end speed should be every player's game plan.

The following breaks down the upper- and lower-body mechanics of linear acceleration.

Upper-Body Mechanics of Acceleration

- *Level head*—The head and eyes are on a level plane and looking forward (not up or down) toward the target.

- *Tall torso*—The torso is upright with the hips underneath the shoulders once top-end speed has been achieved.

- *Elbow flexed*—The elbows must be fixed at a 90-degree angle. The athlete maintains that angle (without a stick in the hand) throughout the event.

- *Shoulder drive*—The athlete drives the arm down and back from the shoulder joint (not the elbow joint), bringing the hand down through the hip. The greater the amount of force generated with the upper body, the greater the force potential of the lower body.

Lower-Body Mechanics of Acceleration

- *Knee punch*—The front knee drives upward toward the target, with the toes up and the foreleg perpendicular to the ground. During this phase, the toes remain dorsi-flexed in preparation for ground contact.

- *Foot strike*—On the downward leg swing, the athlete should plant the foot on the ground just below the hips. This will allow for maximal hip projection and minimize braking forces. Once the foot is planted, the athlete should finish the drive and achieve full extension of the back leg.

- *Recovery*—At the conclusion of the downward leg drive, the heel should rebound upward toward the glutes, the knee should be brought back into the knee punch position with the knee driven upward toward the intended target, and the toes should return to the forward position. This continuous cycle is crucial to achieving substantial forward momentum.

The following exercises improve acceleration mechanics.

1-2-3 Count Wall Drill

Purpose

This exercise teaches the mechanics of top-end linear speed running. It emphasizes keeping the eyes forward and the hips extended while working on the knee-punch and foot-strike stages.

Setup

Assume perfect running posture with the hands against a wall at shoulder height. The hips should be extended and the feet should be closer than shoulder-width apart. Begin with one knee up, holding the toes up in preparation for ground contact and the shin perpendicular to the ground (figure 5.25a).

Procedure

- On the command, switch legs so that the up leg makes contact with the ground under the hip and the down knee punches forward toward the wall (figure 5.25b).
- Do combinations of one-, two-, and three-count (indicating the number of leg exchanges per command) sequences.
- Keep the head and eyes up and focus on a point on the wall; do not watch the lower-body movement.

Figure 5.25 1-2-3 count wall drill.

Form Running

Purpose

This exercise enables the runner to process the technical linear speed information and practice proper mechanics at a tempo that may help eliminate bad habits and formulate new muscle memory patterns.

Setup

The athlete begins behind a designated starting line in a ready position. In most cases, this is a two-point speed stance that is the recommended starting position for most sprint-training drills. The athlete begins upright with the feet underneath the shoulders then drops one foot (either left or right) back so that the toes of the back foot are 12 to 18 inches (30-45 cm) behind the toes of the front foot. Taller athletes may need to stagger the feet more. The front knee is bent approximately 45 degrees, and the back knee is slightly bent (25 degrees). The elbows are flexed 90 degrees, with the hand on the side of the back foot forward and the hand on the side of the front foot back (much like the arms would be placed when running).

Procedure

- Run with perfect technique at a speed less than maximum velocity (typically 70 percent to 80 percent of maximum) for a distance of 25 to 40 yards (figure 5.26).

- Coaches should provide feedback or can perform video analysis so athletes can watch themselves and make the necessary corrections.

- Speed mechanics should be taught at a slower pace before increasing the tempo. A walk, jog, run progression is recommended. This means that the athlete should first do a walk-through to better understand the mechanics. Once those have been mastered, the tempo should increase to a jog (75 percent of maximum). The final stage is a full-speed sprint with an emphasis on proper technique.

Figure 5.26   Form running.

Resisted Run

Purpose

This exercise develops leg drive and stride frequency through simultaneous firing of the hip flexors and extensors.

Equipment

Harness and sled or hill

Setup

If running with a harness or sled, put on the harness or belt and make sure that there is no slack in the tow line. Assume a two-point stance.

Procedure

- Run with proper upper- and lower-body mechanics using the added resistance (figure 5.27).
- The resistance should not be so heavy that the runner's technique deteriorates. Typically a 15- to 30-yard sprint distance is used and the athlete should be allowed 30 to 45 seconds between reps for recovery.

Figure 5.27　Resisted run.

Tennis Ball Drop

Purpose

In the sport of lacrosse, acceleration does not always take place in a linear plane. Quite often acceleration must occur at a variety of angles (e.g., 45-90 degrees) and these should be included in the training program. This exercise teaches acceleration, reactivity, and foot work and challenges the athlete to maximally extend the body in order to catch the ball. This drill is a fun way to simulate chasing ground balls in lacrosse!

Setup

One partner holds a tennis ball and stands 10 to 15 feet (3-5 m) away from the runner (figure 5.28a). The runner may begin in a number of starting positions (e.g., two-point stance, lateral, kneeling) and may either face the partner or stand with the shoulders at 90 degrees to the partner.

Procedure

- The partner drops the ball from shoulder height, and the runner accelerates toward the dropped tennis ball (figure 5.28b).
- The runner attempts to catch the tennis ball after one bounce.

Figure 5.28 Tennis ball drop.

Chase Drill

Purpose

This exercise teaches the athlete to accelerate from a number of starting positions. On game day, athletes must accelerate from a variety of foot-placement positions. This is an excellent way to teach drive mechanics in a fun, competitive environment.

Setup

Three cones should be set up in a straight line. The distance between cones 1 and 2 is 3 to 5 feet and the distance between cones 2 and 3 cones is 15 to 20 feet. One runner stands next to cone 1 and a second runner stands at cone 2 with both runners running toward cone 3. The runners may start in a number of positions (e.g., two-point stance, lateral, kneeling, prone, supine) (figure 5.29a).

Procedure

- On command or on the movement of the front runner, both runners sprint to the finish line.
- The runner in the rear attempts to tag the front runner before the front runner crosses the finish line (figure 5.29b). Exchange positions and repeat.

Figure 5.29　Chase drill.

LATERAL SPEED (CHANGE OF DIRECTION) DEVELOPMENT

Attackers, middies, defensive specialists, and goalies all rely on fast-paced, explosive reactivity to adjust to the external stimuli of the game and perform their skills in open space, often in one-on-one situations. The constant maneuvering of the offense to gain high-quality shot opportunities requires players to be highly skilled in agility movements. The defense has few answers for offensive players who can generate a sudden burst of speed followed by sudden deceleration, a pivot, and the quick release of a shot. Whether a player is on offense or defense, the ability to decelerate and reaccelerate in various planes of movement is critical.

Lateral speed requires the simultaneous integration of a number of skills. Successfully changing directions requires balance, body control, acceleration, deceleration, and foot speed.

Balance

Balance is the ability to maintain positioning while stabilizing against internal and external forces. During a game, the athlete must overcome the force of the body movements as well as the forces of opposing players and gravitational pull. Players must have sufficient balance in order to successfully execute game responsibilities (e.g., absorbing information, making strategic calculations, selecting a shot) while withstanding biomechanical and external forces (i.e., the opposing team).

Deceleration

Deceleration is the ability to decrease movement velocity. Field players must constantly rely on the body's braking system to adjust their speed and must adapt to constantly changing stimuli as the game unfolds.

Initially, change-of-direction skills should be taught at a slower speed and gradually progress to full-speed movements. This will enable the athlete to develop new neural patterns and gain the balance, body control, and confidence necessary for mastering the fundamental mechanics. A lacrosse drill is taught on the field in a walk-through setting before players advance to full-speed execution; the same philosophy should be adopted for lateral skill development. Once a base level of linear speed has been established, the athlete should progress to more complex, multidirectional movement patterns. Once athletes understand the fundamental skills, they may correct themselves when breakdowns occur and know how to fix the techniques in future reps.

In lacrosse, agility movement demands vary based on the athlete's position on the field. For example, an attacker and a goalie are required to execute different lateral movement patterns. Although both must move laterally in a quick, powerful manner, the types of movements executed are a bit different.

The following lateral speed drills are separated into categories based on position-specific movement requirements. All players can use the team drills to improve general agility skills. Drills for offense are appropriate for attackers and offensive midfielders. Drills for defense are appropriate for defenders, defensive midfielders, and goalies. For all of these agility drills, holding a stick can make the drill more realistic and fun.

The first seven drills help develop lateral speed skills for all positions.

Start-Stop-Go Series

Purpose

This drill works on acceleration in a number of planes using a variety of movement skills (linear sprint, shuffle, backpedal) and creates an awareness of false steps and how the upper body, legs, and feet work together.

Setup

Begin behind a designated starting line in a stance appropriate for executing the drill. If the first move is a sprint, assume a two-point speed stance. If the first move is a shuffle, position the shoulders 90 degrees from the starting line. (If multiple athletes are performing the drill at the same time, they must stand five to six yards apart in order to avoid collisions.)

Procedure

- The coach explains in detail the movement patterns that will be executed. Such as:
  - *Run, stop, run:* Accelerate in a linear plane and come to a complete stop on command. After a pause of two to three seconds, reaccelerate on command in either a linear or a lateral plane without taking a false step (i.e., step in the direction opposite the intended objective). The emphasis is on technical precision. Break bad habits and create new neural patterns of movement.
  - *Shuffle, stop, shuffle:* Perform a lateral shuffle in one direction and stop on command. After pausing for two to three seconds to regain balance, continue the shuffle in either the same or the opposite direction. The emphasis is on moving side to side while remaining square on the opponent.
  - *Shuffle, stop, run:* Begin with a lateral shuffle and stop on command. After pausing for two to three seconds to regain balance, perform a crossover run (punch the back knee across the body as it transitions from a lateral run to a forward run) and finish with a linear sprint without taking any false steps. This exercise develops the transition from lateral movement to linear movement.

- *Backpedal, stop, turn, run:* Backpedal on command and then stop on command. After pausing for two to three seconds to gain balance, turn and sprint toward the objective, bringing the head, shoulders, hips, and feet in the direction of the turn. This drill is particularly helpful for midfielders and defensive specialists in unsettled game situations when possession suddenly changes and both teams must transition and set up (offensively or defensively) on the opposite end of the field.

- At the first command, perform the first skill listed.
- At the next command, immediately stop in as few steps as possible.
- While waiting for the third command, lower the center of gravity, stop completely, and maintain balance and body control.
- At the third command, transition to the second movement pattern and then burst through a designated finish line at full speed.
- For each pattern, focus on proper mechanics of linear speed, foot placement, hip and shoulder movement, controlling the center of gravity, and finding the balance point as soon as possible. The balance point is attained when perfect body control is achieved and the runner is in a balanced athletic position (weight shifted slightly on the balls of the feet, knees bent, and hips flexed) and ready for movement in another plane.
- Perform this drill at 80 percent of maximum speed and gradually progress to 100 percent. If athletes are unable to attain the proper mechanics, they should perform at a submaximum capacity until the fundamental skills are improved. The initial time given to achieve a balanced posture (two to three seconds) should be shortened as the athletes learn to control their bodies and come to a sudden, proper balance point.
- As athletes become more proficient in this drill, a third movement component can be added. For example, a "shuffle left, shuffle right, turn, and run" command could be used to train the transition from two lateral movements to a linear movement. Athletes and coaches can get creative with designing options for this drill.

NFL Agility Drill

Purpose

This drill helps develop short-distance lateral speed, balance, and body control. It can also be used to test agility skill.

Setup

Place cones 5 yards apart for 10 consecutive yards (i.e., place one cone on the goal line, one cone on the 5-yard line, and one cone on the 10-yard line) (figure 5.30). Start in a three-point athletic stance with the feet straddling the middle cone and a hand on the middle line.

Procedure

- On the command, run toward one of the outside cones.
- Touch the line with the outside hand and then change direction and run 10 yards toward the other outside line.
- Touch that line with the outside hand.
- Finish by running through the middle starting line.

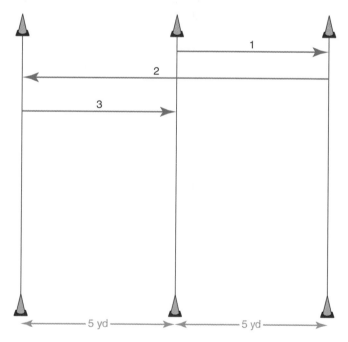

Figure 5.30   NFL agility drill.

60-Yard Shuttle

Purpose

This drill focuses on accelerating, decelerating, and redirecting in a 15-yard zone. These skills are useful because much of the sport takes place in close quarters.

Setup

Mark a starting line and then a line every 5 yards for 15 consecutive yards (figure 5.31). Start in a two- or three-point athletic stance behind the starting line.

Procedure

- On the command, run to the 5-yard line and touch it with either hand. Return to the starting line and touch it with the opposite hand.
- Run to the 10-yard line and touch it with the first hand. Return to the starting line and touch it with the opposite hand.
- Run to the 15-yard line and touch it with the first hand. Return to the starting line and touch it with the opposite hand.

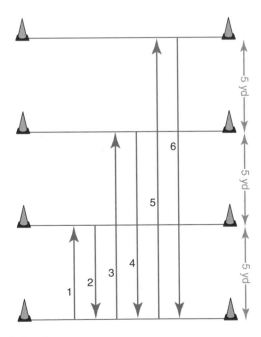

Figure 5.31   60-Yard shuttle.

T Drill

Purpose

This drill focuses on accelerating, decelerating, and quickly changing direction in a compact area.

Setup

Set up the cones in a T shape, with the three cones at the top of the T 10 yards apart and the cone at the base of the T (i.e., the start cone) 5 yards from the middle cone at the top of the T (figure 5.32). Begin in a two-point stance on one side of the start cone.

Procedure

- Sprint to the top middle cone, perform a 90-degree turn, and touch the top of the outside cone with one hand.
- Run across the base of the T to the opposite cone and touch it with the opposite hand.
- Sprint around the top middle cone and return through the starting cone.
- Add variety by changing the starting location (e.g., left or right sides of the cone), starting position (e.g., lying, kneeling), or sequence of movements along the top of the T (e.g., shuffle, carioca).

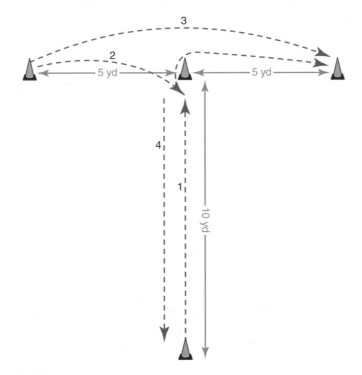

Figure 5.32   T drill.

Illinois Agility Drill

Purpose

This drill combines acceleration, deceleration, foot speed, and body control.

Setup

Use four cones to set up a rectangle that is 10 meters long by 5 meters wide. Inside the rectangle, set four more cones 3.3 meters apart in a line. The top and bottom cones should be even with the outside cones that establish the rectangle. Start in a two- or three-point athletic stance behind the bottom left starting cone.

Procedure

- On the command, run to the cone that is 10 meters from the starting cone. Touch the level of the cone with the left foot and sprint to the first cone in the middle.
- Weave through the cones down and back in the pattern shown in figure 5.33.
- After finishing the weave, sprint toward the cone that is set up 10 meters away, touch the level of the cone with the right foot, and sprint to the final cone.
- To create variety, change up the starting location (e.g., bottom left or bottom right cones) and the starting position (e.g., lying, kneeling, lateral).

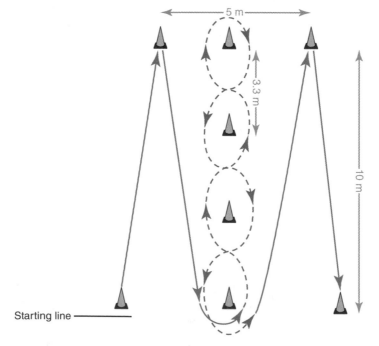

Figure 5.33   Illinois agility drill.

One-Cut Zigzag Drill

Purpose

This drill addresses acceleration, rapid deceleration, and performing quick cuts on one foot. Attackers must be proficient at moving to both the right and the left and must be able to execute quick cuts in either direction.

Setup

Set up the cones in a diagonal pattern 6 to 10 yards apart. Use an even number of cones (usually 8 or 10) in order to have an equal number of cuts (figure 5.34). The first cone is the start cone and the last cone is the finish cone. The others designate the locations of the cuts. Start in a two-point stance behind the first cone.

Procedure

- On the command, accelerate to the second cone.
- Plant the outside foot and go around the cone toward the third cone.
- Follow this pattern around each cone for a total of six to eight cuts.
- At each cone, emphasize technique, body control, and balance. Accelerate with great upper-body mechanics and explosive leg drive when beginning the drill or completing the turn. Decelerate with shorter strides and a lower center of gravity when approaching the next cone and beginning to turn.
- The head, shoulders, and feet should all move together when finishing the deceleration and transitioning to the next acceleration.

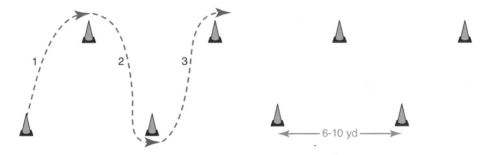

Figure 5.34   One-cut zigzag drill.

Jerry Rice Zigzag Drill

Purpose

This drill addresses acceleration, deceleration, and foot movement in close quarters and helps develop foot speed.

Setup

Set up the cones in a diagonal pattern 6 to 10 yards apart. Use an even number of cones (usually 8 or 10) in order to have an equal number of cuts. The first cone is the start cone and the last cone is the finish cone. The others designate the locations of the cuts. Start in a two-point stance behind the first cone.

Procedure

- On the command, accelerate to the second cone.
- Plant the outside foot and make a circle around the cone toward the third cone.
- Follow this pattern around each cone for a total of six to eight cuts (figure 5.35).
- At each cone, emphasize technique, body control, and balance. Accelerate with great upper-body mechanics and explosive leg drive when beginning the drill or completing the turn. Decelerate with shorter strides and a lower center of gravity when approaching the next cone and beginning to turn.
- The head, shoulders, and feet should all move together when finishing the deceleration and transitioning to the next acceleration.

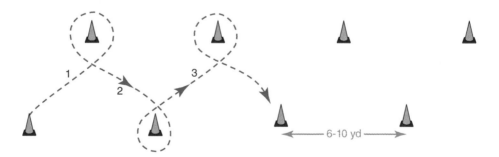

Figure 5.35   Jerry Rice zigzag drill.

Dodge and Pivot Zigzag Drill

Purpose

This drill requires the athlete to learn pivot skills to both the right and the left. This is especially useful for offensive players.

Setup

Set up the cones in a diagonal pattern 6 to 10 yards apart. Use an even number of cones (usually 8 or 10) in order to have an equal number of cuts. The first cone is the start cone and the last cone is the finish cone. The others designate the locations of the cuts. Start in a two-point stance behind the first cone

Procedure

- On the command, accelerate to the second cone.
- Just before arriving at the second cone, perform a roll dodge, pivoting on the inside foot and turning the shoulders completely around. The turn should be tight and enable you to get around as fast as possible. Once the move is complete, keep the head up and locate the next cone.
- Accelerate to the third cone. Just before arriving at the third cone, perform another roll dodge, pivoting again on the inside foot. This move should be in the opposite direction.
- Follow this pattern around each cone for a total of six to eight cuts (figure 5.36).
- At each cone, emphasize technique, body control, and balance. Accelerate with great upper-body mechanics and explosive leg drive when beginning the drill or completing the turn. Decelerate with shorter strides and a lower center of gravity when approaching the next cone and beginning to turn.
- The head, shoulders, and feet should all move together when finishing the deceleration and transitioning to the next acceleration.

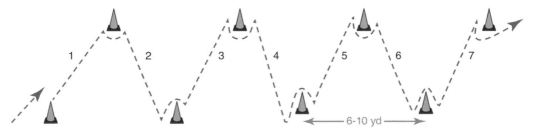

Figure 5.36 Dodge and pivot zigzag drill.

Long Diagonal Six-Cone Drill

Purpose

This drill develops offense-specific agility skills.

Setup

Use six cones to set up a rectangle that is 10 yards long by 5 yards wide. (Place two cones 5 yards apart at the base of the rectangle, two cones 5 yards apart in the middle, and two cones 5 yards apart at the top.) Start in a two-point stance on the outside of the bottom right cone.

Procedure

- Sprint 10 yards to the top right cone.
- Pivot around the top right cone and make a diagonal cut back to the middle left cone.
- Go around the middle left cone and sprint through the top left cone (figure 5.37).
- Repeat in the opposite direction.

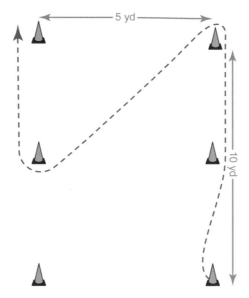

Figure 5.37   Long diagonal six-cone drill.

Loop and Hitch Six-Cone Drill

Purpose

This drill develops offense-specific agility skills.

Setup

Use six cones to set up a rectangle that is 10 yards long by 5 yards wide. (Place two cones 5 yards apart at the base of the rectangle, two cones 5 yards apart in the middle, and two cones 5 yards apart at the top.) Start in a two-point stance on the inside of the bottom right cone.

Procedure

- Sprint to the middle right cone.
- Make a loop around the middle right cone and sprint to the top left cone.
- Pivot on the right foot at the top left cone and sprint through the middle left cone (figure 5.38).
- Repeat in the opposite direction.

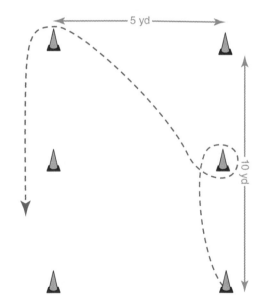

Figure 5.38   Loop and hitch six-cone drill.

Bow Tie Six-Cone Drill

Purpose

This drill develops offense-specific agility skills.

Setup

Use six cones to set up a rectangle that is 10 yards long by 5 yards wide. (Place two cones 5 yards apart at the base of the rectangle, two cones 5 yards apart in the middle, and two cones 5 yards apart at the top.) Start in a two-point stance on the outside of the bottom right cone.

Procedure

- Make a diagonal cut to the middle left cone.
- Make a loop around the middle left cone, keeping the center of gravity low during the turn.
- When the loop is completed, make another diagonal cut and finish through the top right cone (figure 5.39).
- Repeat in the opposite direction.

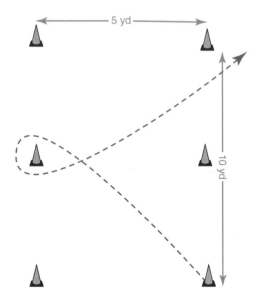

Figure 5.39 Bow tie six-cone drill.

Double Diagonal Six-Cone Drill

Purpose

This drill develops offense-specific agility skills.

Setup

Use six cones to set up a rectangle that is 10 yards long by 5 yards wide. (Place two cones 5 yards apart at the base of the rectangle, two cones 5 yards apart in the middle, and two cones 5 yards apart at the top.) Start in a two-point stance on the outside of the bottom right cone.

Procedure

- Cut diagonally to the middle left cone and make a loop around the middle left cone.
- Sprint to the middle right cone, pivot on the right foot, and go around the middle right cone.
- Make another diagonal cut toward the top left cone and finish through at full speed (figure 5.40).
- Repeat in the opposite direction.

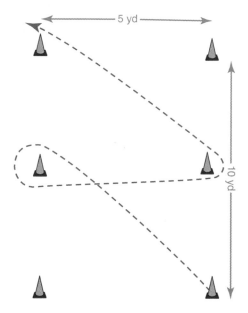

Figure 5.40   Double diagonal six-cone drill.

Inside Figure-8 Six-Cone Drill

Purpose

This drill develops offense-specific agility skills.

Setup

Use six cones to set up a rectangle that is 10 yards long by 5 yards wide. (Place two cones 5 yards apart at the base of the rectangle, two cones 5 yards apart in the middle, and two cones 5 yards apart at the top.) Start in a two-point stance on the inside of the bottom right cone.

Procedure

- Sprint to the inside of the middle right cone.
- Make a figure-8 cut around the middle right cone (right turn) and continue to the middle left cone (left turn).
- Make a diagonal cut toward the top right cone and sprint through the top right cone at full speed (figure 5.41).
- Repeat in the opposite direction.

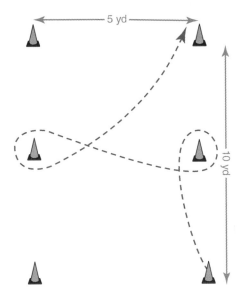

Figure 5.41   Inside figure-8 six-cone drill.

Double Diagonal Shuffle Six-Cone Drill

Purpose

This drill develops defense-specific acceleration and angular shuffle skills.

Setup

Use six cones to set up a rectangle that is 10 yards long by 5 yards wide. (Place two cones 5 yards apart at the base of the rectangle, two cones 5 yards apart in the middle, and two cones 5 yards apart at the top.) Start in a two-point stance on the outside of the bottom right cone.

Procedure

- Sprint forward to the middle right cone.
- At the middle right cone, drop step and perform a backward angle shuffle left toward the bottom left cone.
- At the bottom left cone, sprint to the top left cone.
- At the top left cone, drop step and perform an angle shuffle at 45 degrees toward the middle right cone.
- From the middle right cone, sprint through the top right cone (figure 5.42).
- Repeat in the opposite direction.

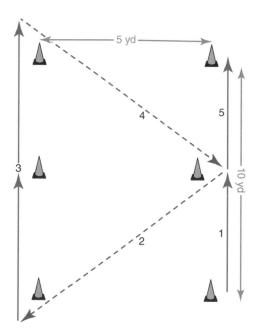

Figure 5.42   Double diagonal shuffle six-cone drill.

High and Low Diagonal Six-Cone Drill

Purpose

This drill develops defense-specific acceleration and angle shuffle skills.

Setup

Use six cones to set up a rectangle that is 10 yards long by 5 yards wide. (Place two cones 5 yards apart at the base of the rectangle, two cones 5 yards apart in the middle, and two cones 5 yards apart at the top.) Start in a two-point stance on the outside of the bottom right cone.

Procedure

- Sprint toward the middle right cone.
- At the middle right cone, drop step and perform a diagonal shuffle toward the bottom left cone.
- At the bottom left cone, sprint to the top right cone.
- At the top right cone, perform a diagonal shuffle to the middle left cone.
- At the middle left cone, plant the outside foot and sprint through the top left cone (figure 5.43).
- Repeat in the opposite direction.

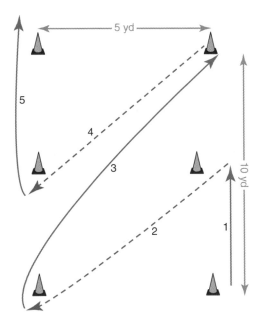

Figure 5.43   High and low diagonal six-cone drill.

Sprint With Lateral Shuffle Six-Cone Drill

Purpose

This drill develops defense-specific sprint, shuffle, and backpedal skills.

Setup

Use six cones to set up a rectangle that is 10 yards long by 5 yards wide. (Place two cones 5 yards apart at the base of the rectangle, two cones 5 yards apart in the middle, and two cones 5 yards apart at the top.) Start in a two-point stance on the outside of the bottom right cone.

Procedure

- Sprint toward the middle left cone and go around the top of the cone.
- Once around the middle left cone, assume a low center of gravity and shuffle toward the middle right cone.
- At the middle right cone, cut on the right foot and immediately sprint full speed through the top left cone (figure 5.44).
- Repeat in the opposite direction.

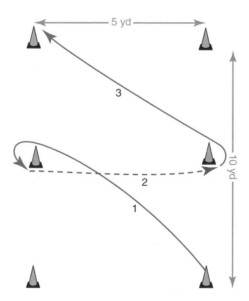

Figure 5.44 Sprint with lateral shuffle six-cone drill.

Shuffle Attack Six-Cone Drill

Purpose

This drill develops defense-specific sprint, shuffle, and backpedal skills.

Setup

Use six cones to set up a rectangle that is 10 yards long by 5 yards wide. (Place two cones 5 yards apart at the base of the rectangle, two cones 5 yards apart in the middle, and two cones 5 yards apart at the top.) Start in a two-point stance on the outside of the bottom right cone.

Procedure

- Shuffle left toward the bottom left cone.
- At the bottom left cone, cut on the left foot and sprint toward the middle right cone.
- Go around the middle right cone and shuffle left toward the middle left cone.
- At the middle left cone, plant with the left foot and sprint full speed through the top right cone (figure 5.45).
- Repeat in the opposite direction.

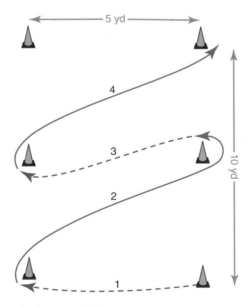

Figure 5.45 Shuffle attack six-cone drill.

Six-Cone Drill

Purpose

This drill develops defense-specific sprint and angle shuffle skills.

Setup

Use six cones to set up a rectangle that is 10 yards long by 5 yards wide. (Place two cones 5 yards apart at the base of the rectangle, two cones 5 yards apart in the middle, and two cones 5 yards apart at the top.) Start in a two-point stance on the outside of the bottom right cone.

Procedure

- Sprint to the middle right cone.
- At the middle right cone, drop step and shuffle at a 45-degree angle left toward the bottom left cone.
- At the bottom left cone, sprint to the top left cone.
- At the top left cone, drop step and shuffle at a 45-degree angle right toward the bottom right cone (figure 5.46).
- Repeat in the opposite direction.

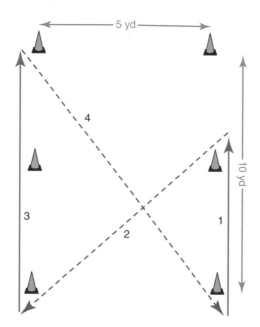

Figure 5.46   Six-cone drill.

Three-Cone Slide Drill

Purpose

This drill challenges the abductors, adductors, and quads. It also develops defense-specific shuffle endurance and the ability to play lower for longer.

Setup

Set up three cones three yards apart in a straight line. The cone on the left is cone 1, the middle cone is cone 2, and the cone on the right is cone 3 (figure 5.47). The athlete starts behind the middle cone in a flexed-knee position.

Procedure

- The coach calls out a cone number (1, 2, or 3) and the athlete shuffles hard toward that cone, attempting to align the hips in front of the cone.
- As the athlete approaches the cone, the coach calls out another number, forcing the athlete to suddenly redirect toward that cone.
- The coach can mix up the order of the commands and call them out in rapid succession. The athlete should always maintain a low defensive position.
- Perform this drill for 10 to 15 seconds.

Figure 5.47   Three-cone slide drill.

Three-Cone Angle Slide Drill

Purpose

This drill challenges the abductors, adductors, and quads. It also develops defense-specific shuffle endurance and the ability to play lower for longer.

Setup

Set up three cones three to four yards apart in a triangle shape. The cone on the left is cone 1, the middle cone is cone 2, and the cone on the right is cone 3 (figure 5.48). The athlete starts behind the middle cone in a flexed-knee position.

Procedure

- The coach calls out a cone number (1, 2, or 3) and the athlete shuffles or runs hard toward that cone, attempting to align the hips in front of the cone.
- As the athlete approaches the cone, the coach calls out another number, forcing the athlete to suddenly redirect toward that cone.
- Players must be able to execute the following skills:
  - Lateral shuffle (cone 1 to 3 or 3 to 1)
  - Drop step and angle shuffle either to the right (2 to 3) or to the left (2 to 1)
  - Acceleration at an angle to the right (1 to 2) or to the left (3 to 2)
- The coach can mix up the order of the commands and call them out in rapid succession. The athlete should always maintain a low defensive position.
- Perform this drill for 10 to 15 seconds.

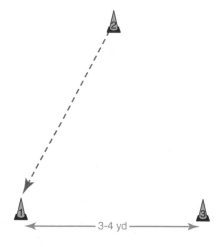

Figure 5.48   Three-cone angle slide drill.

Star Drill

Purpose

This drill works on lateral quickness, balance, and body control.

Setup

Set up five cones approximately six feet (2 m) apart as shown in figure 5.49. Start in a two-point athletic stance behind cone 1.

Procedure

- On the command, shuffle right to a point just behind cone 2 and touch the top of the cone with the right hand.
- Shuffle back to cone 1.
- Backpedal to cone 3 and touch it with either hand before sprinting back to cone 1.
- Shuffle laterally to the left, touch cone 4 with the left hand, and shuffle back to cone 1.
- Sprint through cone 5 to finish.

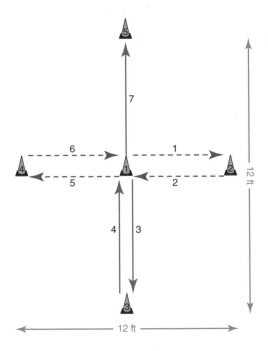

Figure 5.49   Star drill.

GOALIE-SPECIFIC TRAINING

The goalie—the last line of defense—is one of the most crucial positions on the field. A succession of saves by the goalie can inspire teammates and frustrate opponents. In close games, a split-second move by the goalie to stop a shot can create significant shifts in momentum and, ultimately, be the difference between winning and losing. The goalie must have excellent hand–eye coordination, quick reflexes, and precise foot movement to be consistent. To keep team morale high, the goalie should participate in the strength, speed, power, and conditioning exercises with the rest of the team. Position-specific drills can be performed in addition to the team drills, not instead of team drills two to three days per week.

Many of the drills listed above are excellent for goalies such as the NFL agility drill, six-cone drills for defensive players, three-cone slide, three-cone angle slide, and star drill. In addition, existing drills can easily become goalie-specific drills. For example, when performing cone drills, move the cones closer together to simulate the shorter movement patterns used in the crease. For ladder drills, include a second ladder to evoke rapid-fire foot movements on both the left and right sides.

The coach can also incorporate goalie-specific equipment such as a slide board, which helps improve lateral movement in a relatively small area. The slide board is an excellent way to work on quickly changing direction and maintaining a low body position. Goalies can perform lateral slides on a slide board for time (usually 8-20 seconds) or for reps (usually 8-15 reps in each direction).

Lacrosse is dominated by players with explosive speed skills, both linear and lateral. Many of the all-time great players demonstrated such skills on game day and created memorable plays that required power, speed, finesse, and agility. Not all of these players were gifted with natural ability, and all had to work at mastering their craft and train at a high level of intensity. Those special game-day performances come only after putting in time in the weight room, relentlessly pursuing another rep on the track or field, and, as every player knows, spending countless hours playing wall ball—all while working and dreaming of the day when an opportunity will arrive. This is the mind-set required to be successful! With a relentless inner drive, consistency in preparation, and passion to improve, every player can move closer to realizing dreams.

Chapter **6**

Endurance Training

Lacrosse players (and fans!) love to be a part of fast-paced games that move quickly between the offensive and defensive ends of the field. High-speed maneuvering, quick ball movements, and rapid transitions all make for an exciting atmosphere. Because of the intense tempo, lacrosse players must have sufficient energy to perform at the highest level possible in game situations and to avoid physical and mental fatigue during competition.

Gradual adaptation to the stress of competition is necessary if the individual or team is to be successful. Although conditioning is crucial for all players on the field, midfielders in particular need to have the ability to play on, and transition successfully to, both the offensive and defensive zones. Strategic responsibilities, stick skills, footwork, and mental focus can be compromised quickly if the team succumbs to excessive fatigue and does not have adequate physical and mental toughness to execute the game plan in the later stages of competition. This can be addressed only by having a comprehensive game plan for conditioning. Over the course of a year-long training cycle, coaches must learn to manage intensity levels and allow athletes to gradually adapt to substantially increasing levels of stress without causing undue breakdown. When this is done properly, each individual will benefit and, ultimately, give the team the best opportunity to be successful.

The metabolic conditioning demands of lacrosse are extensive and combine elements of the three primary energy systems (aerobic, glycolytic, and ATP-PC). This creates an exciting challenge for athletes and coaches: Maximize strength and power levels while simultaneously building the cardiorespiratory foundation that will lead to successful performance on game day. For field players, absolute speed and agility as measured by performance on a one-repetition maximum are impressive only if those speed and agility levels can be maintained throughout a game. An athlete with great speed for a single rep and poor speed endurance will not be able to perform well in the later stages of the second half. The higher the level of fitness, the better an athlete will perform on game day and the quicker that athlete will recover from activity, whether workouts, practices, or games. A highly efficient, well-maintained fitness level will help athletes avoid late-season breakdown and prevent excessive fatigue, which could be the difference in having a successful season or not. Having a well-planned, thorough training prescription for gradual progression and adaptation is necessary before taking the field.

METABOLIC SYSTEM FUNDAMENTALS

Before discussing conditioning fundamentals, it is essential to have a basic understanding of bioenergetics, which is the way in which the body converts chemical energy to mechanical energy in living organisms. A lacrosse player must have the energy necessary to perform at the highest level for as long as possible during a game. With consistent training, the body can adapt to greater demands and more efficiently produce and utilize the energy needed to execute the required skills.

The body must convert the resources that are taken in as food (carbohydrate, protein, and fat) into a usable source of energy. The crucial element in this process is adenosine triphosphate (ATP), which facilitates muscle activity. Without ATP, muscle function would be impossible. During short-term activities (those lasting less than 30 seconds or so), when power production is at its highest, the body relies on ATP as the primary source of energy. Longer, sustained athletic activity (that lasting from 30 seconds to 3 minutes) also relies on the provision of ATP but requires the breakdown of glucose as the primary means of transporting ATP to the working muscles. During sustained athletic activity within this time window, (known as the anaerobic or glycolytic energy system), if enough oxygen is not present, excessive lactate production may occur, which can impede performance. For low-intensity, long-duration athletic activities lasting between three minutes and two to three hours, more oxygen must be present in order for the ATP to be effectively metabolized. The system utilized in this time period is known as the aerobic (with oxygen) energy system.

Although often identified as distinct, these three systems are interdependent and must be viewed as such. The player must rely on all three energy systems in order to perform well. Although we distinguish them in order to better understand the training needs of a lacrosse player, the systems must be appreciated collectively as the means of energy transportation and conversion during competition.

The metabolic demands of lacrosse are unique based on position. Goalies, defenders, and attackers do not have to run the length of the field and are limited to a specific area of performance. It is estimated that these positions can get up to 80 percent of their energy from the ATP system and 20 percent from the glycolytic system (Plisk and Stenersen 1992). For mid-fielders who must play (and transition) to both ends of the field, 60 percent of their energy may be derived from the ATP system, 20 percent from the glycolytic and 20 percent from the aerobic system (Steinhagen, et. al. 1998). For all players, however, training should consist of elements from all energy systems with a specific emphasis on the ATP system.

Aerobic System

Another energy system is the aerobic system, which sustains the body during low-power activities lasting between three minutes and two to three hours. In the past, many lacrosse coaches emphasized aerobic training, and athletes would perform long-distance running exclusively through-out the off-season. This strategy may be useful at times during the early off-season; however, more of the training focus should be concentrated in working the ATP and gylcolytic systems as those are the primary systems in use during a game. Although not the most important energy system for lacrosse players on game day, the aerobic system does have its place in preparing athletes for competition because a lacrosse player (much like other anaerobic endurance athletes) must have a strong aerobic base in order to perform and recover more effectively from bouts of anaerobic activity. Prolonged, moderate to high-intensity activities can be sustained longer if the aerobic system is sufficiently addressed (Swank 2008). For a lacrosse player, aerobic training is more helpful during recovery than during performance.

Anaerobic System

The next energy system used in lacrosse is the anaerobic, or glycolytic, system. This energy system supports moderate-power, short-duration activity lasting from 30 seconds to 3 minutes and is the most critical for lacrosse players when engaged in long-term, sustained offensive or defensive possessions. Intense physical battles in front of the cage during a man-up situation, prolonged uptempo offensive attack situations, and persistent defensive slides during a sustained possession all require the utilization of energy from this system. When lactate levels increase, the legs get heavier, the feet start to move more slowly, and the will is tested to the limit. It is often in these situations that games are won or lost. Players who can concentrate longer and withstand the build up of lactate have a greater chance at success. This energy system is highly adaptable and can be manipulated through hard work and the progressive imposition of stress during the preparation phase of training. With a proper condition-ing program, athletes can build tolerance to high levels of lactate and will learn to overcome momentary discomfort through training adaptations (Bompa and Calcina 1994).

MENTAL TOUGHNESS

The mental and psychological demands of lacrosse are extensive. Mental focus, consistency, and communication are essential components of success and are challenged daily in preparation, practice, and games. The will to succeed and improve must be cultivated alongside physical preparation. In many cases a player's physical and mental toughness are interwoven and cannot be distinguished from each other. This is where physical training can complement mental and emotional development.

In lacrosse, as in most sports, the deterioration of mental skills coincides with fatigue. Players become overwhelmed with the pace of the game, weather conditions, and other external stresses and become more likely to make mental mistakes. Through training, coaches can reduce the likelihood of skill deterioration by emphasizing the importance of conditioning. As the famous Green Bay Packers coach Vince Lombardi said, "Fatigue makes cowards of us all." Momentary lapses in concentration or a slightly slower reaction to a situation can be costly. Coaches should use training to challenge athletes to perform at their best in all situations. Never allowing mistakes or lack of effort to go unnoticed, always setting expectations higher, and teaching athletes to focus and concentrate despite physical discomfort are all part of the progression to game day. During competition, some athletes tend to succumb to fatigue and lose their mental edge. By teaching athletes that conditioning is as much a mind-set as a physical state, coaches can encourage their athletes to perform through the barriers and potential lulls in a practice or game.

In addition, a proper mindset can be used to level the playing field when the opponent may have more talent, skill, or experience. As teams begin to wear down at an expected pace, better-conditioned teams have the opportunity to outplay opponents during the later portions of the contest. Superior skills can be neutralized by superior training. In other words, hard work can overcome genetics or talent! During the second half of a game, when most competitions are decided, the more physically fit team will have a better chance to execute the game plan than a team that has succumbed to physical and mental deterioration.

ATP-PC System

The most important energy system used in lacrosse is the ATP-PC system. Although cardio-respiratory demands vary depending on a player's position (attacker, defender, midfielder or goalie), most activity performed on game day is supported by this system. Most explosive bursts of speed in lacrosse take place over distances of 10 to 70 yards. These high-power, short-duration bouts of all-out intensity last up to 30 seconds and rely on the ATP-PC system for energy production. When considering the specific cardiorespiratory demands of lacrosse, special attention should be given to activities that result in significant development of this energy system, such as multiple short bursts of activity or interval training that requires the athlete to mix all-out sprint activities with recovery activities between reps. The most common skills of lacrosse—acceleration, rapid deceleration and redirection, fast-paced dodges, and defensive slides—take from within this energy system.

ENDURANCE-TRAINING GUIDELINES

Although all of the energy systems are interrelated and are utilized during competition, coaches may want to isolate specific energy systems during training at certain times of the year. For example, during the early stages of the off-season when a team is beginning its preparation, it may be appropriate to emphasize aerobic training for three to four weeks. This will help to lay the groundwork for conditioning events in the coming weeks. In addition, coaches and athletes may concentrate on training a specific energy system for a period of time in preparation for a fitness test. For example, during the final two to three weeks of the preseason, athletes may perform more anaerobic endurance activities to get ready for the specific energy demands of competition. This two- to three-week cycle may end with a conditioning test just before the start of team practice. Prior to each conditioning training session, a dynamic warm-up should be conducted. Using the guidelines in chapter 3, the athlete should take time before the session to prepare for the stress of the training session. Afterward, a cooldown and static stretch should be conducted.

Aerobic Focus

As a training calendar is developed, athletes can establish an endurance base through aerobic training. For lacrosse, aerobic training is usually performed in the early off-season. After a period of adaptation, it does not need to be addressed more than occasionally during the remainder of the off-season. To establish a fitness base, training sessions (one to two days per week) can focus on aerobic training at the conclusion of strength or movement skill development.

Aerobic training is necessary to increase work capacity, prepare the athlete for more intense sprint and agility training, and to allow for more efficient recovery. These can include sustained activities at a low intensity or continuous interval training in which the athlete performs short, intense bursts of activity with a brief recovery period in between. These short bursts can take place for a predetermined length of time or distance and are spaced between lower-intensity activities that allow for recovery in preparation for the next high-intensity activity (Bompa and Calcina 1994). For lacrosse players, this training phase includes work-capacity circuits or other events (e.g., jogging or cycling for a specific length of time or distance without the pressure of making a specific goal or time) that enable the athlete to transition gradually from light activity during a postseason recovery interval or an active rest period. Once this baseline work capacity has been established, more intense aerobic work may then be introduced. As the athlete moves from the introductory phase, aerobic training should become more lacrosse specific. Sustained, long-distance events (running, cycling, etc.) should be replaced by interval training to enhance maximal oxygen uptake and includes brief, intense sprints with shorter rest intervals between reps (Swank 2008). With this type of training, the aerobic benefits may be realized in a manner that mimics lacrosse game-day cardio-respiratory demands. Thus, after the first several weeks of training, aerobic training can be performed on a semiregular basis (e.g., every other week) with no need for a more substantial time investment. As the training cycle progresses and the season nears, repeat short sprints events will become a more substantial part of the endurance training program.

Several common sample aerobic-training protocols are as follows.

- One-, two-, or three-mile (1.6, 3.2, or 4.8 km) runs on a track at a fairly high level of intensity to simulate the metabolic demands of the game. Mileage longer than this is not necessarily beneficial and, if performed for an extended period of time, may be detrimental to strength and power gains. The athlete should begin behind the designated start line on an Olympic track. On the start command, run the distance prescribed without stopping. The timer should call out the run time as the runners cross the finish line and record the results.

- Bike, elliptical, or stair climber workouts with the heart rate at or beyond 150 beats per minute or approximately 75 percent of maximum heart rate (220 – age = maximum heart rate) for 30 to 45 minutes. Continuous, steady-state activity on a cardio piece of equipment can be an occasional alternative for lacrosse training, especially during the pre-season.

- Cross-country course for one to two miles (1.6-3.2 km). To add energy and intensity to the drill, split the group into smaller teams and have them compete against each other. The athlete should begin behind the designated start line. On the start command, run the course without stopping. The timer should call out the run time as the runners cross the finish line and record the results.

Bike Workouts

Stationary-bike interval workouts are an excellent means for developing the aerobic energy system. Although a healthy lacrosse player should perform running drills as often as possible, biking can be a way to change up what can be a monotonous routine. In addition, from an injury prevention standpoint, occasional (i.e., one day per week) biking is a way to challenge the heart, lungs, and legs without overtaxing the knee, hip, and ankle joints.

The easiest way to perform these workouts is with the use of a heart rate monitor. The athlete can then focus on the training routine without having to stop and measure the heart rate after every sprint. In order to follow the routines, the athlete must know the approximate maximum heart rate (220 – age = maximum heart rate) and calculate the prescribed percentages beforehand.

For each routine, follow the length and intensity level prescribed for each interval. For example, if the workout calls for 75 percent of maximum heart rate for 6 minutes, a 20-year-old athlete would ride at a sustained heart rate of 150 beats per minute for 6 minutes. If an all-out sprint is prescribed, the athlete would ride as fast as possible for the length of the interval. See tables 6.1 through 6.4 for sample routines.

Table 6.1 Heart Rate Interval Bike Workout

Warm up	5 min
75% of maximum heart rate	6 min
All-out sprint × 1-3 reps	30 sec; 1-min recovery
80% of maximum heart rate	6 min
All-out sprint × 1-3 reps	30 sec; 1-min recovery
85%+ of maximum heart rate	6 min
All-out sprint × 1-3 reps	30 sec; 1-min recovery
Cool down	3 min

Table 6.2   Graduated Interval Bike Workout

Warm up	5 min
75% of maximum heart rate	5 min
80% of maximum heart rate	4 min
85% of maximum heart rate	3 min
60% of maximum heart rate	2 min
75% of maximum heart rate	4 min
80% of maximum heart rate	3 min
85% of maximum heart rate	2 min
60% of maximum heart rate	2 min
75% of maximum heart rate	3 min
80% of maximum heart rate	2 min
85% of maximum heart rate	1 min
Cool down	3 min

Table 6.3   Game Simulation Bike Workout

Warm up		5 min
Quarter 1 × 2 rounds	Sprint at 100% of max effort	1 min
	Easy ride at 50% of max effort	1 min 30 sec
Quarter 2 × 3 rounds	Sprint at 100% of max effort	45 sec
	Easy ride at 50% of max effort	1 min
Quarter 3 × 4 rounds	Sprint at 100% of max effort	30 sec
	Easy ride at 50% of max effort	45 sec
Quarter 4 × 4 rounds	Sprint at 100% of max effort	30 sec
	Easy ride at 50% of max effort	30 sec
Cool down		3 min

Anaerobic Focus

Anaerobic (glycolytic) activities are those lasting between 30 seconds and 3 minutes and sustained at a high level of intensity. Athletes who can resist the pain and mental fatigue of acidosis can perform at a higher level of concentration, focus, and technical precision for longer periods of time (Bompa 1994). Through proper training and preparation, lacrosse players can withstand the barrage of lactic acid that builds during sustained activity and work through it more efficiently. This system can then be addressed up to and during the in-season phase. Coaches should gradually work up to anaerobic training events and should encourage athletes to have a base of conditioning before undertaking this type of training in order for the training to be most effective.

An anaerobic focus can be incorporated into training sessions (one to two days per week) after strength and skill development. It should be the final event of the training session. On occasion, training in this zone can be followed by team competitions (e.g., tug of war, races, relays) to emphasize hard work and mental toughness when fatigue is near its peak. Several common sample anaerobic-training protocols are as follows.

Repeat Track Sprints

The combination of a target time along with the length of the sprints can make this event particularly challenging. For coaches, track workouts can be an opportunity to determine not only which players are in shape but who is willing to fight through the mental barriers as well.

This event requires an Olympic size track. Each athlete (or group of athletes) should begin behind a designated start time. On command, the prescribed distance is run with a timer at the finish line calling out the time. An example of a track sprint workout is as follows.

800 meters × 1 rep as fast as possible. A sample run time is 3:30 minutes with a rest period of 5:00 minutes.

400 meters × 1 rep as fast as possible. A sample run time is 1:35 minutes with a rest period of 3:00 minutes.

200 meters × 2 reps as fast as possible. A sample run time is 40 seconds with 2:00 minutes of rest between reps.

Repeat Shuttles

If training space is an issue during the off-season, athletes and coaches can be creative in utilizing available facilities such as a basketball court. The following is a way to run intermediate distances in a confined area. Repeat shuttles of varying distances are performed utilizing a 25-yard space between lines or cones. The distance for each rep is different and can follow a pattern of increasing, then decreasing volume or can be in random order (much like the demands of a lacrosse game). The athlete(s) should begin behind the start line and wait for the start command. When the command is given, the athlete should run to the line 25 yards away, touch the line with the foot and return to the start line for a total of 50 yards. If (for example) the prescribed length is 150 yards, the athlete should repeat the down-back event 3 times. An example of a fixed pattern 1,500-yard shuttle workout is as follows:

150-yard interval × 1 at 100% intensity with a 1:00 recovery.
200-yard shuttle × 1 at 100% intensity with a 1:30 recovery.
250-yard shuttle × 1 at 100% intensity with a 2:00 recovery.

300-yard shuttle × 1 at 100% intensity with a 2:30 recovery.

250-yard shuttle × 1 at 100% intensity with a 2:00 recovery.

200-yard shuttle × 1 at 100% intensity with a 1:30 recovery.

150-yard interval × 1 at 100% intensity with a 1:00 recovery.

An example of a random order 1,500-yard shuttle workout is as follows:

200-yard shuttle × 1 at 100% intensity with a 1:30 recovery.

150-yard interval × 1 at 100% intensity with a 1:00 recovery.

200-yard shuttle × 1 at 100% intensity with a 1:30 recovery.

250-yard shuttle × 1 at 100% intensity with a 2:00 recovery.

250-yard shuttle × 1 at 100% intensity with a 2:00 recovery.

300-yard shuttle × 1 at 100% intensity with a 2:30 recovery.

150-yard interval × 1 at 100% intensity with a 1:00 recovery

3 × 300-Yard Shuttles

This event is a great way to emphasize the glycolytic energy system and can be used as training event or as a conditioning test. Athletes can be asked to run each rep under a specific time or attain an average time for all three reps. Either way, progress can be measured from week to week as the athlete should gradually reduce the amount of time taken to run each rep.

Using a 50-yard course, the athlete should begin behind a starting line and wait for the start command. When the start command is given, the athlete sprints 50 yards (to a designated line or cone) and returns to the starting line. This down-back for 50 yards should be repeated two more times for a total of 300 yards. After a recovery period of 2 or 3 minutes, the athlete should repeat the event two more times.

A sample target time might be 65 seconds per rep meaning the athlete should perform each rep under 65 seconds. If an average of 65 seconds is used, the athlete should average 65 seconds for all three reps.

One way to make the event even more challenging is to reduce the distance between lines from 50 yards to 25 yards. Instead of three trips down-back, there are now six.

ATP-PC Focus

Lacrosse is a game of speed and speed endurance. Sudden breakaways, fast-paced offensive systems that force the defense to react to split-second movements, and defensive slides or switches to cover offensive attackers are all performed in the ATP-PC zone. The athlete who can accelerate, dodge, slide, and pivot at the highest level of intensity for the longest period of time has the greatest opportunity to be successful. Most activities on game day require the activation of this energy system, thus making it the most important element in the training plan. Speed is properly addressed in a progressive, gradual manner with longer rest intervals between reps. Coming to a state of almost complete recovery is necessary—especially early on—to develop high-quality adaptation. As levels of absolute acceleration and speed are improved, a gradual introduction of speed endurance events will properly transition the athlete to competition mode. Patience, preparation, and thoughtful design are necessary to elicit the desired response: speed!

In the initial stages of training, it may be necessary to work on speed before deterioration of the central nervous system occurs in order to maximize the mind–body connection and develop running technique and muscle memory. As the training phase progresses, speed endurance can be addressed at any time during the workout to improve speed under conditions of stress. Several common training protocols focused on the ATP-PC system are as follows.

Repeat Hill or Stadium Sprints

Another way to intensify the sprint conditioning is to use a hill or stadium steps. Depending on the distance available, the resisted sprints can include short, intermediate or longer distances (or a combination). In a team setting, coaches can split the team into smaller groups and race up the hill or steps (with a walk-down afterward) either among individuals or as a relay. The athlete should begin at the bottom of the hill or stadium at the start line and wait for the command. Once the command is given, sprint the distance to the finish line and sprint through the finish line. For safety purposes, walk down (don't run) to the start line and prepare for the next rep.

An example of a hill workout is as follows:

10 yards × 4 reps as fast as possible with a walk-down and a :45 rest between reps.

25 yards × 3 reps as fast as possible with a walk-down and a 1:00 rest between reps.

50 yards × 2 reps as fast as possible with a walk-down and a 1:30 rest between reps.

25 yards × 3 reps as fast as possible with a walk-down and a 1:00 rest between reps.

10 yards × 4 reps as fast as possible with a walk-down and a :45 rest between reps.

Repeat Linear Sprints

Repeat linear sprints without resistance are performed at 100 percent of intensity over a distance of 10 to 50 yards with sufficient recovery given between reps so that the athlete can maintain as close to 100 percent intensity as possible. Early in the training process, the athlete should be given at least 5 seconds of recovery for every second of activity (a 1:5 work to rest ratio). The athlete should select the distance based on the space available. A shorter distance is used for these intervals because the ATP-PC energy system is targeted. The number of reps could be as few as 6 to 8 or as many as 18 to 20. A sample repeat linear sprint workout is as follows.

30 yards × 2 reps (100% of sprint capacity with :25 rest)
20 yards × 4 reps (100% of sprint capacity with :15 rest)
10 yards × 6 reps (100% of sprint capacity with :10 rest)
20 yards × 4 reps (100% of sprint capacity with :15 rest)
30 yards × 2 reps (100% of sprint capacity with :25 rest)

Repeat Linear Sprints With Resistance

For developing speed endurance, resistance sprints can be incorporated into the training progression. Sleds, Prowlers, and other resistance-based equipment can add intensity and require the athlete to be mentally strong to handle the added stress. The sprints are performed at 100 percent of intensity for a distance of 10-50 yards.

The athlete begins behind the designated starting line and, at the command, sprints at 100 percent of intensity through the finish line, turns the sled or Prowler in the opposite direction and waits for the start of the next rep. For these types of sprints, the work to rest ratio is usually between 1:3 and 1:5.

An example of a sled pull workout is as follows:

30 yards × 4 reps (each rep is at 100% of sprint capacity with a 1:5 work:rest ratio)

20 yards × 6 reps (each rep is at 100% of sprint capacity with a 1:4 work:rest ratio)

10 yards × 8 reps (each rep is at 100% of sprint capacity with a 1:3 work:rest ratio)

Variable-Length Short Shuttles

Short shuttles of variable length help develop the ATP-PC system. Cones are placed on the goal line and the 25-yard line. The athlete stands behind the starting line. At the command, the athlete sprints 25 yards and either runs through (if a 25-yard interval is prescribed) or touches the 25-yard line, returns to the starting line, and continues to run the 25-yard length to complete the prescribed distance for each rep. Between reps, the athlete rests for the prescribed amount of time and waits for the next interval to begin. A sample short-shuttle interval workout with the reps in random order is as follows.

25 yards × 1 rep (at 100% intensity with :15 rest)

75 yards × 1 rep (<:14 with :45 rest ratio)

100 yards × 2 reps (each rep <:19 with 1:00 rest)

50 yards × 2 reps (each rep <:09 with :30 rest)

25 yards × 2 reps (at 100% intensity with :15 rest)

100 yards × 1 rep (<:19 with 1:00 rest)

50 yards × 1 rep (<:09 with :30 rest)

25 yards × 3 reps (at 100% intensity with :15 rest)

100 yards × 1 rep (<:19 with 1:00 rest)

Fixed-Length Repeat Shuttles

Repeat shuttles with a fixed length also help develop the ATP-PC system. Cones are placed on the goal line and the 25-yard line. The athlete stands behind the starting line. At the command, the athlete sprints to the 25-yard line and touches it with the foot, runs back to the starting line and touches it with the foot, runs back to the 25-yard line and touches it with the foot, and then returns to the starting line for a total of 100 yards. Between reps, the athlete rests for the prescribed amount of time and waits for the next interval to begin. A sample repeat-shuttle interval workout with a fixed length is as follows.

100 yards × 10-16 reps (each rep <:19 with a :45 rest between)

Half Gasser

Half gassers are a good tool for both off-season and in-season development of the ATP-PC system. The athlete begins behind one sideline of the lacrosse field. At the command, the athlete sprints across the width of the field to the far sideline, touches it with the foot, and returns to the starting sideline. Between reps, the athlete rests for the prescribed amount of time and waits for the next interval to begin. A sample in-season half gasser workout is as follows.

Half gassers × 6 reps (each rep <:20 with a :45 rest between)

Sprint–Walk Intervals

Sprint–walk intervals are performed on the field and combine the intensity of sprinting with the recovery of walking. The sprint portion should be performed at 100-percent intensity and the walk interval should be performed at 50 percent of maximum speed. Using the dimensions of a football field, the athlete begins on one goal line and sprints toward the far goal line for the prescribed length (measured in yards; see figure 6.1). The athlete then decelerates and begins walking at 50 percent of sprint speed for the prescribed length. The sprint distances will vary each rep and can last from 50 to 200 yards. The walk intervals will vary from 50 to 100 yards. Upon reaching the far goal line, the athlete turns and heads back toward the starting goal line. The athlete follows this continuous run–walk pattern for the entire prescribed distance for each quarter

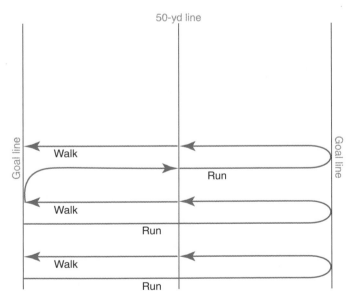

Figure 6.1   Sprint–walk interval setup.

before the rest interval begins. A sample sprint-walk intervals workout is as follows (distances in yards):

Quarter 1: run 150, walk 50, run 150, walk 100, run 100, walk 50, rest 2 min (see figure 6.1)

Quarter 2: run 100, walk 50, run 100, walk 50, run 100, walk 50, run 100, walk 50, rest 2 min

Quarter 3: run 200, walk 100, run 100, walk 50, run 100, walk 50, rest 2 min

Quarter 4: run 50, walk 100, run 150, walk 50, run 100, walk 50, run 50, walk 50

Blended Conditioning

Although classified primarily as an anaerobic sport, lacrosse engages all three energy systems at different times throughout the game or season. For example, against an offense that emphasizes shot frequency, a significant amount of sprinting might occur between ends of the field and on both the offensive and defensive ends. Against a slower, more methodical team that maximizes possession time and works for high-quality shot opportunities, the flow may be slower and sprint opportunities may be minimal. Conditioning during the off-season must reflect the need to prepare for all situations, ranging from highly aerobic to almost exclusively ATP-PC. The following examples of blended conditioning, which combines elements of all energy systems and truly mimics the demands of game day.

Blended Shuttle Ladder

To prepare for a game-like situation in which multiple energy systems are utilized, the shuttle ladder is a very useful training tool. Cones are placed on lines 25 yards apart and the athlete begins behind the start line. On command, the athlete sprints the 25-yard course and touches the far line and returns to the start line for a total of 50 yards. The number of reps should correspond with the distance prescribed.

An example of a blended shuttle ladder is as follows:

50 yards × 1 rep <:09 with a :20 recovery
100 yards × 1 rep <:19 with a :45 recovery
150 yards × 1 rep <:30 with a 1:00 recovery
200 yards × 1 rep <:43 with a 1:30 recovery
300 yards × 1 rep <:66 with a 2:00 recovery
200 yards × 1 rep <:43 with a 1:30 recovery
150 yards × 1 rep <:30 with a 1:00 recovery
100 yards × 1 rep <:19 with a :45 recovery
50 yards × 1 rep <:09 with a :20 recovery

One-Mile Sprint

In the one-mile (1.6 km) sprint, the athlete begins on the starting line of an Olympic track. At the command, the athlete completes the prescribed distance around the track and finishes through the starting line. The event should be timed, and the athlete should strive to improve throughout the off-season. The athlete begins behind the start line and waits for the start command. Sprint the designated distance and finish through the end line. An example is as follows.

400 meters × 1 rep with a 3:00 recovery
200 meters × 2 reps with a 2:00 recovery
100 meters × 8 reps with a 1:00 recovery

Perimeters

When space is limited, running the perimeter of a 25-yard × 25-yard square can be a useful (indoor) training event. In addition, if athletes are placed at all four corners, they can run simultaneously in the same direction. The number of athletes performing the event can be multiplied by having some athletes run while others are resting inside the box and cheering for their teammates. Perimeter training allows the athlete to combine ATP-PC training with elements from the glycolytic energy system.

Mark off a 25-yard × 25-yard square with cones (see figure 6.2). The athlete begins at one cone, runs a lap around all four cones for a distance of 100 yards, ends at the starting cone, and rests for the prescribed time. The athlete then completes two laps around all four cones for a total distance of 200 yards. This continues for the prescribed distance. An example is as follows.

100 yards × 2 reps (1 lap) with a :45 recovery

200 yards × 1 rep (2 laps) with a 1:30 recovery

300 yards × 1 rep (3 laps) with a 2:00 recovery

200 yards × 1 rep (2 laps) with a 1:30 recovery

100 yards × 2 reps (1 lap) with a :45 recovery

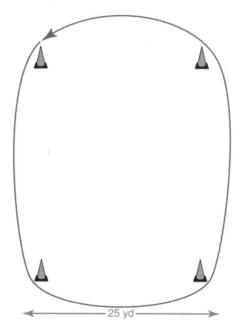

Figure 6.2   Perimeter training setup.

Regardless of an athlete's experience or skill level, conditioning plays a major role in the development of a lacrosse player. If the coach can provide a vision of game-day performance during the preseason, players will accept the discomfort of training and focus on the big-picture objective of success on game day. If properly prepared, athletes will be mentally sharp and able to execute the game-plan details rather than focusing on their physical state during a game.

Chapter 7

Off-Season Program Development

Thoughtful, progressive, comprehensive training—along with a lot of hard work—will help produce the winning edge that all lacrosse players hope to achieve. In this chapter I discuss putting together a lacrosse-specific off-season training program that will help each athlete achieve goals. When merging training concepts in a practical, cohesive manner, the desired outcome is always injury prevention and performance enhancement. These two objectives go hand in hand and should be considered throughout the progression regardless of time of year or training season. The health and safety of the athlete is paramount in program design. Safe, effective, efficient training is the goal! In addition, awareness of the injury history of the team and individual athletes must be a consideration. Some of the lacrosse injuries most frequently reported in the past several years include knee injuries (e.g., anterior cruciate ligament, meniscus), shoulder subluxations and separations, back injuries (e.g., muscle strains, disc issues), and concussions. Strength-development exercises, movement skills, and drills that help prevent or reduce the severity of these injuries must be included in the prescription. For example, change-of-direction drills, plyometric movements (unilateral and bilateral), joint-stabilization exercises, and core strengthening before the season all help reduce the number and severity of injuries once competition begins.

Ultimately, game-day performance improvement is a key element in program design. What are the specific needs of the sport, team, and individual? Speed, agility, speed endurance, strength, power, and flexibility are some general categories in which lacrosse players desire to improve. For example, a defensive player may work on foot speed and change of direction to better execute man-to-man coverage. A midfielder may want to improve upper-body strength for enhanced stick handling, ball control, and checking. A goalie may need mental toughness and improved quickness to endure close-quarter defensive barrages. If considering the specific shortcomings of a team, a coach might want to implement a year-round conditioning program to avoid physical and mental breakdown in the latter stages of the game.

Whatever the weaknesses, coaches and athletes must learn to evaluate prior performance and be willing to honestly address shortcomings in order to transform the individual into a more skilled lacrosse player. The off-season is the ideal time of year to address these shortcomings. The athlete has plenty of time to devote to a detailed, comprehensive training program so that he or she has made the necessary improvements once the season begins.

The manner in which training occurs is also of great importance. Many young, immature athletes are concerned with demonstrating their strengths to their peers rather than addressing their weaknesses. For example, players who are naturally gifted with linear speed skills may like to perform movement skills and avoid the weight room. Those gifted with natural strength may not have the linear and lateral speed skills needed to perform well and therefore may avoid speed and agility training. Although good for the ego, this strategy is bad for performance! A realistic understanding of specific needs and a willingness to risk having weaknesses temporarily exposed are necessary elements of the training process. A humble athlete who is willing to accept the advice of parents, coaches, or teachers tends to be the most successful when it comes to preparation and development. Throughout my career, I've witnessed athletes who were open to the honest suggestions of coaches and, with hard work and diligence during the off-season months, were able to elevate their game and reach their genetic potential once competition began. Having this attitude is one of the key components of success!

OFF-SEASON PROGRAM DESIGN

Before the start of any training program, the athlete or coach must understand some fundamental concepts that will allow for success. Without these, the training may be ineffective and the outcome flawed. Coaches and athletes should think about each of the following as they develop the substance of the off-season protocol.

Practical Considerations

Some practical barriers may exist and should be considered before developing the training prescription. Do the training resources match the workout requirements? Have the practical matters (e.g., time, location, equipment availability) been resolved before proceeding? If they have not, the results may be compromised due to a lack of sufficient preparation. The following are a few examples of issues that must be addressed.

Training Time

The first practical consideration is simply deciding the amount of time available for training. How much time will be allotted per session? How many days per week? These simple questions are often overlooked when designing a program. For example, an athlete might create a lengthy program that takes too long to complete and, after a few days or weeks of trying to make it work, may quit in frustration. It is best to be conservative when estimating time availability. Most people tend to devote substantial time to academic commitments, family, and other interests. Having a mind-set of "less is better" will allow the athlete to complete the workout in a reasonable amount of time.

Another very important—and often overlooked—element of training is building recovery time into the tactical plan. Rest, proper nutrition, and psychological and emotional recovery are crucial pieces in the puzzle. Without allowing for adequate recovery, workouts may become dull and less productive and result in diminished outcomes. In some extreme cases, overtraining may result, which will take a considerable amount of time to overcome. If overtraining occurs, the athlete will become frustrated and may experience negative physiological symptoms such as extreme fatigue, muscle soreness, and an inability to adapt (Hoffman 2002). In order to avoid such breakdown, a progressive escalation in volume and intensity is suggested. Start slow and gradually increase workout duration, intensity, or both. When it comes to nutrition and proper rest, the athlete is in training every day regardless of time of year!

Training Type

The next practical concern is how training will be conducted. Will the individual train with the team, in small groups, or individually? The answer to this question has implications in many areas of team dynamics. Is there an opportunity for team building, or will the athletes work separately during the training phase? If the athletes are training together, there will be more of a team-building atmosphere in which athletes will be more likely to push and challenge one another to achieve goals. Discipline, accountability, and workout pace can be established because everyone is working as a unit. If training alone, the athlete must be intrinsically disciplined and motivated to execute all of the movements with great precision and effort. As in many endeavors, having one or more partners will increase the likelihood of mutual accountability because the partners can help spot, oversee technique, and motivate each other.

Training Equipment

Next, the athlete must decide what training equipment is available and determine whether he or she is familiar with using those pieces. Will the athlete have access to a school facility, home gym, or commercial gym and equipment such as free weights, selectorized machines, suspension devices, medicine balls, Swiss balls, and any other necessary equipment? For optimal results, the training program should include a blend of modalities that incorporate a variety of training devices. A prescription with substantial training resources will vary greatly from one with limited resources in terms of volume, intensity, and duration. However, regardless of the sophistication of the equipment available, any successful program must include the sweat equity of the athlete in order to create gains. Hard work, consistency, and gradual progression are key! Modest facilities in which the athlete pushes to the limit during every session will beat state-of-the-art facilities and inadequate effort every time.

Training Safety

Another major element of every training program is safety. Every athlete should consider this crucial phrase during the design period. The goal is performance improvement, and anything that detracts from this goal should be avoided. If the athlete lacks experience, maintaining a simple routine with great technique would be advised. In all cases, strict attention to basic principles involving common sense will ensure a safe, productive training atmosphere.

- The first safety consideration is proper programming. Progression, assessment, and motivation are key elements to a safe and effective training program.
- A spotter should always be present during training, especially if the lifter is using barbells and dumbbells. A spotter can assist if the lifter is unable to complete the movement. From a safety perspective, spotters play a critical role in ensuring that the movements are completed with proper technique and motivation.
- Someone should be available to evaluate skill progression in speed and agility training. Each movement skill should be performed with technical precision and attention to detail. If technique breaks down, the movement will become counterproductive and potentially unsafe. Safe training conditions are a must!
- The training environment should be safe (well lit and well ventilated with a nonslip floor), and the equipment checked for damage or potential hazards. Injury may result if the equipment is inadequate.
- Before performing heavier sets on multijoint exercises, be sure to engage in one to three warm-up sets of three to five reps. Start with light weights and gradually increase to the desired training weight.

Design Fundamentals

The design and progression of the training routine play a major role in the outcome. The results may be less than optimal if the exercises do not fit together in a cohesive manner or if the volume, intensity, and frequency are not properly manipulated. Experience level (beginner, intermediate, or advanced), training state (well trained or detrained), health status (injured or healthy), motivation, and facility availability all play a role in program design. Exercise selection should begin with these variables in mind. As a general rule, lighter loads (low intensity and volume) should be prescribed at the beginning of a training cycle, especially if the athlete is detrained or a beginner. As adaptation occurs and the athlete acclimates to increasingly greater training loads, he should be challenged to then adapt to and overcome greater levels of stress.

Training Volume

Volume is the amount of work performed in any one time period (e.g., day, week). The number of sets and reps, which varies depending on the athlete's age, experience, and training cycle emphasis, should be taken into consideration. In most cases, 2 to 4 sets of 3 to 15 reps are appropriate for lacrosse players. This number will allow for sufficient adaptation. The team or individual should also consider how much time is available, and the training prescription should be completed within that time frame. Athletes and coaches frequently overestimate the amount of time available and become frustrated if the workout cannot be completed in the time allotted. If the athlete has only 30 minutes for training, a brief, intense workout would be in order. Workouts that last no longer than 90 minutes are most effective, even for more mature athletes.

Training Intensity

Intensity is the amount of resistance used during a training period (e.g., day, week). When beginning a training cycle, lighter weights with higher reps are recommended. This will allow for physical and psychological adaptation to occur. Even for more mature, experienced athletes, beginning a training program with lighter weights is recommended until readaptation occurs (usually in two to three weeks). In addition, the percentage of maximum used when performing speed, agility, and conditioning training should be taken into consideration. Conditioning should be light to moderate until sufficient work capacity is formed. For injury prevention, speed work should be graduated until the athlete's musculature (quads, hamstrings, hip flexors, and low back) and cardiorespiratory system have been acclimated to more intense work.

Training Outcome

The next design consideration is the desired outcome. What specific goals does the athlete hope to attain at the conclusion of the training cycle? Keep in mind that the ultimate goal is success on the field and that training must be viewed as a means to an end. The coach must take into consideration injury prevention, performance, and team or individual weaknesses. Which events will be tested and become the main focus of the workouts?

The goals and objectives should match the desired outcomes. For example, to measure acceleration, an athlete would perform the 10-yard dash test as well as drills that improve acceleration, such as starts, 1-2-3 count wall drill (chapter 5), and sled pulls. If an athlete is trying to improve strength levels, a bench press or squat maximum would be significant elements of the training prescription.

Training Level

The athlete's current training level must be realistically evaluated. Is the athlete beginner, intermediate, or advanced? Athletes often classify themselves as intermediate or even advanced with very little significant experience and without a true appreciation for the time commitment and investment necessary for achieving a higher classification. Very few athletes actually achieve advanced status, which is earned over many years of dedicated, comprehensive, year-round training.

Level of experience is related more to one's training age than to one's chronological age. Training age is the number of years of training—which includes some form of resistance training, speed and agility experience, and a year-round commitment to a cardio conditioning program—completed. Training age should take into consideration sport specificity (i.e., how many years has the athlete played organized lacrosse?) and training specificity (i.e., how many years has the athlete trained specifically for lacrosse?). One weakness is that this formula does not take into account the quality of training. A poor-quality program performed with inconsistent effort will not yield the same results as a high-quality program performed in the same amount of time. In addition, those who are naturally gifted with strength, speed, power, and skill may not need as much time for skill development as those who don't have the same gifts.

Nevertheless, adjustments to the program may be required based on the quantity and quality of prior experience. A beginner is usually someone who has zero to two years of training experience. This experience should include total-body lifts (not just bench presses and biceps curls) and a succession of movement skill cycles (not just a few weeks during the preseason). An intermediate athlete is someone with two to five years of high-quality experience. Advanced athletes are those with five or more years of training to their credit. Using these definitions, the amount of experience dictates the training prescription.

Training Progression

Workout progression must be developed in order to ensure a productive cycle. Every workout should begin with a dynamic warm-up to increase the athlete's core temperature, increase blood flow, and prepare the neurological system for more intense activity. The warm-up should last between 5 and 15 minutes and should include multiple range-of-motion activities.

The second concept is progression. Training sessions should move from complex (typically, more demanding) movements to simple (less complex) movements. Multijoint movements that require sophisticated movement patterns and multiple muscle groups (e.g., plyometrics, Olympic lifts, squats) should be performed earlier in the workout, when the neurological system is fresh and before fatigue has set in. These movements should be followed by single-joint exercises (e.g., shoulder shrugs, calf raises, triceps extensions), which may not require the same muscle recruitment and may involve only one muscle group.

The third design consideration is power before strength, which is the typical pattern for workouts unless there is a specific rationale for doing otherwise. Explosive movements (e.g., plyometrics, Olympic lifts, medicine ball power exercises) are generally reserved for the beginning of the session. In some cases, as athletes get closer to the in-season, coaches may want to work on power under conditions of modified fatigue. This would take place after absolute power development has been incorporated into the cycle. The workout would then include strength-development exercises. In any one workout session, three to seven main lifts are considered to be sufficient for building the type of strength needed for lacrosse. Any more than that may lead to fatigue and may not be productive. Injury-prevention movements can be incorporated either before or after the main movements for that day. Working on joint stability and muscle integrity is crucial, and such exercises should be performed with the same intensity and focus as other exercises whenever they are incorporated into the routine.

The next training category is core training. In most routines for beginner or intermediate athletes, core exercises are performed near the end of the session. It may not be as valuable to train the core early in the session due to fatigue. For example, when performing a squat, lunge, Olympic lift, or other exercise that requires extensive core engagement, it would be unwise to train the abs and obliques beforehand because the core muscles may break down during these exercises and result in injury if the back is unable to remain stable.

Finally, each workout should conclude with some sort of static (in place) stretch. Ending formal activity with 5 to 10 minutes of static stretching will improve flexibility if done consistently and will begin the process of restoration. Individual, partner, and towel or band stretches are all excellent for facilitating the recovery process in anticipation of the next day's events.

OFF-SEASON TRAINING PROGRAMS

Before going into greater detail and providing a sample 14-week off-season program (12 weeks of training and 2 weeks of recovery), an overview of training theory must be given. When designing a training program, the coach must consider when and how the program will progress as the athlete adapts to the training stimuli. Initially, there will be a low to moderate amount of stress on the body's system as the individual transitions from a detrained state to a training state. As the athlete becomes stronger, faster, and better conditioned, he or she will need to be exposed to increasingly greater amounts of stress in order to make physiological progress and for the training effect to take place. The best way to do this is to implement a systematic means of organizing the training weeks that precede the competition season (i.e., an off-season).

Periodization is a system of regulating stress on the body while gradually and methodically imposing greater demands to bring about optimal gains in performance. Using this cyclical progression, a larger, specific period of time (as short as several weeks or as long as several years) is broken into smaller units of time (usually two to five weeks). These shorter intervals, or cycles, have a specific emphasis and allow for adaptation to the imposed stimuli (Plisk 2008). As training progresses, the cycles become more intense and culminate in a peaking phase, after which the athlete ends the off-season training and transitions to the performance season.

For our purposes, we specifically focus on a 14-week preseason period that includes 12 weeks of work and 2 weeks of recovery. The breakdown is as follows.

General Preparation Phase

The initial three-week phase is the preparation phase in which the athlete begins to lay the foundation for more intense activity that will follow. This phase includes readaptation to training and begins with using lower levels of intensity and higher volume during resistance-training and aerobic-training activities and focusing on technique with linear and lateral speed development.

Hypertrophy Phase

The second three-week phase is the hypertrophy phase in which the athlete continues to perform with higher volume during resistance training but begins to challenge herself with higher intensity levels. The speed and agility workouts begin to increase in volume and intensity as the athlete becomes accustomed to doing more work at a higher level of stress. Focusing on the glycolytic energy system should be a priority in conditioning during this phase.

Recovery Phase

If the overall schedule allows, a one-week recovery phase is suggested after these two cycles have been performed. The athlete can perform a modified workout plan with lower volume and intensity or take time off to allow for regeneration. This phase can help rejuvenate the mind and body and prepare the athlete for more intense work in the last six weeks. In addition, integrating testing at this time is a great way to mark the halfway point in the off-season. Feedback from testing will reveal where adjustments to the program are needed and will motivate and inspire the athlete during the second half of the off-season.

Strength Phase

The third three-week cycle of training is the strength phase. The development of higher strength levels should be the goal in weight training, and at this time the athlete should be ready to handle higher intensity levels as the volume decreases to a more moderate level. Speed and agility training is emphasized during this period, and the athlete should be able to handle fairly high levels of training volume and intensity. Conditioning should focus on developing explosive power, speed and speed endurance as the season draws near.

Power Phase

The final three-week cycle is the power phase, after which the athlete will be ready to begin the season. The resistance used in the weight room will be at the highest levels and the volume will be fairly low with an emphasis on power. Speed and agility work will begin to peak, and the athlete should be ready to handle a high volume of linear and lateral speed work. Because the physiological demands of lacrosse require the activation of all energy systems, conditioning should include elements of all three (aerobic, glycolytic and ATP-PC systems), with an emphasis on the ATP-PC system. It is usually a good idea to allow for some recovery before testing during this final phase.

Final Recovery Phase

After the last two cycles have been performed, a one-week recovery phase is suggested before the start of the season. If accompanied by proper dietary practices, this phase can reduce stress on the muscles and joints. In many cases, an athlete has few opportunities to fully recover once the season begins. Making the last week of the off-season a light or off week will give the body and mind the opportunity to rejuvenate.

Here are three sample training programs:

- A sample 14-week off-season training cycle for a beginner with 0 to 2 years of experience
- A sample 14-week off-season training cycle for an intermediate athlete with 2 to 5 years of experience
- A sample 14-week off-season training cycle for an advanced athlete with more than 5 years of experience

SAMPLE BEGINNER 14-WEEK OFF-SEASON TRAINING CYCLE

Table 7.1 provides an overview of the setup and focus of an off-season training plan for a beginner athlete. Tables 7.2 through 7.5 describe the specific training prescription for each phase. For all tables in this chapter, exercises with reps listed as a number plus a number (e.g., 10 + 10) are unilateral; the prescribed reps are for the right and left sides.

Table 7.1 Beginner Off-Season Training Overview

Phase		General preparation phase	Hypertrophy phase	Recovery phase	Strength phase	Power phase	Final recovery phase
Strength and power	Number of weeks	3	3	1	3	3	1
	Sets per exercise	2 or 3	3 or 4	0	3 or 4	3 or 4	3 or 4
	Reps per set	8-15	8-12	0	6-10	3-8	3-10
	Intensity	Low	Moderate		High	High	Low
	Volume	High	High		Moderate	Low	Low
	Emphasis	Build a base	Increase intensity	Recovery	Develop strength	Transition to power	Reset
Speed and agility	Number of weeks	3	3	1	3	3	1
	Intensity	Low	Moderate		High	High	Low
	Volume	Low	Low		Moderate	High	Low
	Emphasis	Technique	Increase volume and tempo	Recovery	Pure speed	Endurance; prepare for competition	Low volume, low intensity
Conditioning	Number of weeks	3	3	1	3	3	1
	Intensity	Low	Low		Moderate	High	Low
	Volume	Low	Moderate		Moderate	Low	Low
	Emphasis	Work capacity	Aerobic base	Recovery	Glycolytic	ATP-PC; prepare for competition	Light activity (e.g., pool)

Table 7.2 Beginner Off-Season Training: General Preparation Phase Weeks 1-3

Monday			Wednesday			Friday			Saturday		
Dynamic warm-up	Pg 46	10 min	Dynamic warm-up	Pg 46	10 min	Dynamic warm-up	Pg 46	10 min	Dynamic warm-up	Pg 46	10 min
Selected ladder drill	Pg 170	10-12 reps	Push-up	Pg 51	3 × 6-10	Two-cone drill	Pg 178	6-8 reps	Athletic activity		Bike, swim, jog, row for 20-30 min
1-2-3 count wall drill	Pg 197	6 reps	Single-arm dumbbell row	Pg 128	3 × 12 + 12	Tennis ball drop	Pg 200	6 reps	Static stretch	Pg 77	10 min
NFL agility drill	Pg 205	2 reps at 90%	Dumbbell shrug	Pg 126	2 × 12	Form running	Pg 198	6 reps for 20-40 yds at 90%-95%			
T drill	Pg 207	2 reps at 90%	Dumbbell lateral raise	Pg 135	3 × 12	Leg press	Pg 107	3 × 15			
Reverse pull-up	Pg 131	5, 5, max	Reverse dip	Pg 138	3 × 12	Suspension row	Pg 132	3 × 8			
Bodyweight squat	Pg 49	3 × 15	Reverse curl	Pg 141	3 × 12	Walking lunge	Pg 62	3 × 12 + 12			
Upright row	Pg 127	3 × 15	Distance run		15-20 min	Dumbbell shoulder press	Pg 122	3 × 12			
Swiss ball hamstring curl	Pg 114	3 × 12	Static stretch	Pg 77	10 min	Band slide	Pg 117	3 × 12 + 12			
Dumbbell alternating biceps curl	Pg 139	3 × 10 + 10				Sit-up	Pg 144	2 × 15			
Front plank	Pg 142	2 × 30 sec				Static stretch	Pg 77	10 min			
Static stretch	Pg 77	10 min									

Table 7.3 Beginner Off-Season Training: Hypertrophy Phase Weeks 4-6

Monday			Wednesday			Friday			Saturday		
Dynamic warm-up	Pg 46	10 min	Dynamic warm-up	Pg 46	10 min	Dynamic warm-up	Pg 46	10 min	Dynamic warm-up	Pg 46	10 min
Selected ladder drill	Pg 170	10-12 reps	Box jump	Pg 155	2 × 5	Low-hurdle drill	Pg 185	8-10 reps	Aerobic conditioning	Pg 228	1-mile run
Illinois agility drill	Pg 208	6 reps	Double-leg lateral hurdle hop	Pg 159	2 × 10 each side	Chase drill	Pg 201	6 reps	Static stretch	Pg 77	10 min
One-cut zigzag drill	Pg 209	2 reps	Dumbbell bench press	Pg 120	3 × 10	Form running	Pg 198	6 reps for 20-40 yds at 90-95%			
Jerry Rice zigzag drill	Pg 210	2 reps	Single-arm dumbbell row	Pg 128	3 × 10 + 10	Leg press	Pg 107	3 × 10			
Dodge and pivot zigzag drill	Pg 211	2 reps	Shoulder shrug	Pg 152	3 × 10	Suspension row	Pg 132	3 × 10			
Chin-up	Pg 124	3 × 10	Suspension reverse fly	Pg 133	3 × 10	Swiss ball hamstring curl	Pg 114	3 × 10			
Dumbbell bench press	Pg 120	3 × 10	Suspension push-up	Pg 134	3 × 10	Lat pulldown	Pg 129	3 × 10			
Goblet squat	Pg 103	3 × 10	Dumbbell hold	Pg 140	:30, max	Dumbbell lateral squat	Pg 115	3 × 10 + 10			
Swiss ball hamstring curl	Pg 114	3 × 10	Aerobic bike intervals		See chapter 6	Resisted crunch	Pg 143	2 × 25			
Dumbbell alternating biceps curl	Pg 139	3 × 8 + 8	Static stretch	Pg 77	10 min	Static stretch	Pg 77	10 min			
Front plank	Pg 142	2 × 40 sec									
Static stretch	Pg 77	10 min									

Table 7.4 Beginner Off-Season Training: Strength Phase Weeks 8-10

Monday			Wednesday			Friday			Saturday		
Dynamic warm-up	Pg 46	10 min	Dynamic warm-up	Pg 46	10 min	Dynamic warm-up	Pg 46	10 min	Dynamic warm-up	Pg 46	10 min
Selected ladder drill	Pg 170	10-12 reps	Box jump	Pg 155	3 × 6	Low-hurdle drill	Pg 185	8-10 reps	Repeat track sprints with 1:3 work:rest ratio	Pg 234	800M × 1, 400M × 2, 200M × 2
NFL agility drill	Pg 205	4 reps	Split jump	Pg 157	3 × 6 + 6	Resisted run	Pg 199	6 reps for 20-30 yds	Static stretch	Pg 77	10 min
Illinois agility drill	Pg 208	2 reps	Barbell bench press	Pg 119	4 × 8	Romanian deadlift	Pg 104	4 × 6			
Chin-up	Pg 124	3 × 8	Single-arm dumbbell row	Pg 128	3 × 8 + 8	Lat pulldown	Pg 129	3 × 8			
Front squat	Pg 101	4 × 6	Dumbbell shrug	Pg 126	3 × 8	Dumbbell elevated split squat	Pg 111	3 × 8 + 8			
Dumbbell alternating incline press	Pg 121	3 × 8 + 8	Dumbbell lateral raise	Pg 135	3 × 8	Dumbbell shoulder press	Pg 122	3 × 8			
Glute-ham raise	Pg 108	3 × 8	Dumbbell lying triceps extension	Pg 136	3 × 10	Calf raise	Pg 112	3 × 15			
Dumbbell alternating biceps curl	Pg 139	3 × 6 + 6	Four-way neck strengthening	Pg 150	1 × 6 each way	Band torso rotation	Pg 145	3 × 10 + 10			
Swiss ball roll-out	Pg 149	3 × 12	300-yd shuttle for best time	Pg 234	2 reps with 3-min rest	Static stretch	Pg 77	10 min			
Static stretch	Pg 77	10 min	Static stretch	Pg 77	10 min						

Table 7.5 Beginner Off-Season Training: Power Phase Weeks 11-13

Monday			Wednesday			Friday			Saturday		
Dynamic warm-up	Pg 46	10 min	Dynamic warm-up	Pg 46	10 min	Dynamic warm-up	Pg 46	10 min	Dynamic warm-up	Pg 46	10 min
Selected ladder drill	Pg 170	10-12 reps	Single-leg lateral hurdle hop	Pg 160	3 × 6 + 6	Low-hurdle drill	Pg 185	8-10 reps	Half gasser × 8 reps	Pg 239	1:2 work:rest ratio
NFL agility drill	Pg 205	4 reps	Ice skater	Pg 158	3 × 6 + 6	Six-cone drill	Pg 221	8 reps with 1-min rest between reps	Static stretch	Pg 77	10 min
60-yard shuttle	Pg 206	2 reps	Barbell bench press	Pg 118	4 × 5	Single-leg Romanian deadlift	Pg 105	4 × 6 + 6			
Towel pull-up	Pg 125	6, 6, max	Single-arm dumbbell row	Pg 128	4 × 6 + 6	Suspension row	Pg 132	10, 10, max			
Back squat	Pg 100	5, 4, 3, 3	Shoulder shrugs	Pg 152	3 × 8	Band snap-down	Pg 161	3 × 8 + 8			
Dumbbell bench press	Pg 120	4 × 5	Suspension reverse fly	Pg 133	3 × 10	Dumbbell shoulder press	Pg 122	3 × 6			
Nordic curl	Pg 113	3 × 6	Triceps dip	Pg 137	5, 5, max	Barbell lateral slide	Pg 116	3 × 10 + 10			
Dumbbell alternating biceps curl	Pg 139	3 × 5 + 5	Reverse curl	Pg 141	2 × 15	Medicine ball torso toss	Pg 147	3 × 10 + 10			
Swiss ball stabilization	Pg 148	3 × 45 sec	Four-way neck strengthening	Pg 150	1 × 6 each way	Static stretch	Pg 77	10 min			
Static stretch	Pg 77	10 min	Blended ladder conditioning at 25-yd intervals with 1:3 work:rest ratio	Pg 241	50 yds × 1, 100 yds × 1, 150 yds × 1, 300 yds × 1, 150 yds × 1, 100 yds × 1, 50 yds × 1						
			Static stretch	Pg 77	10 min						

SAMPLE INTERMEDIATE 14-WEEK OFF-SEASON TRAINING CYCLE

Table 7.6 provides an overview of the setup and focus of an off-season training program for an intermediate athlete. Tables 7.7 through 7.10 describe the specific training prescription for each phase.

Table 7.6   Intermediate Off-Season Training Overview

Phase		Preparation phase	Hypertrophy phase	Recovery phase	Strength phase	Power phase	Final recovery phase
Strength and power	Number of weeks	3	3	1	3	3	1
	Sets per exercise	3	3 or 4	0	3 or 4	4 or 5	3 or 4
	Reps per set	10-15	8-12	0	3-8	1-6	3-10
	Intensity	Low	Moderate		High	Very high	Low
	Volume	High	High		Moderate	Low	Low
	Emphasis	Build a base	Increase intensity	Recovery	Develop strength	Transition to power	Reset
Speed and agility	Number of weeks	3	3	1	3	3	1
	Intensity	Low	Moderate		High	High	Low
	Volume	Low	Moderate		Moderate	High	Low
	Emphasis	Technique	Increase volume and tempo	Recovery	Pure speed	Endurance; prepare for competition	Low volume, low intensity
Conditioning	Number of weeks	3	3	1	3	3	1
	Intensity	Low	Moderate	Low	High	High	Low
	Volume	Low	Moderate	Low	Moderate	High	Low
	Emphasis	Aerobic	Glycolytic	Recovery	ATP-PC	Blended conditioning; prepare for competition	Light activity (e.g., pool)

Table 7.7 Intermediate Off-Season Training: General Preparation Phase Weeks 1-3

Monday			Wednesday			Friday			Saturday		
Dynamic warm-up	Pg 46	10 min	Dynamic warm-up	Pg 46	10 min	Dynamic warm-up	Pg 46	10 min	Dynamic warm-up	Pg 46	10 min
Selected ladder drill	Pg 170	10-12 reps	Barbell bench press	Pg 119	3 × 10	Two-cone drill	Pg 178	6-8 reps	Aerobic activity		20-30 min
1-2-3 count wall drill	Pg 197	6 reps	Shoulder shrug	Pg 152	3 × 15	Tennis ball drop	Pg 200	6 reps	Static stretch	Pg 77	10 min
NFL agility drill	Pg 205	3 reps	Single-arm dumbbell row	Pg 128	3 × 12 + 12	Form running technique 20-40 yds at 90%-95%	Pg 198	8-10 reps			
T drill	Pg 207	3 reps	Upright row	Pg 127	3 × 10	Dumbbell hang snatch	Pg 167	3 × 5			
Back squat	Pg 100	3 × 10	Dumbbell lateral raise	Pg 135	3 × 10	Dumbbell lunge	Pg 109	3 × 10 + 10			
Chin-up	Pg 124	3 × 6	Dumbbell lying triceps extension	Pg 136	3 × 15	Towel pull-up	Pg 125	6, 6, max			
Dumbbell step-up	Pg 110	3 × 10 + 10	Resisted crunch	Pg 143	2 × 20	Calf raise	Pg 112	3 × 15			
Dumbbell shoulder press	Pg 122	3 × 10	Distance run		20-30 min	Machine low row	Pg 130	3 × 12			
Band slide	Pg 117	3 × 10 + 10	Static stretch	Pg 77	10 min	Band torso rotation	Pg 145	3 × 10 + 10			
Plank (front and side)	Pg 142	3 × 30 sec				Reverse curl	Pg 141	3 × 12			
Plate hold	Pg 140	30 sec, max				Static stretch	Pg 77	10 min			
Static stretch	Pg 77	10 min									

Table 7.8 Intermediate Off-Season Training: Hypertrophy Phase Weeks 4-6

Monday			Wednesday			Friday			Saturday		
Dynamic warm-up	Pg 46	10 min	Dynamic warm-up	Pg 46	10 min	Dynamic warm-up	Pg 46	10 min	Dynamic warm-up	Pg 46	10 min
Selected ladder drill	Pg 170	10-12 reps	Barbell bench press	Pg 119	4 × 8	Low-hurdle drill	Pg 185	8-10 reps	Aerobic conditioning	Pg 228	2-mile run
Illinois agility drill	Pg 208	6 reps	Dumbbell shrug	Pg 126	3 × 15	Start-stop-go drill	Pg 203	6 reps	Static stretch	Pg 77	10 min
One-cut zigzag drill	Pg 209	2 reps	Single-arm dumbbell row	Pg 128	3 × 10 + 10	Three-cone slide drill	Pg 222	3 reps			
Jerry Rice zigzag drill	Pg 210	2 reps	Suspension push-up	Pg 134	3 × 10	Double-leg lateral hurdle hop	Pg 179	3 × 8 + 8			
Dodge and pivot zigzag drill	Pg 211	2 reps	Suspension reverse fly	Pg 133	3 × 10	Split jump	Pg 157	3 × 6 + 6			
Box jump	Pg 155	3 × 6	Reverse dip	Pg 138	3 × 20	Hang clean	Pg 165	4 × 5			
Front squat	Pg 101	3 × 8	Sit-up	Pg 144	2 × 25	Hex bar deadlift	Pg 106	4 × 8			
Chin-up	Pg 124	6, 6, max	Four-way neck strengthening	Pg 150	1 × 6 each way	Reverse pull-up	Pg 131	6, 6, max			
Dumbbell step-up	Pg 110	3 × 8 + 8	300-yd shuttle	Pg 234	3 reps with 2:00 rest	Swiss ball hamstring curl	Pg 114	3 × 10			
Dumbbell shoulder press	Pg 122	3 × 8	Static stretch	Pg 77	10 min	Lat pulldown	Pg 129	3 × 10			
Dumbbell lateral squat	Pg 115	3 × 10 + 10				Barbell rotation	Pg 146	3 × 10 + 8			
Swiss ball stabilization	Pg 148	3 × 50 sec				Dumbbell hold	Pg 140	:30, max			
Plate hold	Pg 140	30 sec max				Static stretch	Pg 77	10 min			
Static stretch	Pg 77	10 min									

Table 7.9 Intermediate Off-Season Training: Strength Phase Weeks 8-10

Monday			Wednesday			Friday			Saturday		
Dynamic warm-up	Pg 46	10 min	Dynamic warm-up	Pg 46	10 min	Dynamic warm-up	Pg 46	10 min	Dynamic warm-up	Pg 46	10 min
Selected ladder drill	Pg 170	10-12 reps	Barbell bench press	Pg 119	8, 6, 5, 5, 5	Two-cone drill	Pg 178	8-10 reps	Track sprint	Pg 234	800M × 1, 400M × 1, 200M × 2 with 1:3 work:rest ratio
Star drill	Pg 224	4 reps	Shoulder shrug	Pg 152	8, 6, 5, 5, 5	Chase drill	Pg 201	6 reps	Static stretch	Pg 77	10 min
Illinois agility drill	Pg 208	2 reps	Single-arm dumbbell row	Pg 128	3 × 8 + 8	Sled pull × 15-25 yds	Pg 237	8-10 reps			
Box jump	Pg 155	4 × 4	Dumbbell alternating incline press	Pg 121	3 × 6 + 6	Ice skater	Pg 158	3 × 6 + 6			
Back squat	Pg 100	4 × 5	Dumbbell lateral raise	Pg 135	3 × 8	Single-leg lateral hurdle hop	Pg 160	3 × 6 + 6			
Weighted chin-up	Pg 124	4 × 5	Triceps dip	Pg 137	6, 6, max	Hang clean	Pg 165	5, 4, 3, 3			
Dumbbell elevated split squat	Pg 111	4 × 5 + 5	Resisted crunch	Pg 143	3 × 25	Romanian deadlift	Pg 104	5 × 5			
Dumbbell shoulder press	Pg 122	4 × 6	Four-way neck strengthening	Pg 150	3 × 15	Chin-up (with added resistance)	Pg 124	4 × 6			
Barbell lateral slide	Pg 116	3 × 10 + 10	Repeat shuttle × 100 yds	Pg 238	25-yd intervals × 10-12 reps with 1:3 work:rest ratio	Glute ham raise	Pg 108	3 × 10			
Plank (front and side)	Pg 142	3 × 1 min	Static stretch	Pg 77	10 min	Suspension row	Pg 132	10, 10, max			
Reverse curl	Pg 141	2 × 15				Band torso rotation	Pg 145	3 × 10 + 10			
Static stretch	Pg 77	10 min				Plate hold	Pg 140	:30, max			
						Static stretch	Pg 77	10 min			

Table 7.10 Intermediate Off-Season Training: Power Phase Weeks 11-13

Monday			Wednesday			Friday			Saturday		
Dynamic warm-up	Pg 46	10 min	Dynamic warm-up	Pg 46	10 min	Dynamic warm-up	Pg 46	10 min	Dynamic warm-up	Pg 46	10 min
Selected ladder drill	Pg 170	10-12 reps	Barbell bench press	Pg 119	5, 4, 3, 3, 3	Low-hurdle drill	Pg 185	8-10 reps	100-m sprint × 14-16 reps	Pg 234	1:3 work:rest ratio
NFL agility drill	Pg 205	3 reps	Dumbbell shrug	Pg 126	3 × 15	Six-cone drill; rest 45 sec between reps	Pg 221	8 reps	Static stretch	Pg 77	10 min
60-yard shuttle	Pg 206	4 reps	Single-arm dumbbell row	Pg 128	3 × 6 + 6	Single-leg lateral hurdle hop	Pg 160	3 × 8 + 8			
Box jump	Pg 155	5 × 3	Dumbbell bench press	Pg 120	4 × 5	Single-leg power hop	Pg 156	3, 2, 1, 1, 1			
Front squat	Pg 101	5, 4, 3, 3, 3	Suspension reverse fly	Pg 133	3 × 10	Hang clean	Pg 165	3, 2, 1, 1, 1			
Towel pull-up	Pg 125	8, 8, max	Triceps dip (with added resistance)	Pg 137	3 × 6	Single-leg Romanian deadlift	Pg 105	4 × 6 + 6			
Band snap-down	Pg 161	3 × 10 + 10	Resisted crunch	Pg 143	3 × 25	Lat pulldown	Pg 129	3 × 6			
Dumbbell shoulder press	Pg 122	5 × 5	Blended Conditioning Ladder × 25-yd intervals with 1:3 work:rest ratio	Pg 234	50 yds, 100 yds, 150 yds, 200 yds, 300 yds, 200 yds, 150 yds, 100 yds, 50 yds	Machine low row	Pg 130	4 × 6			
Dumbbell lateral squat	Pg 115	3 × 10 + 10	Static stretch	Pg 77	10 min	Barbell lateral slide	Pg 116	3 × 10 + 10			
Swiss ball roll-out	Pg 149	3 × 12				Medicine ball torso toss	Pg 147	3 × 10 + 10			
Dumbbell hold	Pg 140	30 sec max				Reverse curls	Pg 141	2 × 15			
Static stretch	Pg 77	10 min				Static stretch	Pg 77	10 min			

SAMPLE ADVANCED 14-WEEK OFF-SEASON TRAINING CYCLE

Table 7.11 provides an overview of the setup and focus of an off-season training program for an advanced athlete. Tables 7.12 through 7.15 provide the specific training prescription for each phase.

Table 7.11 Advanced Off-Season Training Overview

Phase		Preparation phase	Hypertrophy phase	Recovery phase	Strength phase	Power phase	Final recovery phase
Strength and power	Number of weeks	3	3	1	3	3	1
	Sets per exercise	3	3-5	0	3-5	3-5	3 or 4
	Reps per set	10-15	8-12	0	4-10	1-10	3-10
	Intensity	Low	Moderate		High	Very high	Low
	Volume	High	High		Moderate	Low	Low
	Emphasis	Build a base	Increase intensity	Recovery	Develop strength	Transition to power	Reset
Speed and agility	Number of weeks	3	3	1	3	3	1
	Intensity	Low	Moderate		High	High	Low
	Volume	Low	Moderate		Moderate	High	Low
	Emphasis	Technique	Increase volume and tempo	Recovery	Pure speed	Endurance; prepare for competition	Low volume, low intensity
Conditioning	Number of weeks	3	3	1	3	3	1
	Intensity	Moderate	Moderate		High	Very high	Low
	Volume	Low	Moderate		High	High	Low
	Emphasis	Aerobic	Glycolytic	Recovery	ATP-PC	Blended; prepare for competition	Light activity (e.g., pool)

Table 7.12 Advanced Off-Season Training: General Preparation Phase Weeks 1-3

Monday			Tuesday			Thursday			Friday		
Dynamic warm-up	Pg 46	10 min	Dynamic warm-up	Pg 46	10 min	Dynamic warm-up	Pg 46	10 min	Dynamic warm-up	Pg 46	10 min
Selected ladder drill	Pg 170	10-12 reps	Hang clean	Pg 165	5 × 5	Two-cone drill	Pg 178	6-8 reps	Barbell bench press	Pg 119	4 × 12
1-2-3 count wall drill	Pg 197	6 reps	Dumbbell bench press	Pg 120	4 × 12	Tennis ball drop	Pg 200	6 reps	Shoulder shrug	Pg 152	3 × 15
NFL agility drill	Pg 205	3 reps	Dumbbell shrug	Pg 126	3 × 15	Form running	Pg 198	8-10 reps for 20-40 yds at 90%-95%	Dumbbell shoulder press	Pg 122	3 × 10
T drill	Pg 207	3 reps	Medicine ball chest pass	Pg 164	3 × 10	Hex bar deadlift	Pg 106	4 × 8	Dumbbell lateral raise	Pg 135	3 × 12
Back squat	Pg 100	4 × 10	Suspension reverse fly	Pg 133	3 × 10	Suspension row	Pg 132	8, 8, max	Suspension push-up	Pg 134	10, 10, max
Chin-up	Pg 124	8, 8, max	Dumbbell alternating biceps curl	Pg 139	3 × 10 + 10	Dumbbell lunge	Pg 109	3 × 10 + 10	Front plank	Pg 142	2 × :30
Swiss ball hamstring curl	Pg 114	3 × 10	Resisted crunch	Pg 143	3 × 15	Single-arm dumbbell row	Pg 128	3 × 12 + 12	Band torso rotation	Pg 145	2 × 10 + 10
Reverse pull-up	Pg 131	8, 8, max	Distance run	Pg 198	20-30 mins	Band slide	Pg 117	3 × 10 + 10	Aerobic conditioning	Pg 228	2-mile run
Calf raise	Pg 112	3 × 15	Static stretch	Pg 77	10 min	Plate hold	Pg 140	:30, max	Static stretch	Pg 77	10 min
Reverse curl	Pg 141	2 × 15				Four-way neck strengthening	Pg 150	1 × 6 each way			
Static stretch	Pg 77	10 min				Static stretch	Pg 77	10 min			

Table 7.13 Advanced Off-Season Training: Hypertrophy Phase Weeks 4-6

Monday			Tuesday			Thursday			Friday		
Dynamic warm-up	Pg 46	10 min	Dynamic warm-up	Pg 46	10 min	Dynamic warm-up	Pg 46	10 min	Dynamic warm-up	Pg 46	10 min
Selected ladder drill	Pg 170	10-12 reps	Hang clean	Pg 165	5, 4, 3, 3	Low-hurdle drill	Pg 185	8-10 reps	Barbell bench press	Pg 119	10, 8, 6, 6
One-cut zigzag drill	Pg 209	2 reps	Dumbbell alternating incline press	Pg 121	4 × 8 + 8	Start-stop-go drill	Pg 203	6 reps	Dumbbell shrug	Pg 126	3 × 15
Jerry Rice zigzag drill	Pg 210	2 reps	Shoulder shrug	Pg 152	3 × 15	Three-cone slide drill	Pg 222	3 reps	Dumbbell shoulder press	Pg 122	3 × 8
Dodge and pivot zigzag drill	Pg 211	2 reps	Medicine ball overhead toss	Pg 162	3 × 10	Single-leg lateral hurdle hop	Pg 160	3 × 6 + 6	Suspension reverse fly	Pg 133	2 × 10
Box jump	Pg 155	3 sets	Dumbbell lateral raise	Pg 135	3 × 10	Hex bar deadlift	Pg 106	10, 8, 6, 6	Dumbbell lying triceps extension	Pg 136	3 × 20
Split jump	Pg 157	3 × 6 + 6	Dumbbell alternating biceps curl	Pg 139	3 × 10 + 10	Lat pulldown	Pg 129	3 × 10	Barbell rotation	Pg 146	3 × 10 + 10
Back squat	Pg 100	10, 8, 6, 6	Sit-up	Pg 144	3 × 20	Dumbbell step-up	Pg 110	3 × 8 + 8	Aerobic conditioning	Pg 228	3-mile run
Chin-up	Pg 124	5 × 5	300-yd Shuttles (50-yd interval)	Pg 234	3 reps with 2-min rest	Single-arm dumbbell row	Pg 128	3 × 10 + 10	Static stretch	Pg 77	10 min
Nordic curl	Pg 113	3 × 10	Static stretch	Pg 77	10 min	Dumbbell lateral squat	Pg 115	3 × 10 + 10			
Machine low row	Pg 130	3 × 10				Dumbbell shrug	Pg 126	3 × 15			
Calf raise	Pg 112	3 × 15				Four-way neck strengthening	Pg 150	1 × 6 each way			
Reverse curl	Pg 141	2 × 15				Static stretch	Pg 77	10 min			
Plate hold	Pg 140	30 sec, max									
Static stretch	Pg 77	10 min									

Table 7.14 Advanced Off-Season Training: Strength Phase Weeks 8-10

Monday			Tuesday			Thursday			Friday		
Dynamic warm-up	Pg 46	10 min	Dynamic warm-up	Pg 46	10 min	Dynamic warm-up	Pg 46	10 min	Dynamic warm-up	Pg 46	10 min
Selected ladder drill	Pg 170	10-12 reps	Hang clean	Pg 165	4, 3, 2, 2, 2	Two-cone drill	Pg 178	8-10 reps	Barbell bench press	Pg 119	8, 6, 5, 5
NFL agility drill	Pg 205	4 reps	Barbell bench press	Pg 119	10, 8, 6, 5, 5	Chase drill	Pg 201	6 reps	Shoulder shrug	Pg 152	3 × 15
Illinois agility drill	Pg 208	2 reps	Dumbbell shrug	Pg 126	3 × 15	Single-leg lateral hurdle hop	Pg 160	3 × 6 + 6	Barbell military press	Pg 123	4 × 6
Box jump	Pg 155	3 × 6	Medicine ball chest pass	Pg 164	3 × 10	Split jump	Pg 157	3 × 6 + 6	Dumbbell lateral raise	Pg 135	3 × 10
Ice skater	Pg 158	3 × 6 + 6	Suspension reverse fly	Pg 133	3 × 10	Hex bar deadlift	Pg 106	8, 6, 5, 5, 5	Triceps dip	Pg 137	6, 6, max
Back squat	Pg 100	8, 6, 5, 5, 5	Dumbbell alternating biceps curl	Pg 139	3 × 8 + 8	Towel pull-up	Pg 125	8, 8, max	Swiss ball stabilization	Pg 148	2 × :45
Weighted chin-up	Pg 124	5 × 6	Sit-up (with added resistance)	Pg 144	3 × 20	Dumbbell step-up	Pg 110	4 × 6 + 6	Medicine ball torso toss	Pg 147	3 × 10+10
Glute-ham raise	Pg 108	3 × 12	Repeat shuttle × 100 yds at 25-yd interval	Pg 238	10-12 reps with 1:3 work:rest ratio	Single-arm dumbbell row	Pg 128	4 × 6 + 6	400-m sprint	Pg 234	4 reps with 1:3 work: rest ratio
Suspension row	Pg 132	10, 10, max	Static stretch	Pg 77	10 min	Barbell lateral slide	Pg 116	3 × 10 + 10	Static stretch	Pg 77	10 min
Calf raise	Pg 112	3 × 15				Reverse curl	Pg 141	2 × 15			
Dumbbell hold	Pg 140	30 sec, max				Four-way neck strengthening	Pg 150	1 × 6 each way			
Static stretch	Pg 77	10 min				Static stretch	Pg 77	10 min			

265

Table 7.15　Advanced Off-Season Training: Power Phase Weeks 11-13

Monday			Tuesday			Thursday			Friday		
Dynamic warm-up	Pg 46	10 min	Dynamic warm-up	Pg 46	10 min	Dynamic warm-up	Pg 46	10 min	Dynamic warm-up	Pg 46	10 min
Selected ladder drill	Pg 170	10-12 reps	Hang clean	Pg 165	3, 2, 1, 1, 1	Low-hurdle drill	Pg 185	8-10 reps	Barbell bench press	Pg 119	5, 4, 3, 3, 3
NFL agility drill	Pg 205	4 reps	Alternating dumbbell incline press	Pg 121	5 × 3 + 3	Six-cone drill; rest 45 sec between reps	Pg 221	8 reps	Dumbbell shrug	Pg 126	3 × 15
60-yard shuttle	Pg 206	2 reps	Shoulder shrugs	Pg 152	3 × 15	Single-leg lateral hurdle hop	Pg 160	3 × 6 + 6	Barbell military press	Pg 123	5, 4, 3, 3
Ice skater	Pg 158	3 sets 3 × 6 + 6	Medicine ball overhead toss	Pg 162	3 × 12	Single-leg power hops	Pg 156	3 × 10 + 10	Suspension reverse fly	Pg 133	3 × 12
Split jump	Pg 157	3 × 6 + 6	Dumbbell lateral raise	Pg 135	3 × 10	Hex bar deadlift	Pg 106	5, 4, 3, 3	Triceps dip (with added resistance)	Pg 137	4 × 5
Back squat	Pg 100	5, 4, 3, 3	Dumbbell alternating biceps curl	Pg 139	3 × 6 + 6	Towel pull-up	Pg 125	8, 8, max	Swiss ball rollout	Pg 149	2 × 12
Chin-up (with added resistance)	Pg 124	5, 4, 3, 3	Sit-up (with added resistance)	Pg 144	3 × 25	Dumbbell elevated split squat	Pg 111	4 x 5 + 5	Band torso rotation	Pg 145	2 × 10 + 10
Romanian deadlift	Pg 104	4 × 5	Blended Ladder Conditioning × 50 yds, 100 yds, 150 yds, 200 yds, 300 yds, 200 yds, 150 yds, 100 yds, 50 yds	Pg 241	25-yd intervals with 1:3 work:rest ratio	Single-arm dumbbell row	Pg 128	4 × 5 + 5	400-m sprint	Pg 234	1 rep with 1:3 work:rest ratio
Machine low row	Pg 130	10, 8, 6, 6	Static stretch	Pg 77	10 min	Band slide	Pg 117	3 × 10 + 10	200-m sprint	Pg 234	2 reps with 1:3 work:rest ratio
Calf raise	Pg 112	3 × 15				Plate hold	Pg 140	:30, max	100-m sprint	Pg 234	8 reps with 1:3 work:rest ratio
Reverse curl	Pg 141	2 × 15				Four-way neck strengthening	Pg 150	1 × 6 each way	Static stretch	Pg 77	10 min
Static stretch	Pg 77	10 min				Static stretch	Pg 77	10 min			

By putting into practice the helpful hints included in this chapter, every lacrosse player can improve. A thoughtful, well-planned, comprehensive off-season program will have a significant effect on performance and help the athlete prepare for the rigors of the in-season phase. With a greater understanding of some basic theoretical and practical guidelines, every lacrosse player can start to build the right individual program. These principles, combined with hard work and consistency, are the keys to improving performance on the field. For athletes committed to becoming their very best, taking the time to train in the off-season is not optional! The investment made in the weight room and on the field or track will enable every player to become more athletic, explosive, and durable. These improved physical skills, along with the confidence that begins to grow, can have amazing results on game day!

Chapter **8**

In-Season Program Development

For a lacrosse player, the training conducted during the in-season phase is the most important. It is during this time that the athlete must be at his or her physiological best and be able to perform at a high level of proficiency on game day. In order to do this, the player must be strong, powerful, in peak physical condition, and able to resist injuries. Over the course of the season, which typically lasts 12 weeks or more, it is crucial to continue to train for strength and power and avoid muscle breakdown and deterioration. Practice alone will not get the job done! An element of resistance training must complement the activities on the field. Without this, lacrosse players tend to lose strength and muscle mass during the season due to the overall volume of activity required in practice and games. Body weight decreases due to loss in lean mass, and strength levels plummet. The results of the time invested during the preseason may decrease gradually, and, after a period of just a few weeks without resistance training, the athlete may lose much of what was built.

For most teams, the majority of the conference schedule, playoffs, and championship tournaments are held closer to the end of the season. If strength and power levels are not sustained, the hard work done in the off-season may not pay dividends when the athlete needs them the most. One of the main objectives of training is for the athlete to be at his or her physical best when peak performance is required. Taking the time to work total-body strength and power is a must for those who want to sustain consistent performance during the entire season!

IN-SEASON PROGRAM DESIGN

When designing an in-season program, the athlete must keep in mind some fundamental guidelines to ensure the success of the training program. During this phase, the overall volume of training activity (e.g., off-field workouts, practices, games, travel) must be considered. The resistance and conditioning programs should always complement, not interfere with, on-field skill development.

Practical Considerations

When designing specific workout protocols, the athlete must keep in mind some practical issues that will influence the outcome of the program.

Training Time

During the season, skill development on the field must be the priority when it comes to scheduling. Practices, games, and individual technique sessions must take precedence over other activities. Personnel adjustments, strategy, and skill preparation must be fine-tuned, which requires a great deal of time. School-related activities, family time, personal time, and physical and mental preparation for game day must be considered as well. For the serious lacrosse player, making time to train within the confines of these numerous obligations is challenging but possible! If efficient, strength and power training done with the proper level of intensity should take no more than 20 to 40 minutes per session. Training can be done earlier in the day before practice begins (allowing enough time to recover afterward) or at the end of practice.

The weekly schedule will depend on when games and practices are scheduled. The athlete with an allotment of three to five days between games should plan on training two times during that period. If a midweek game is also on the schedule, the athlete may be able to train only once that week. With proper scheduling, two training days per week (an optimal number of workout days per week) can have a tremendous effect on strength, muscle mass, and power levels and enable the athlete to remain at his best throughout the season.

Most players commit extensive time to preparation during the season. Games, skill sessions, meetings (team and unit), video review, and practice consume a great deal of mental and physical energy. Having a balanced approach to training and recovery is essential in order to avoid a late-season collapse in performance. The energy required to accomplish all of this must be a major consideration in the overall planning scheme. Proper nutrition, adequate rest, and flexibility maintenance are all part of the recovery cycle and must be a priority during this time. Without returning to a point of complete recovery, the athlete may experience a deterioration of lean muscle mass, which over the course of a season may compromise performance. The athlete must do a great job of taking care of his body between training sessions.

Training Type

During the in-season phase of training, speed and agility training outside of practice may not be necessary. For most lacrosse players, especially those who get a lot of reps at practice during the week, the total volume of sprinting and cutting at practice is sufficient. Too much running volume may result in diminished performance. The only exception might be the inclusion of some foot speed drills (ladder, cone, or hurdle drills) in practice after the dynamic warm-up and before lacrosse drills. This is a way to supplement foot speed training, prepare the neurological system for the demands of practice, and prepare the athlete for the physiological demands that will follow.

Multijoint exercises (e.g., squat, power clean, lunge, pull-up) enable the athlete to be efficient in training multiple muscle groups with only a few exercises. Using these types of movements as the primary means of training will help performance and strengthen the joints used in lacrosse. The goal is to create balance in the body (top and bottom, left and right, front and back), and the athlete and coach should be mindful of this when designing the program. Upper- and lower-body movements, unilateral (one leg or arm at a time) and bilateral (both arms or legs at once) movements, and anterior (front of the body) and posterior (back of the body) exercises should be included in each training session. A training prescription that focuses on the "show" muscles (biceps, triceps, and chest) will have some effect on performance, but not as much as addressing the "go" muscles (hamstrings, glutes, low back, core, and shoulders). Neglecting the lower body, trunk, and core muscles will result in physiological deterioration and diminished performance in the long run.

Maintaining an appropriate fitness level during the season is crucial for players in all positions. On most lacrosse teams, the team coach conducts fitness conditioning at the end of practice when appropriate. On other teams, conditioning may not be a part of the practice routine. These coaches may feel that the tempo and volume of running at practice is enough and that additional conditioning may inhibit performance. For other teams, on days with a lighter running volume at practice or if the number of reps for the individual is lower, additional conditioning (especially for midfielders) may be appropriate. Regardless of whether extra conditioning is part of a team's routine, the athlete must make a decision about including additional conditioning. This chapter includes some in-season conditioning routines, but the athlete, along with the coach, will have to decide if and when this conditioning is necessary.

Training Equipment

As in the off-season, equipment availability may be an issue in program design, especially if access to a training facility is limited. This may present a significant problem for some and may require the athlete to become creative in an effort to resolve the issue. If access to a weight room during the season is challenging, bodyweight options may have to suffice. If executed with a high level of intensity and proper form, bodyweight alternatives—which do not require the athlete to travel to and from a weight facility—can be an excellent means of addressing strength and power. If a facility is inconvenient, the athlete may choose to perform one workout per week in a weight room and perform the other workout using only body weight or a partner for resistance. Gains can be made with proper intensity and technique. Some in-season bodyweight routines are included at the end of this chapter.

Injury Prevention

One major consideration is the inclusion of joint-stability and strengthening exercises in the in-season training routine. These exercises should focus on the lacrosse hot spots—those joints or muscle groups that are more susceptible to injury in the sport. Exercises for stabilizing the knees, shoulders, low back, and neck will help reduce the chances of injury and enable the athlete to stay stronger throughout the playing season. Without including these, the routine will not be as effective. Addressing these areas is crucial to helping the athlete resist injury, especially during the latter part of the season when fatigue begins to play a more prominent role in the training equation.

Design Fundamentals

Before putting together the in-season workout, the athlete and coach must decide what training volume and intensity are necessary to elicit the desired results. Ultimately, all decisions regarding training must be understood in the context of how to maximize lacrosse game-day performance. Keep in mind that with the added stress of practice, games, travel, and less daily recovery time, the athlete may not be able to handle the same amount of work that she performed in the off-season. In-season sessions tend to be shorter, and athletes are typically unable to manage the higher loads that were tolerated during the off-season due to these added stressors. Coaches and athletes should consider the following when planning a workout.

Training Volume

The total number of exercises, sets, and reps constitutes the training volume during a session. Although typically lower than the off-season volume, in-season training volume must be high enough to elicit a training effect.

One time-efficient strategy during the season is to pair exercises together. This technique enables the athlete to rest one body part or muscle group while another is working. For example, an athlete may pair a pulling movement (e.g., row) with a core movement (e.g., band torso rotation). Pairing two or three exercises allows the athlete to perform the same total number of sets in less time. This is a great time-saving strategy, especially during the season when training time may be more limited. The following guidelines can help the coach and athlete develop an in-season resistance-training program.

- *Sets*. The total number of sets performed during the season will vary. On multijoint exercises (e.g., squat, bench press), the athlete must have a plan that will complement what is being done on the field and should not detract from performance in practice or games. Some level of fatigue is to be expected during in-season training and moderate muscular soreness is acceptable during the early part of the week. By game day, however, the athlete should be recovered enough to play at 100 percent of maximal capacity for the entire length of the game. Generally, 12 to 25 total work sets (excluding warm-up sets) per workout are enough to address strength and power needs in-season. Fewer sets may be insufficient for making meaningful gains, whereas more sets may be unnecessary, especially for those who play a lot of minutes. The key is to train at a volume that will complement on-field performance.

- *Reps*. Depending on the exercise and the training age of the athlete, the athlete may perform as few as 1 rep (especially on multijoint movements) or as many as 15 reps during each set. Typically, 1 to 10 reps is ideal for strength and power movements, whereas higher reps may be performed on supplementary movements (e.g., single-joint lifts, grip, and core).

- *Rest*. The athlete may not need more than 30 to 45 seconds of rest between warm-up sets. On work sets, however, rest time between sets ranges from 90 to 150 seconds. Using heavier weights in a session necessitates longer recovery periods.

- *Tempo*. As in all other times during the training year, the tempo for most exercises (with the exception of Olympic lifts and plyometrics, which are performed at a high rate of speed) is controlled, meaning 1 to 2 seconds during the eccentric (lengthening) phase and 1 to 2 seconds during the concentric (shortening) phase. The athlete must try to avoid jerking, bouncing, or using excessive momentum to throw the weight in any way. The muscles should control the weight in both directions of the movement in order to maximize the benefits of the movement. Any abuse of proper technique will limit gains and may lead to injury.

Training Intensity

The intensity of a workout is determined by the percentage of the one repetition maximum (1RM) used during training. For multijoint movements (e.g., power clean, squat, bench press), the typical training intensity during the season ranges from 75 percent to 95 percent. Most of the time, training in that window will elicit gains in strength and power and will allow the athlete to retain the joint integrity needed to resist injury. For other movements used in the workout, the typical training intensity ranges from 60 percent to 90 percent, and higher (6-15) rep ranges are used. The supplementary movements used in addition to multijoint exercises support the primary lifts or isolate a specific region (e.g., a lateral raise to strengthen the medial deltoids) for injury-prevention purposes. A combination of higher rep, lower intensity and lower rep, higher intensity movements should be included. Table 8.1 shows the relationship between specific rep ranges, percentages of 1RM, and intended outcomes.

Training Level

The athlete should evaluate his level of training experience and decide on the routine that is most appropriate. The training program the athlete selects during the preseason should be followed throughout the in-season phase as well. For example, if the athlete classified himself as a beginner during the off-season, he should continue the beginner training protocol during the season as well. The best time to upgrade to another level (e.g., move from beginner to intermediate status) is the conclusion of an entire year's program. If the adjustment is made during the off-season, the athlete can better manage upgrades in intensity and complexity when the added physical demands of practice and games are not as much of an issue.

Training Progression

During the early part of the season, the athlete may be able to handle more training volume (i.e., a greater number of sets and reps and a higher percentage of 1RM). Fatigue is not as much of an issue because the athlete's body has not yet been through many practices or games. As the season wears on, reducing the overall volume in both conditioning and resistance training is recommended. This strategy will allow the body to continue to

Table 8.1　Volume and Intensity Guidelines

Reps	% 1RM	Goal
1-3	90%-100%	Power
4-6	75%-90%	Strength
8-12	60%-75%	Hypertrophy
15+	<60%	Endurance

adapt to the external stresses placed on it and recover sufficiently. In the sample 12-week training cycle, the final 3 weeks (10, 11, and 12) include fewer exercises, sets, and reps. Using this approach will allow for continued development of strength while simultaneously tapering the overall volume as the season draws to a conclusion.

Training Recovery

If competition takes place on a weekend, having a day off after competition can be a great way to recover. Dynamic movements, static stretches, foam rolling, yoga, or taking an ice bath on the postgame day can have a tremendous effect on the recovery process. Depending on when the next game will be played, the athlete may consider adding a resistance-training session the day after an off day. If the subsequent competition is three or more days after the weekend game, the athlete will have sufficient recovery time between competitions so that any soreness or fatigue will not affect game-day performance. Saturday is typically a competition day for many clubs or teams. If this is the case, Sunday can be the off, or recovery, day and Monday can be the first lift day of the week. If the next game isn't until the following weekend, Wednesday could potentially be the second lift day of the week. If a midweek (e.g., Wednesday) game is scheduled, the athlete can either perform only one lift (Monday) or do a second lift the day after the midweek game (Thursday). Whatever days are selected, the athlete should use discretion in determining what movements to use and what effect the movements will have on performance (especially the lower body). Performing lower-body lifts of higher intensity and volume within the 48 hours before the next contest is not recommended.

IN-SEASON TRAINING PROGRAMS

Throughout each phase of the in-season program, an inverse relationship exists between on-field activity and off-field activity. As the season progresses, the athlete must continually adapt off-field training to the stresses placed on the body and adjust the resistance-training program so that the emphasis transitions from a higher volume of training to a lower volume of training. At the end of the season there are typically more conference games, playoffs, and championship tournaments, thus increasing the intensity level of game-day performance. It is at this time that the athlete's skills should peak on the field. Lacrosse skill development should be the primary focus, and off-field training tends to shorten; brief workouts of lower volume are recommended. As each of the four phases (weeks 1-3, weeks 4-6, weeks 7-9, and weeks 10-12) of the in-season progresses, the idea is to gradually reduce the volume and allow for maximum recovery. The following sections provide sample in-season training programs for beginner, intermediate, and advanced athletes.

SAMPLE BEGINNER IN-SEASON TRAINING PROGRAM

Table 8.2 provides an overview of the setup and focus of an in-season training plan for a beginner athlete. Tables 8.3 through 8.6 describe the specific training prescription for each phase. For all tables in this chapter, exercises with reps listed as a number plus a number (e.g., 10 + 10) are unilateral; the prescribed reps are for the right and left sides.

Table 8.2 Beginner In-Season Training Overview

	Early in-season	Midseason	Late in-season	Playoff phase
Strength and power				
Number of weeks	3	3	3	1-3
Sets per exercise	2-3	2-3	2-3	2-3
Reps per set	8-15	6-12	6-10	6-10
Intensity	Moderate	Moderate	Moderate	Moderate
Volume	Moderate	Moderate	Moderate	Low
Emphasis	Adapt to practice	Strength, injury prevention	Strength, injury prevention	Finish strong
Conditioning				
Number of weeks	3	3	3	1-3
Intensity	Moderate	Moderate	Moderate	No extra conditioning
Volume	High	Moderate	Low	No extra conditioning
Emphasis	Work capacity	Speed endurance	Speed endurance	Recovery

Table 8.3 Beginner In-Season Training Program Weeks 1-3

Day 1			Day 2		
Dynamic warm-up	Pg 46	5 min	Dynamic warm-up	Pg 46	5 min
Dumbbell lunge	Pg 109	3 × 10 + 10	Box jump	Pg 155	3 × 5
Chin-up	Pg 124	3 × 6	Barbell bench press	Pg 119	3 × 10
Dumbbell lateral raise	Pg 135	3 × 10	Machine low row	Pg 130	3 × 12
Dumbbell lateral squat	Pg 115	3 × 8 + 8	Dumbbell shrug	Pg 126	2 × 15
Sit-up	Pg 144	2 × 15	Four-way neck strengthening	Pg 150	1 × 6 each way
Static stretch	Pg 77	5 min	Static stretch	Pg 77	5 min

Table 8.4   Beginner In-Season Training Program Weeks 4-6

Day 1			Day 2		
Dynamic warm-up	Pg 46	5 min	Dynamic warm-up	Pg 46	5 min
Dumbbell elevated split squat	Pg 111	3 × 8 + 8	Medicine ball squat throw	Pg 163	3 × 6
Reverse pull-up	Pg 131	6, 6, max	Barbell bench press	Pg 119	3 × 8
Dumbbell shoulder press	Pg 122	3 × 8	Single-arm dumbbell row	Pg 128	3 × 8 + 8
Dumbbell lateral squat	Pg 115	3 × 8 + 8	Shoulder shrug	Pg 152	2 × 15
Medicine ball torso toss	Pg 147	2 × 10 + 10	Four-way neck strengthening	Pg 150	1 × 6 each way
Static stretch	Pg 77	5 min	Static stretch	Pg 77	5 min

Table 8.5   Beginner In-Season Training Program Weeks 7-9

Day 1			Day 2		
Dynamic warm-up	Pg 46	5 min	Dynamic warm-up	Pg 46	5 min
Goblet squat	Pg 103	3 × 10	Split jump	Pg 157	3 × 5 + 5
Towel pull-up	Pg 125	3 × 6	Dumbbell bench press	Pg 120	3 × 6
Triceps dip	Pg 137	6, 6, max	Dumbbell lateral raise	Pg 135	3 × 10
Dumbbell lateral squat	Pg 115	3 × 8 + 8	Dumbbell shrug	Pg 126	2 × 15
Band torso rotation	Pg 145	2 × 10 + 10	Four-way neck strengthening	Pg 150	1 × 6 each way
Static stretch	Pg 77	5 min	Static stretch	Pg 77	5 min

Table 8.6   Beginner In-Season Training Program Weeks 10-12

Day 1			Day 2		
Dynamic warm-up	Pg 46	5 min	Dynamic warm-up	Pg 46	5 min
Swiss ball hamstring curl	Pg 114	3 × 10	Double-leg lateral hurdle hop	Pg 179	3 × 6 + 6
Suspension row	Pg 132	3 × 10	Dumbbell alternating incline press	Pg 121	3 × 6 + 6
Lying dumbbell triceps extension	Pg 136	3 × 10	Suspension reverse fly	Pg 133	3 × 10
Swiss ball stabilization	Pg 148	2 × 30 sec	Four-way neck strengthening	Pg 150	1 × 6 each way
Static stretch	Pg 77	5 min	Static stretch	Pg 77	5 min

SAMPLE INTERMEDIATE IN-SEASON TRAINING PROGRAM

Table 8.7 provides an overview of the setup and focus of an in-season training plan for an intermediate athlete. Tables 8.8 through 8.11 describe the specific training prescription for each phase.

Table 8.7 Intermediate In-Season Training Overview

	Early in-season	Midseason	Late in-season	Playoff phase
Strength and power				
Number of weeks	3	3	3	1-3
Sets per exercise	2-4	2-4	2-4	2-4
Reps per set	6-10	5-8	4-8	3-8
Intensity	Moderate	Moderate	Low	Moderate
Volume	High	Moderate	Moderate	Low
Emphasis	Adapt to practice	Strength, injury prevention	Strength, injury prevention	Finish strong
Conditioning				
Number of weeks	3	3	3	1-3
Intensity	Moderate	Moderate	Moderate	No extra conditioning
Volume	High	Moderate	Low	No extra conditioning
Emphasis	Work capacity	Speed endurance	Speed endurance	Recovery

Table 8.8 Intermediate In-Season Training Program Weeks 1-3

Day 1			Day 2		
Dynamic warm-up	Pg 46	5 min	Dynamic warm-up	Pg 46	5 min
Hang clean	Pg 165	3 × 5	Barbell bench press	Pg 119	10, 8, 6
Back squat	Pg 100	10, 8, 6	Nordic curl	Pg 113	3 × 10
Chin-up	Pg 124	6, 6, max	Machine low row	Pg 130	3 × 10
Dumbbell step-up	Pg 110	3 × 8 + 8	Front plank	Pg 142	2 × 30 sec
Barbell rotation	Pg 146	2 × 8 + 8	Dumbbell shrug	Pg 126	2 × 15
Dumbbell hold	Pg 140	1 × max	Four-way neck strengthening	Pg 150	1 × 6 each way
Static stretch	Pg 77	5 min	Static stretch	Pg 77	5 min

Table 8.9   Intermediate In-Season Training Program Weeks 4-6

Day 1			Day 2		
Dynamic warm-up	Pg 46	5 min	Dynamic warm-up	Pg 46	5 min
Hang clean	Pg 165	5, 4, 3	Barbell bench press	Pg 119	8, 6, 5
Front squat	Pg 101	8, 6, 5	Dumbbell lateral squat	Pg 115	3 × 8 + 8
Towel pull-up	Pg 125	6, 6, max	Single-arm dumbbell row	Pg 128	3 × 8 + 8
Dumbbell lunge	Pg 109	3 × 6 + 6	Medicine ball torso toss	Pg 147	2 × 8 + 8
Band torso rotation	Pg 145	2 × 8 + 8	Shoulder shrug	Pg 152	2 × 15
Plate hold	Pg 140	As long as possible	Four-way neck strengthening	Pg 150	1 × 6 each way
Static stretch	Pg 77	5 min	Static stretch	Pg 77	5 min

Table 8.10   Intermediate In-Season Training Program Weeks 7-9

Day 1			Day 2		
Dynamic warm-up	Pg 46	5 min	Dynamic warm-up	Pg 46	5 min
Hang clean	Pg 165	3, 2, 1	Barbell bench press	Pg 119	6, 5, 4
Back squat	Pg 100	6, 5, 4	Glute-ham raise	Pg 108	3 × 10
Reverse pull-up	Pg 131	6, 6, max	Lat pulldown	Pg 129	3 × 8
Dumbbell elevated split squat	Pg 111	3 × 6 + 6	Swiss ball stabilization	Pg 148	2 × 30 sec
Sit-up	Pg 144	2 × 15	Dumbbell shrug	Pg 126	2 × 15
Reverse curl	Pg 141	1 × 15	Four-way neck strengthening	Pg 150	1 × 6 each way
Static stretch	Pg 77	5 min	Static stretch	Pg 77	5 min

Table 8.11   Intermediate In-Season Training Program Weeks 10-12

Day 1			Day 2		
Dynamic warm-up	Pg 46	5 min	Dynamic warm-up	Pg 46	5 min
Box jump	Pg 121	3 × 5	Dumbbell alternating incline press	Pg 155	3 × 6 + 6
Front squat	Pg 101	5, 4, 3	Band slide	Pg 117	3 × 8 + 8
Suspension row	Pg 132	10, 10, max	Single-arm dumbbell row	Pg 128	3 × 6 + 6
Calf raise	Pg 112	2 × 15	Dumbbell shrug	Pg 126	2 × 15
Resisted crunch	Pg 143	2 × 15	Four-way neck strengthening	Pg 150	1 × 6 each way
Static stretch	Pg 77	5 min	Static stretch	Pg 77	5 min

SAMPLE ADVANCED IN-SEASON TRAINING PROGRAM

Table 8.12 provides an overview of the setup and focus of an in-season training plan for an advanced athlete. Tables 8.13 through 8.16 describe the specific training prescription for each phase.

Table 8.12 Advanced In-Season Training Overview

	Early in-season	Midseason	Late in-season	Playoff phase
Strength and power				
Number of weeks	3	3	3	1-3
Sets per exercise	3-4	3-4	3-4	3-4
Reps per set	5-15	3-12	2-10	1-10
Intensity	Moderate	Moderate	Low	Moderate
Volume	High	Moderate	Moderate	Low
Emphasis	Adapt to practice	Strength, injury prevention	Strength, injury prevention	Finish strong
Conditioning				
Number of weeks	3	3	3	1-3
Intensity	Moderate	Moderate	Moderate	No extra conditioning
Volume	High	Moderate	Low	No extra conditioning
Emphasis	Work capacity	Speed endurance	Speed endurance	Recovery

Table 8.13 Advanced In-Season Training Program Weeks 1-3

Day 1			Day 2		
Dynamic warm-up	Pg 46	5 min	Dynamic warm-up	Pg 46	5 min
Hang clean	Pg 165	3 × 5	Barbell bench press	Pg 119	10, 8, 6, 5
Back squat	Pg 100	10, 8, 6, 5	Dumbbell step-up	Pg 110	3 × 8 + 8
Chin-up (with added resistance)	Pg 124	3 × 6	Lateral squat	Pg 115	3 × 8 + 8
Glute-ham raise	Pg 108	3 × 10	Single-arm dumbbell row	Pg 128	3 × 8 + 8
Dumbbell bench press	Pg 120	3 × 10	Front plank	Pg 142	3 × 30 sec
Barbell rotation	Pg 146	3 × 10 + 10	Dumbbell shrug	Pg 126	2 × 15
Dumbbell hold	Pg 140	2 × max	Four-way neck strengthening	Pg 150	1 × 6 each way
Static stretch	Pg 77	5 min	Static stretch	Pg 77	5 min

Table 8.14 Advanced In-Season Training Program Weeks 4-6

Day 1			Day 2		
Dynamic warm-up	Pg 46	5 min	Dynamic warm-up	Pg 46	5 min
Hang clean	Pg 165	5, 4, 3, 3	Barbell bench press	Pg 119	8, 6, 5, 4
Front squat	Pg 101	8, 6, 5, 4	Romanian deadlift	Pg 104	3 × 6
Chin-up (with added resistance)	Pg 124	3 × 5	Band slide	Pg 117	3 × 8 + 8
Dumbbell elevated split squat	Pg 111	3 × 8 + 8	Machine low row	Pg 130	3 × 10
Barbell bench press (with close grip)	Pg 119	10, 8, 6, 6	Resisted crunch	Pg 143	3 × 15
Medicine ball torso toss	Pg 147	3 × 8 + 8	Shoulder shrug	Pg 152	2 × 15
Plate hold	Pg 140	2 × max	Four-way neck strengthening	Pg 150	1 × 6 each way
Static stretch	Pg 77	5 min	Static stretch	Pg 77	5 min

Table 8.15 Advanced In-Season Training Program Weeks 7-9

Day 1			Day 2		
Dynamic warm-up	Pg 46	5 min	Dynamic warm-up	Pg 46	5 min
Hang clean	Pg 165	4, 3, 2, 2	Barbell bench press	Pg 119	6, 5, 4, 3
Back squat	Pg 100	6, 5, 4, 3	Goblet squat	Pg 103	3 × 10
Suspension row	Pg 132	10,10, max	Barbell lateral slide	Pg 116	3 × 8 + 8
Dumbbell lunge	Pg 109	3 × 6 + 6	Suspension reverse fly	Pg 133	3 × 10
Dumbbell alternating incline press	Pg 121	4 × 6 + 6	Swiss ball rollout	Pg 149	3 × 12
Barbell rotation	Pg 146	3 x 10 +10	Dumbbell shrug	Pg 126	2 × 15
Reverse curl	Pg 141	2 × 15	Four-way neck strengthening	Pg 150	1 × 6 each way
Static stretch	Pg 77	5 min	Static stretch	Pg 77	5 min

Table 8.16 Advanced In-Season Training Program Weeks 10-12

Day 1			Day 2		
Dynamic warm-up	Pg 46	5 min	Dynamic warm-up	Pg 46	5 min
Hang clean	Pg 165	3, 2, 1, 1	Barbell bench press	Pg 119	5, 4, 3, 1
Front squat	Pg 101	5, 4, 3, 1	Box jump	Pg 155	3 × 5
Suspension row	Pg 132	10, 10, max	Band slide	Pg 117	3 × 8 + 8
Calf raise	Pg 112	3 × 15	Lateral raise	Pg 135	3 × 10
Suspension push-up	Pg 134	3 × 10	Suspension reverse fly	Pg 133	2 × 15
Swiss ball stabilization	Pg 148	3 × 30 sec	Four-way neck strengthening	Pg 150	1 × 6 each way
Static stretch	Pg 77	5 min	Static stretch	Pg 77	5 min

SAMPLE IN-SEASON BODYWEIGHT TRAINING PROGRAMS

Some athletes may not have access to weight-training equipment or a dedicated facility during the season. Team practice facilities may not be in close proximity to a weight room, or availability may be limited due to team practices, video sessions, travel, and game schedules. If the athlete is sufficiently motivated, strength development may continue with the assistance of little or no equipment. Bodyweight resistance exercises can help the athlete maintain strength and avoid injury, especially during the season. The sample circuits in tables 8.17 and 8.18 allow the athlete or team to continue to work and gain a competitive edge. These exercises can be done either during the day before practice begins (allowing for some recovery time in between) or after practice during the week leading up to game day. If done with sufficient intensity, these exercises can be a great way to continue the training regimen during the season!

Table 8.17 Sample In-Season Bodyweight Circuit Program 1

Day 1			Day 2		
Dynamic warm-up	Pg 46	5 min	Dynamic warm-up	Pg 46	5 min
Vertical jump	Pg 27	3 × 6	Split jump	Pg 157	3 × 6 + 6
Walking lunge (without added resistance)	Pg 62	3 × 12 + 12	Step-up (without added resistance)	Pg 110	3 × 10 + 10
Nordic curl	Pg 113	3 × 6	Medicine ball chest pass	Pg 164	3 × 6 + 6
Push-up	Pg 51	10, 10, max	Lateral squat (without added resistance)	Pg 50	3 × 10 + 10
Sit-up	Pg 144	3 × 15	Medicine ball torso toss	Pg 147	3 × 10 + 10
Static stretch	Pg 77	5 min	Static stretch	Pg 77	5 min

Table 8.18 Sample In-Season Bodyweight Circuit Program 2

Day 1			Day 2		
Dynamic warm-up	Pg 46	5 min	Dynamic warm-up	Pg 46	5 min
Box jump	Pg 155	3 × 6	Ice skater	Pg 158	3 × 6 + 6
Elevated split squat (without added resistance)	Pg 111	3 × 15 + 15	Bodyweight squat	Pg 49	3 × 15
Calf raise (without added resistance)	Pg 112	3 × 20	Medicine ball overhead toss	Pg 162	3 × 6 + 6
Reverse dip	Pg 138	10, 10, max	Lateral squat (without added resistance)	Pg 50	3 × 10 + 10
Front plank	Pg 142	3 × 30 sec	Swiss ball stabilization	Pg 148	3 × 30 sec
Static stretch	Pg 77	5 min	Static stretch	Pg 77	5 min

SAMPLE IN-SEASON ENDURANCE PROGRAMS

Table 8.19 provides a template for an extra in-season conditioning program that can be performed two days per week. If athletes or coaches determine that extra conditioning is appropriate, the following guidelines will help determine the overall volume of conditioning. These extra conditioning events can be administered at the end of practice or at a time separate from practice (usually earlier in the day, allowing for ample recovery afterward). A number of topics must be considered before making a final decision about whether or not to perform in-season endurance training in addition to practices and competitions.

Strategic Implementation

Extra conditioning—if implemented properly—can be a valuable way to improve a team's or individual's ability to perform in a game, especially during the latter stages. When should an individual or team do extra running? Generally, if a team has recovered properly, two days per week of extra conditioning is most appropriate. For example, if a team played a game on Saturday and doesn't have another game until the following Saturday, Monday and Tuesday might be great opportunities to get in some extra work. Enough time has elapsed since the last game, and the legs have enough time to bounce back before the next game. With proper implementation, the added benefits of postpractice conditioning can give a team the conditioning edge on game day!

Athlete Age

Younger athletes may not be able to handle the volume listed. The recommend volume can always be scaled to a more appropriate level. More volume might be appropriate for older (college age) athletes, and less volume might be appropriate for athletes in elementary school or junior high.

Preceding Volume

If an athlete performed a considerable amount of running during the most recent game (e.g., in overtime), the volume can be reduced to a level that the athlete or coach thinks is appropriate. Adequate recovery since the last game must take place in order for extra conditioning to be beneficial. If athletes are fatigued and unable to practice at a high rate of speed and with sufficient energy, the volume of extra conditioning may be reduced. A high volume of running during practice will also influence the recommended amount of extra conditioning postpractice. For example, midfielders who have performed numerous full-field drills may not need extra conditioning on that particular day.

Interpret the sample program in table 8.19 as follows:

- There are 12 weeks in the sample season, and two days of conditioning per week is suggested (if no midweek contest is scheduled).
- A combination of energy systems are utilized, but most events should include work using short-intermediate distance intervals, the ATP and glycolytic energy system, or both. Because these two systems are the most frequently utilized on game day, they should be the primary focus.
- Athletes and coaches should track the total volume of extra conditioning (usually measured in yards) for each event as well as the total volume in a week. This method allows the coach to examine how running volume affects the athletes' performance on game day. If the athletes are explosive, fast, and powerful on game day, the extra running has proven to be successful. If the athletes are sluggish and slow on game day, the problem may be that the athletes did not recover sufficiently.
- Over the course of the season, the volume of conditioning should be reduced as the athletes adapt to greater loads of stress on the field.

Table 8.19 Sample In-Season Conditioning Program

Week	Day 1 events	Volume (yd)	Day 2 events	Volume (yd)	Weekly volume (yd)
1	Repeat shuttle × 100, 150, 200, 150, 100	700	Linear short sprint 10 × 2, 20 × 2, 30 × 3, 20 × 2, 10 × 2	210	910
2	Half gasser × 5	550	Short shuttle at 25-yd intervals × 50, 75, 100, 75, 50	350	900
3	Perimeters × 3 laps, 2 laps, 1 lap	600	Repeat 100-yd shuttle × 3	300	900
4	110-yd linear sprint × 6	660	Short shuttle 25 × 2, 50, 75, 50, 25 × 2	275	935
5	Repeat shuttle × 100, 150, 200, 150, 100	700	Linear short sprint 10, 20 × 2, 30 × 3, 20 × 2, 10	190	890
6	Half gasser × 5	550	Perimeter 3 × 1	300	850
7	110-yd linear sprint × 6	660	No extra conditioning	0	660
8	Repeat 100-yd shuttle × 6	600	No extra conditioning	0	600
9	Repeat shuttle 50 × 2, 100, 150, 100, 50 × 2	550	No extra conditioning	0	550
10	No extra conditioning	0	No extra conditioning	0	0
11	No extra conditioning	0	No extra conditioning	0	0
12	No extra conditioning	0	No extra conditioning	0	0

The total yardage declines throughout the season and tapers from two days per week during the early part of the season to one day per week and finally is dropped completely, allowing for more recovery as the season draws to an end. If the extra conditioning was administered properly, the athletes should feel a sense of extra energy during this crucial time of the season.

Regardless of position or level of experience, all lacrosse players should incorporate strength and power training into their in-season training routine. It's easy to make excuses—fatigue, the excessive time requirements, and muscular soreness—about why not to train. Every lacrosse player has some degree of fatigue and muscle soreness, and a well-prepared, thoughtful in-season resistance-training program can allow the athlete to work through the soreness in order to avoid muscle deterioration. Brief, intense workouts can be beneficial in the long run and, as the season wears on, will help maintain the strength and joint integrity the athlete needs to perform well and avoid injury. Including resistance training in the in-season routine will make for a healthier, stronger, and more explosive player on game day!

Becoming a better player is a choice. It is simply a matter of hard work, discipline and patience. By taking advantage of every opportunity to develop your physical skills, you can become a faster, quicker and more effective player. If you make the decision to work on your game (both on the field and off the field) every day and wait patiently for your body to adapt, you will see dramatic results! It's up to you to make it happen!

References

Baechle, T., and R.W. Earle (Eds.) 2008. *Essentials of strength and conditioning.* 3rd ed. Champaign, IL: Human Kinetics. 151.

Bompa, T.O., and O. Calcina. 1994. *Theory and methodology of training: The key to athletic performance.* Dubuque, IA: Kendall/Hunt.

Chu, D., and A. Faigenbaum. 2002. Plyometric training for children and adolescents. American College of Sports Medicine. www.acsm.org/docs/current-comments/plyo-metrictraining.pdf?sfvrsn=4.

Chu, D. and G. Myer 2013. *Plyometrics: Dynamic strength and explosive power.* Champaign, IL: Human Kinetics.

Ebben, W.P., and R.L. Jensen. 1998. Strength training for women: Debunking myths that block opportunity. *Physician and Sports Medicine* 26(5):86-97.

Epley, B. 1985. Poundage chart. In *Boyd Epley workout.* Lincoln: University of Nebraska.

Gambetta, Vern. May 28, 2015. Athleticism. Perform better. N.p., n.d.

Hoffman, J. 2002. Metabolic system and exercise. *Physiological aspects of sport training and performance.* Champaign, IL: Human Kinetics.

Knuttgen, H.G., and W.J. Kraemer. 1987. Terminology and measurement in exercise performance. *Journal of Strength and Conditioning Research* 1(1):1-10.

Plisk, S., and S.B. Stenersen. 1992. The lacrosse face-off. NSCA Journal 14(2):6-8, 77-91.

Plisk, S. 2008. Speed, agility, and speed-endurance development. In T.R. Baechle and R.W. Earle (eds.), *Essentials of strength training and conditioning.* Champaign, IL: Human Kinetics.

Steinhagen, M.R., M.C. Meyers, H.H. Erickson, L. Noble, and M.T. Richardson. 1998. Physiological profile of college club-sport lacrosse athletes. *Journal of Strength and Conditioning Research* 12 (4) 226-231.

Swank, A. 2008. Adaptations to aerobic endurance training programs. In T.R. Baechle and R.W. Earle (eds.), *Essentials of strength training and conditioning.* Champaign, IL: Human Kinetics.

About the Author

Tom Howley has been the strength and conditioning coach at Cornell University since 1995. He oversees the design and implementation of athletic performance programs for 32 of Cornell's varsity sports.

From 1991 to 1995, Howley was the assistant director of strength and conditioning at East Carolina University. While there, the Pirates participated in two football bowl games (the 1992 Peach Bowl and the 1995 Liberty Bowl), qualified for the 1994 NCAA baseball regional tournament, and played in the 1993 NCAA basketball tournament.

From 1989 to 1991, Howley was a graduate assistant strength and conditioning coach and assistant football coach at Auburn University, where he earned his master's degree in education. During that time Auburn's football team was the 1989 Southeastern Conference co-champion, 1990 Hall of Fame Bowl champion, and 1991 Peach Bowl champion.

In 1988 Howley earned a bachelor of arts degree in history from Tulane University, where he was a three-year letterman and two-year starting offensive lineman on the football team. As a senior he received the New Orleans Quarterback Club Student-Athlete Award.